THE ANTI-CULT MOVEMENT
IN AMERICA

SECTS AND CULTS IN AMERICA:
BIBLIOGRAPHICAL GUIDES
(General editor: J. Gordon Melton)
Vol. 2

GARLAND REFERENCE LIBRARY
OF SOCIAL SCIENCE
Vol. 130

THE ANTI-CULT MOVEMENT
IN AMERICA
A Bibliography and
Historical Survey

Anson D. Shupe, Jr.
David G. Bromley
Donna L. Oliver

GARLAND PUBLISHING, INC. • NEW YORK & LONDON
1984

REFERENCE

Library of Congress Cataloging in Publication Data

Shupe, Anson D.
   The anti-cult movement in America.

   (Sects and cults in America. Bibliographical
guides ; v. 2) (Garland reference library of social
science ; v. 130)
   Includes index.
   1. Cults—United States—Controversial literature—
Bibliography.   2. Cults—Controversial literature—
History and criticism.   I. Bromley, David G.
II. Oliver, Donna L.   III. Title.   IV. Series.
V. Series: Garland reference library of social science ;
v. 130.
Z7835.C86S55   1984   [BL2530.U6]   016.291′0973   82-49028
ISBN 0-8240-9214-7

Cover design by Laurence Walczak

Printed on acid-free, 250-year-life paper
Manufactured in the United States of America

CONTENTS

INTRODUCTION

In this book we shall examine the most significant and influential religious countermovement of the twentieth century, the anti-cult movement (hereafter ACM). This volume balances other volumes in this series since it focuses on the opposition that virtually every major new religious movement in American history has encountered. While a wealth of information has been accumulated on the histories of many new religions (and indeed that is what makes such a bibliographic series valuable), there has not been a similar compilation of materials on religious countermovements. Yet it is certainly the case that the fortunes of new religions usually have been substantially influenced by their opponents. The impact of opposition has been mixed. Persecution has increased the internal solidarity of oppressed groups as well as the fervor and commitment of individual members. Campaigns against new religions also have been a rallying point for established churches and evangelical groups which have been rejuvenated by the perceived threat to their doctrines and lifestyles. And, finally, in the long run countermovements usually have contributed to the "moderation" of new religions (although cases with the opposite outcome can be found) as the price of protracted conflict, persecution and lack of legitimacy have proven to be a heavy burden.

The ACM, as we shall describe, is composed of three separate but interrelated components. The anti-cult associations consist of local and regional groups of family members of converts to new religions and former members of new religions. The ACM also has formed national level organizations, which essentially have been federations of local groups on several occasions, but it has always been strongest at the grassroots level. The anti-cult associations have largely initiated and coordinated the campaign against new religions. They have formed support and information networks for family members of converts, sought publicity in order to air their grievances and gain public support, and actively lobbied for legislation which would enable parents to legally extricate their offspring from cults and cut off the flow of vital resources to cults.

Parents of converts to the new religions not only have been the backbone of the anti-cult associations, they also have provided the financial base for the second component of the ACM, the deprogrammers. Deprogrammers operate as a loose network of individuals who contract with parents to "rescue" their children from cults. Although there have been both amateur (usually former members of new religions) and professional deprogrammers, it has been the latter group which has been most visible. To the anti-cultists these entrepreneurs are heroic figures who rescue their brainwashed children, risking lawsuits and imprisonment in the process. To the new religions and civil libertarians deprogrammers are "hired guns" who exploit family conflicts to line their pockets. Deprogrammers have played an important role in the ACM directly through their sensational, controversial exploits and indirectly through the personal testimonies of individuals who have been "successfully" deprogrammed. It has been such personal accounts, verifying ACM allegations against the new religions, which have been the single most influential factor in shaping public opinion about the new religions.

The third component of the ACM is a network of religious groups. While a number of mainline churches have spoken out against the new religions and Jewish opposition has been strong, it has been evangelistic and fundamentalist Christian groups which have led the religious opposition. In general, the religious groups opposing cults have been more supportive of the anti-cult associations (indeed there are many cross-memberships) than of the deprogrammers because of the far-reaching implications of allowing religious affiliation to be determined by force. For the most part, however, these religious groups have operated independently, condemning the heretical doctrines of various new religions and seeking to warn both the fallen and the faithful of the dangers they pose. The evangelical groups have produced a torrent of literature condemning cults while the mainline churches have been more likely to issue reports or "educational" materials. Their impact has not been inconsequential, for their unified rejection of the new religions has denied new religions legitimacy as churches.

The final impact of the ACM remains unclear as this volume is prepared. The new religious movements against which it mobilized (such as the Unification Church, Hare Krishna, Children of God, The Way International, the Divine Light Mission, and Scientology) experienced considerably greater popularity in the 1970's than they had in the preceding decade, and it was their increased growth and visibility that triggered the development of the ACM in the early 1970's. Now, a decade later, the heyday of most of the new religions seems to be over. Although none of the major new religions has disappeared, particularly those that are organized communally and involve the greatest break with conventional lifestyles, they have not continued to grow at their mid-1970's rate. Furthermore, a great deal of their energies and resources have been expended in countering ACM attacks and in trying to gain public legitimacy.

For its part, the ACM has succeeded in discrediting the new religions. There seems to be widespread agreement that there has been a sudden upsurge of dangerous, destructive cults that threaten innocent young adults, legitimate religions and even cherished values and institutions. The widespread public fear and hostility toward new religions has permitted their systematic harassment, but final victory has eluded the ACM. There have been hearings and investigations, terrible tales of defectors, condemnations by major public figures representing a broad range of powerful institutions, kidnappings and deprogrammings. Still, the anti-cultists have not been able to secure the passage of legislation that would allow systematic, legal repression of new religions nor have they been able to win the unwavering support of any major institution. And so the battle goes on. At this juncture, it appears that the struggle will be a protracted one. The ACM has become better organized over time, and, correspondingly, the new religions have become more entrenched. While there are some signs of accommodation among the new religions, it does not appear that they will soon be accepted as legitimate churches. What may well transpire is a gradual reduc-

tion in the visibility and intensity of the conflict as the size of the
most controversial new religions declines and these groups show
signs of preliminary accommodation to the conventional social
order. It is still possible, however, for specific historical events,
such as the tragedy at Jonestown, or the excesses of yet another
new religion, to trigger renewed vigor in the anti-cult campaign.

The organization of this volume flows out of both the structure of the ACM and the issues the movement has raised. Chapter One places the ACM in historical perspective by reviewing
the receptions earlier new religions received and similarities between present and past anti-cult campaigns. The following three
chapters outline the history and structure of the ACM. In contrast to the religiously based anti-cult groups which have produced a prodigious literature, the family based anti-cult associations are much more difficult to trace through written records.
The history of anti-cult associations therefore is traced through
the authors' field interviews, newsletters and internal documents, public hearings, court records and the like. The actions
of deprogrammers are even more difficult to trace. Indeed, only
the careers of the few nationally prominent deprogrammers, like
Ted Patrick, can be reconstructed with any degree of certainty.
The religiously based wing of the ACM can be traced more easily
through its literature, for literature production has been central
to its efforts. With the exception of the Spiritual Counterfeits
Project, the most prominent evangelical opponent of the cults,
the organizational history of most other such groups remains
unrecorded.

Chapters Five and Six trace the social science and legal responses to the ACM. The centerpiece of ACM ideology is the
brainwashing thesis, for without the allegation of mind control,
it would be difficult to justify the legal and extra-legal actions
against cults promoted by the ACM. As a result, social science
research has been dominated by this issue. Psychologists have
interviewed and tested members and former members of new
religions and assessed the consequences of prolonged meditation. Sociologists have studied the conversion process and compared the organizational structure within which members function. Furthermore, a variety of social scientists has sought to
understand the socio-cultural significance and implications of

the emergence and popularity of these groups. By and large, scientific research has not supported the extreme allegations of the ACM, but the more controversial and sensational conclusions have received the greatest fanfare. Chapter Five considers these and other related issues.

Chapter Six focuses on the court cases generated by parental attempts to extricate their offspring from new religions. ACM allegations that converts are brainwashed, attempts to secure passage of legislation granting parents custody over their offspring and vigilante style actions by deprogrammers have produced a myriad of court cases. As the number of cases has grown, analyses of the legality and implications of legislative, judicial and extra-legal actions have been produced. These form the basis for an assessment of the legal implications of the ACM.

Chapter Seven reviews other major institutional responses to the ACM. Although the political, legal, religious and familial institutions have been the primary actors in the new religions' controversy, a number of other institutions have become involved in the dispute. The educational system, for example, has been forced to consider a whole range of issues. Colleges have had to decide whether to allow recruiters from new religions on campus, whether to allow new religions to start student organizations on campus and whether to accept transfer credits from colleges and seminaries started by new religions. High schools and PTA's have debated what kind of counseling and literature should be provided to students concerning new religions. The media, of course, found in the family crises and exploits of deprogrammers consummate human drama. Beyond the exciting copy this controversy yielded, however, the media had to decide how to portray this emotional and sometimes bitter conflict. Both sides sought to control the agenda of issues which were discussed in the media and, as we shall see, media decisions played no small role in shaping public opinion. Finally, both the legal and medical professions were drawn into the fray. In the medical profession psychiatrists were most involved as several new religions (e.g., Transcendental Meditation, Scientology) made mental health claims for themselves while the anti-cultists were touting deprogramming as a therapy to counter coercive mind control. Lawyers were embroiled in the controversy both as prosecution and defense attorneys and as analysts of the rapidly growing number of cases generated as the conflict between families and new religions developed.

Also in Chapter Seven we consider the response by the new religions and civil libertarians to the ACM. The response of new religions to the hostility they have experienced (and to some degree provoked) has varied considerably. The Children of God departed for Europe early in the 1970's; Scientology has filed numerous legal suits and engaged in harassment of proclaimed "enemies" as well as criminal violations to defend itself. At the same time, all of the new religions have tried in one way or another to counter the allegations made against them through public relations campaigns. A sample of these documents will be reviewed and discussed. The only defenders of new religions, besides the groups themselves, have been civil libertarians. Warnings of the danger for civil liberties if ACM remedies are formally or tacitly accepted have come from a variety of sources including religious leaders and newspaper editorialists. In this sense it would be incorrect to depict the churches or the media as monolithic opponents of new religions. Nevertheless, it has been civil liberties groups which have most consistently and vocally warned of ACM abuses of civil rights. Reports on coercive deprogrammings and opposition to repressive legislation have been a central civil liberties concern. The book concludes with a consideration of these issues, which seems appropriate in light of the variety of excesses and personal tragedies associated with the controversy over new religions.

Finally, a word is in order concerning the types of sources included in and excluded from the bibliographic references at the end of each chapter. In Chapter One we have cited only major sources, principally books, which illustrate the nature of the response by established religious groups to new religious movements. Any systematic treatment of this literature (which includes books, periodicals, sermons, tracts and cassette tapes) would require a separate volume. The bibliographic materials following Chapters Two and Three, by contrast, specifically do include more obscure materials ranging from state legislative hearings transcripts and bills to fugitive materials produced by the ACM. The items referenced in Chapter Four parallel the entries in Chapter One but are much more detailed. References include both monographs and a representative sampling of the vast periodical literature. Mainline Christian, Jewish and evangelical Christian literatures are represented. Scholarly literature addressing various facets of the cult controversy is listed at the end of Chapter Five. Most of this research has been produced by scholars in the disciplines of sociology, psychology, psychiatry and religion. Unpublished papers have been included to incorporate the most recent research developments. Chapter Six includes references to legal scholars' assessments of issues related to the cult controversy, particularly brainwashing and deprogramming. These assessments focus on the precedent setting cases in what has become a major area of litigation. Chapter Seven reviews some of the documents produced by institutions not discussed in earlier chapters (e.g., medical, educational, media) which have been drawn into the cult controversy. In Chapter Seven we also list statements produced by civil libertarians and spokespersons for new religions, the two chief defenders of new religions. A great deal of this material has not been published or widely circulated.

CHAPTER ONE

ANTI-CULT CAMPAIGNS IN HISTORICAL PERSPECTIVE

In this chapter we shall attempt to place the anti-cult campaign launched in the early 1970's in proper historical context.
American religious history has witnessed a steady succession of new
religious movements which certainly number in the hundreds and very
probably in the thousands. Most new religious movements have not
achieved great size or visibility and have eventually simply disappeared. The more successful ones usually have attracted intense
opposition in the form of countermovements like the ACM. It is
clearly beyond the scope of this chapter to review the histories of
these countermovements. Not only have there been a large number of
them but also information is much more readily available on new
religious movements than on their countermovement opponents.

Those new religions which have established themselves as major
churches (e.g., Mormons) have gone back and recorded their own
histories and have also been the objects of study by scholars in a
number of disciplines. Religious countermovements usually have not
survived and prospered. On the one hand, if the new religion they
opposed failed, the countermovement probably succumbed with it since
countermovements were single issue protest groups. On the other
hand, if the new religion succeeded in gaining legitimacy, the
countermovements gradually lost its target. It is also important to
note that religion has become less and less central as a source of
political conflict and decision making over the last century and
hence anti-cult type movements have rarely been successful in mobilizing powerful political coalitions. For the most part, these
countermovements have remained struggling, fledgling organizations,
and the records of their organization and activities are therefore
few and scattered. Thus, even in those anti-cult campaigns that
spanned a considerable period of time (e.g., against Catholics),
countermovements rarely supported robust organizations although it
is in such cases that the most systematic data are available
(Billington, 1963; Higham, 1963).

The response of Christians of various persuasions to new religions can be more easily traced. Each new religion which enjoyed
any real measure of success triggered a response from the Christian
community, for each posed a challenge to some aspect of Christian
doctrine or practice. Since there are a limited number of basic
tenets professed by Christians, the clashes between established
Christian churches and new religious movements have tended to

focus on a few central issues. As a result, the responses to new
religions have been remarkably similar, and a genre of literature
has developed in which only the identities of the challenging
groups have changed. The steady flow of new religions and the need
to warn the faithful as well as the fallen in each case have yielded
a prodigious literature. In this chapter we shall concentrate primarily on the major new religions which appeared in the United
States during the nineteenth century (Seventh Day Adventism,
Jehovah's Witnesses, Mormonism, Christian Science, Spiritualism,
Unity). There were, of course, earlier waves of new religions, but
many of these groups (Shakers, Quakers, Amish, Oneidas, Mennonites,
Hutterites) had either disappeared or accommodated sufficiently to
conventional society for opposition to have abated. We shall therefore make only occasional reference to these latter groups.

    In light of the available historical resources on anti-cult
movements, the remainder of the chapter will be divided into two
major segments. First, we shall examine some common parallels between the contemporary ACM and some of its historical counterparts.
Although information on earlier countermovements is scattered, there
are sufficient materials to illustrate these parallels and lend some
perspective to the later chapters dealing with the contemporary ACM.
Second, we shall review the Christian response to earlier new religions. Because the themes remain fairly constant across time, we
shall defer a detailed analysis of those themes for Chapter Four.
Furthermore, we can cite only a small part of the historical Christian literature denouncing new religions. However, the brief survey we will present and the sample of sources cited will establish
the repetitive nature of the clash between Christian churches and
"cults."

CONTINUITIES IN ANTI-CULT MOVEMENTS

    By definition, social movements are organized attempts to ini-
tiate social change. Since established social arrangements represent the outcome of efforts by individuals and groups to create
equitable or advantageous exchanges (of goods, services, sentiments)
with others, it follows that any social movement will evoke some degree of tension. Quite simply put, social movements reorganize and
reorient behavior in ways that movement members find rewarding but
outsiders may well oppose. For this reason countermovements frequently are formed by those whose interests are most directly challenged by emergent social movements. In the case of the anti-cult
type movements with which we are concerned here four major continuities can be observed: (1) a conflict of interest between the new
religion and one or more established groups, (2) the formation of
one or more anti-cult organizations, (3) allegations of clear and
present danger and (4) efforts to mobilize powerful allies to combat
the perceived dangers posed by the new religion.

Conflicts of Interest

    Each of the new religions that has aroused significant opposi-
tion has sought a major change in traditional values and in the

established institutional order. While there has been a response
from the established churches in each case, these conflicts have
often taken on the appearance of intra-mural religious disputes.
However, when more than one powerful group has felt its interests to
be threatened then the conflict has been more visible and repression
more severe. The anti-Catholic campaign nicely illustrates this
point.

Overt hostility toward Catholics can be traced to the early
days of the American colonies. Even though there were relatively
few Catholics in Colonial America, Protestant-Catholic hatreds were
quickly transplanted from Europe. Later, when large numbers of
Catholic immigrants began pouring into the United States following
the advent of the industrial revolution, smoldering anti-Catholic
sentiments flared once again. The longevity and intensity of the
anti-Catholic movement can be traced to the fact that Catholics
posed a threat to several powerful groups. In addition to fears of
attempted papal domination of America there was widespread public
animosity toward the waves of lower-class Catholic immigrants whose
values and lifestyles clashed with those of the dominant native
Protestants and fear of bloc voting leading to Catholic political
hegemony in urban-industrial centers. A series of other issues,
ranging from Catholic-Protestant intermarriage to public support for
parochial schools, grew out of these basic conflicts of interest.
Mistrust of Catholics lingered on well into the twentieth century
and was still evident in the 1960 presidential campaign when questions were raised about John F. Kennedy's independence of papal
authority.

Like the Catholics, the Mormons became the center of a controversy which has spanned well over a century and lingers on particularly in the western regions of the United States. The belief that
existing churches were flawed and that God's chosen people were to
gather together to build Zion in America in anticipation of the return of the messiah was central to Mormon doctrine. Such separatism
and rejection of established religion and the conventional order
historically have been among the principal sources of hostility to
new religions. This was not the only source of conflict however;
there also were fears of Mormon political power. Their numbers grew
quickly, they were tightly organized, and they prospered financially. As a result, by the time the main contingent of Mormons had
arrived in Nauvoo, Illinois (after having been driven out of New
York and Ohio), the group was large and well organized enough to
constitute a swing vote in that state. The Mormons developed considerable political autonomy within those areas where the Mormon
population was concentrated, even to the point of maintaining their
own separate militia. This combination of political power and separation fueled public mistrust; these feelings were further inflamed
when Joseph Smith declared his candidacy for President of the United
States. Probably the most volatile issue of all, however, was the
Mormon practice of polygamy. It was this issue that became a light-
ningrod for anti-Mormon sentiment. Charges of immorality, destruction of family life and exploitation of wives were widely publicized. And cases in which Mormon wives separated from their hus-
bands and were not allowed custody of their children only confirmed

the darkest suspicions of Mormon opponents. In recent years, opposition to Mormons has centered around their aggressive proselytization tactics, which have produced dramatic membership growth rates,
and strong Mormon political influence in Utah and surrounding
states.

The Jehovah's Witnesses provide a third illustration of the
conflict between new religions and gatekeepers of the conventional
social order. According to Jehovah's Witnesses' theology, a coalition of religious, political and commercial institutions has wielded
Satan's power and worked together to oppress the righteous. Established churches are defined as tools of Satan which in concert with
the commercial class have dominated and exploited the poor. The
wealthy have been protected by satanically coordinated governments.
Not surprisingly, this theology both angered the mainline churches
and led to conflict with the government. The conflicts have centered on issues such as Witnesses' refusal to salute the flag or to
serve in the armed forces. More recently the Jehovah's Witnesses
have aggressively and successfully proselytized large numbers of new
members, and current opposition to them has centered on this issue,
particularly among family members of converts.

Anti-Cult Organizations

Each major new religion in the United States has been greeted
by organized opposition. Anti-cult type organizations typically
have played a leading role in initiating, fueling and coordinating
campaigns against new religious movements. Sometimes anti-cult
groups have arisen in response to a single new religion; sometimes
these groups have attacked a whole range of new religions (as the
ACM has) and sometimes the anti-cult campaigns have constituted part
of a larger countermovement (e.g., nativism). The anti-Catholic and
anti-Mormon organizations typify anti-cult organizations; nineteenth
century organizations have been chosen to illustrate the former and
contemporary organizations to exemplify the latter.

The late 1880's saw a revival of anti-Catholicism, which had
waned somewhat after fears of a papal conspiracy to subvert and take
over the United States during the 1830's had subsided. The 1880's
witnessed a spate of new anti-Catholic organizations (United Order
of Deputies; Minute Men of 1886; Red, White and Blue; United Order
of Native Americans; American Patriotic League; Get There American
Benefit Association; and Loyal Men of American Liberty) of which the
American Protective Association (APA) was the most prominent and
powerful (Desmond, 1969; Kinzer, 1964). Recruits to the APA took an
oath never to vote for, employ or go out on strike with Catholics
(Higham, 1963:62-108). By 1893, the APA achieved national prominence. Its activities included aiding the election campaigns of
candidates who sympathized with its cause, organizing boycotts of
Catholic merchants and lecturing on the dangers of Catholicism.
The APA's national legislative agenda included reduction of immigration; extension of time for naturalization; educational qualifications for suffrage; denial of public funds for sectarian purposes;
taxation of all non-public property; and public inspection of private schools, convents and monasteries (Kinzer, 1964:203). There

were legislative initiatives in a number of states as well. For
example, bills were presented to the Michigan legislature in 1894 to
rescind a previous law giving a Catholic bishop control over the
property of his diocese and to prohibit the commitment of youths to
a Catholic run home for children, the house of Good Shepherd, in
Detroit (Kinzer, 1964:163-4). Both passed the Michigan Senate but
failed in the lower house. A bill supported by the APA which required the display of the national flag over all school buildings
did become law but ultimately proved unenforceable. In the state of
Washington proclamations were passed to recommend that the federal
government institute a longer residence period prior to naturalization, permit entry into the country only for those who desired to
become citizens and terminate immigration for two years to reduce
job competition with the native labor force. Furthermore, a bill
was enacted into law which had the effect of requiring that churches
make financial reports available to state and local officials in
order to be eligible for tax exemption, but it also proved unenforceable (Kinzer, 1964:167-8).

There have been a series of anti-Mormon groups since opposition
began during the nineteenth century. Anti-Mormonism did not achieve
the intensity and longevity of anti-Catholicism, however, and this
is reflected in the organization of anti-Mormon groups. Anti-Mormon
sentiment is largely concentrated in the western United States for
that is where Mormon population, wealth and political power are concentrated. As a result, it has been difficult for anti-Mormon
organizations to generate a viable coalition of opponents to the
Mormon Church. In the West, particularly Utah, it would be difficult to mount a serious political challenge to the Mormons; elsewhere there simply is little interest in the controversy. Conse-
quently, most of the anti-Mormon groups (such as Utah Missions,
Utah Christian Tract Society, Ex-Mormons for Jesus, and the Modern
Microfilm Company) concentrate on issuing warnings about the continuing threat of Mormonism, witnessing to Mormons, seeking to discredit Mormon theology and providing a public platform for ex-
Mormons. The Modern Microfilm Company, for example, publishes a
monthly newsletter, Salt Lake City Messenger, and Utah Missions publishes The Utah Evangel, both of which contain such themes. These
newsletters very much resemble the anti-cult materials reviewed in
Chapter Three. They monitor Mormon activities (e.g., proselytization activities in the U.S. and abroad, land purchases, pronounce-
ments by church leaders), feature apostate accounts, report the
latest discoveries of irregularities in official Mormon histories,
offer anti-Mormon literature for sale and "expose" the presence or
influence of Mormons in national political arenas. In addition, of
course, these groups distribute a wide variety of tracts, pamphlets,
tape cassettes to both Mormons and non-Mormons.

Allegations of Danger

One recurrent feature of all anti-cult campaigns has been a
flood of propaganda initiated or coordinated by the anti-cult organizations. The objectives of the "atrocity stories" circulated by
the anti-cultists have been to build public support for their position, build fear and suspicion about the new religions, and reduce

public or official concern about any persecution these movements
might suffer. In view of the limited success anti-cult organizations have achieved in securing the passage of repressive legislation, propaganda successes have assumed major importance. Even if
substantive sanctions could not be imposed, public rejection of new
religions would leave them discredited and help to preserve the dominance and public legitimacy of the established churches.

The two major sources of sensational allegations against the new
religions have been leaders of anti-cult organizations and former
members of new religions. In many cases these two sources were
identical since former members have frequently served as leaders of
anti-cult groups. Personal testimony of ex-members of new religions
who made sensational allegations and swore "I was there and I saw it
happen" often has been uncritically accepted and widely circulated.
The most convincing evidence of the importance of such testimony to
anti-cult movements and of its effectiveness is that when apostates
willing and able to condemn the groups with which they had been affiliated have not been available, anti-cultists have simply created
such individuals. The most celebrated cases of this kind were Maria
Monk and Rebecca Reed, both of whom claimed to have been "escaped"
nuns. There is solid historical evidence that in fact neither had
been a nun and that their stories were largely fabricated and ghost
written by the leaders of anti-Catholic organizations (Billington,
1963:90-101).

The emergence of each major new religion has been accompanied
by a spate of apostate accounts. The anti-Catholic movement, for
example, inspired a series of personal testimonies by ex-nuns and
ex-priests (in addition to the almost wholly fictional accounts of
Monk and Reed) which alleged that all kinds of atrocities were being
committed behind convent and monastery walls (Billington, 1933). It
was alleged that nuns were grossly deceived about the true nature of
convent life, became virtual slaves, were physically abused if they
failed to conform to a superior's orders and were treated as sexual
objects by frustrated priests. A number of such accounts were published between the 1830's and the 1850's. Representative titles
include Scipio de Ricci's Female Converts: Secrets of Nunneries Dis-
closed (1834), Reed's Six Months in a Convent (1835), Samuel Smith's
The Wonderful Adventures of a Lady of the French Nobility, and the
Intrigues of a Romish Priest, her Confessor, to Seduce and Murder
Her (1836), Monk's Awful Disclosures of the Hotel Dieu Nunnery of
Montreal (1836), Sister Agnes; or, the Captive Nun; a Picture of
Convent Life (1854), and Bunkley's The Testimony of an Escaped
Novice from the Sisterhood of St. Joseph, Emmetsburg, Md. Of
course, there were numerous more general condemnations of Catholic-
ism as well (Billington, 1933).

Similar sensational literatures developed around other new religions. The polygamous lifestyle of the Mormons led to charges
that Mormon wives were virtual slaves and created the impression
that no Mormon marriages were voluntary. Representative titles include Green's Fifteen Years Among the Mormons: Being the Narrative
of Mrs. Mary Ettie V. Smith (1857), Ward's Female Life Among the
Mormons: A Narrative of Many Years Personal Experience, By the Wife

of a Mormon Elder, Recently Returned from Utah (1857), Young's Wife
No. 19; or, the Story of a Life in Bondage, Being a Complete Expose
of Mormonism (1875) and Froiseth's The Women of Mormonism; or, the
Story of Polygamy as Told by the Victims Themselves (1882). In the
case of religions which were not organized communally apostate accounts have dwelt more heavily on themes such as deception of re-
cruits and members, fallacies in the group's doctrines and unsavory
practices by members and leaders. A sample of this literature in-
cludes Dencher's Why I Left Jehovah's Witnesses (1966), Schnell's 30
Years a Watchtower Slave (1971), Tomsett's Watchtower Chaos (1974),
Joe Hewitt's I was Raised a Jehovah's Witness (1979), Canright's
Seventh-Day Adventism Renounced; After an Experience of Twenty-Eight
Years by a Prominent Minister and Writer of that Faith (1978) and
Adair and Miller's We Found Our Way Out (1964), a collection of
apostate testimonials from former members of groups, ranging from
Theosophy to agnosticism to Rosicrucianism.

      Apostate accounts have been one of the most potent weapons in
anti-cult campaigns throughout history. In using these accounts and
other allegations to arouse public concern, anti-cultists frequently
have sought to portray a common threat from several such groups
which emerged during the same historical era. Since some new
religions were small, since some possessed only one or a few traits
that might arouse opposition and since some were concentrated in a
single geographic region, building a national campaign was
facilitated by somehow linking the alleged threats posed by several
new religious movements. As we shall see in later chapters, this
tactic has been employed by the contemporary ACM, which has linked
together a series of very disparate groups under the label of
"cults." A similar phenomenon occurred during the time period
under consideration in this chapter. During the mid-nineteenth
century opposition had arisen to Catholics and Mormons for rather
different reasons. Nevertheless, these two groups were lumped
together with Masonry and presented as posing a common threat to the
American way of life. As David Davis (1960:205-208) commented:

           The movements of counter-subversion differed
           markedly in historical origin, but as the im-
           age of an un-American conspiracy took form in
           the nativist press, in sensational exposes,
           in the countless fantasies of treason and
           mysterious criminality, the lines separating
           Mason, Catholic and Mormon became almost in-
           distinguishable.... If Masons, Catholics and
           Mormons bore little resemblance to one an-
           other in actuality, as imagined enemies they
           merged into a nearly common stereotype.

Combining groups in this fashion created the aura of a conspiracy
and provided at least one group which could be used to defend the
stereotypical set of subversive qualities.

Impact of Anti-Cult Campaigns

      The success achieved by anti-cult campaigns has varied consid-

erably. There have been numerous cases in American history where
the degree of violence against members of new religions has far ex-
ceeded the abduction and deprogramming activities of the contemporary ACM. Four Quakers were hanged in public between 1659 and 1661;
later other Quakers were sentenced to death for pacifism (although
their sentences were commuted). The Mormons were driven from New
York and went to Ohio, Missouri and Illinois before finally settling
in Utah. In 1844, the leader of the Mormon Church, Joseph Smith,
was attacked and slain in a jail cell while awaiting trial in
Nauvoo, Illinois. There were numerous instances of anti-Catholic
rioting during the nineteenth century. For example, in 1834, the
Ursuline Convent in Charlestown, Massachusetts, was burned to the
ground by a mob after rumors circulated that a young woman was being
held there against her will. In 1844, mobs attacked Catholic neigh-
borhoods in Kensington, Pennsylvania; riots left thirteen people
dead and two Catholic churches destroyed. Members of Jehovah's Witnesses have suffered persistent persecution; property destruction
has been common and a few members have been castrated.

There were numerous instances of attempts at legal repression
as well. Prior to the American Revolution, for example, the civil
liberties of Catholics were severely limited in several colonies;
later a number of laws were passed that were aimed at Catholics although no specific group was designated in the legislation. Attempts were made to curtail the distribution of literature by
Jehovah's Witnesses and imprison Quakers and Jehovah's Witnesses for
refusal to serve in the armed forces. Even though most overt legal
repression has not been supported when challenged in the courts,
legal challenges consume time and resources as well as keep new religions on the defensive.

Ultimately the success of anti-cult campaigns must be traced
not to a single factor, but to a combination of factors. Conflicts
with several powerful groups meant that new religions had few potential allies but a number of potential enemies. The allegations
raised by ex-members in particular and anti-cult groups in general
had the effect of arousing public fear and suspicion. If there was
no merit to these charges, why were there so many apostates warning
of imminent danger and why were so many "legitimate" institutions at
constant odds with these groups? Civil suits and criminal proceedings, public hearings and proposed legislation, whatever their
final disposition only served to reinforce public negativity. The
groups whose histories we have reviewed here did survive and have
gained some measure of legitimacy, but these gains have come at high
cost. For decades their resources were substantially committed to
self-preservation and self-defense.

                          THE CHRISTIAN RESPONSE

The challenges to established Christian churches from new religious movements have been both continuous and diverse. Although new
religions typically have received less than a warm welcome, still it
has been possible for large numbers of new religious groups to take
root. Some of these groups have been indigenous (e.g., Mormonism,

Christian Science) while others have been imported (e.g., Shakers, Swedenborgianism). Some have drawn on Christianity for their doctrinal inspiration (e.g., Jehovah's Witnesses); others arose out of one or more of the other major world religions (e.g., Baha'ism). The only quality that all such new religions possessed in common was some combination of doctrine and practice which clashed with orthodox Christianity. Thus, the deviant beliefs and practices attributed to new religions can best be understood not so much as inherent qualities of these movements but as relational qualities vis-a-vis mainline Christian doctrine and practice. By focusing primarily on new religions which emerged during the nineteenth century we shall be able to show the continuity in the response to a diverse array of new religions and the continuity in response across time to those religions which have continued to pose a challenge to the established churches. The relatively uniform response to the motley assortment of new religions is important to demonstrate the socially constructed nature of religious deviance. The continuities over time are important to understand the contemporary ACM, for a number of anti-cult groups originally dedicated to combatting nineteenth-century vintage new religions have rejuvenated their campaigns by taking on contemporary new religions as well. We shall only highlight the conflicts between mainstream Christianity and new religions in this chapter since these themes will be explored in detail in Chapter Four. The bibliography contains a representative, but not exhaustive, set of references. In general, books rather than pamphlets, tracts, and reprinted speeches and sermons have been emphasized in the bibliography.

It would be incorrect to characterize all of the Christian literature as hostile to new religions. There have been a number of authors who have written sympathetic treatments rather than simply comparing them to predetermined criteria of heretical qualities. Among the best known of these more moderate works are Atkins' Modern Cults and Religious Movements (1923), Bach's They Have Found a Faith (1947), Strange Sects and Curious Cults (1961), Strangers at the Door (1971), Braden's These Also Believe: A Study of Modern American Cults and Minority Religious Movements (1949) and Peterson's Those Curious New Cults (1973). Braden (1949:xi), for example, stated in the Preface to his volume that he "holds no brief for any particular cult nor is he violently opposed to any." He went on to conclude that "cults represent the earnest attempt of millions of people to find the fulfillment of deep and legitimate needs of the human spirit." Bach (1946:21-22) began his book with a similar statement:

> Let others turn ecclesiastical microscopes on
> them and weigh them in the sensitive scale of
> final truth. I would content myself with the
> age-old verdict of Gamaliel, "If this work be
> of men, it will come to nought; but if it be
> of God, ye cannot overthrow it."

He went on to conclude that "All roads that lead to God are good," a statement with which less tolerant Christians might agree only because they believed there is but a single road.

In general, however, Christian authors have been less charitable in their assessment of the new religions. There have been literally thousands of critical works on "cults" if all published materials are included. Among the best known of the book length compendia criticisms of new religions are Ferguson's The Confusion of
Tongues (1931); Binder's Modern Religious Cults and Society (1933);
Sanders' Heresies and Cults (1962), which was originally published
in 1948; various Van Baalen's works such as The Chaos of Cults
(1938), The Gist of the Cults (1944) and Christianity versus the
Cults (1956); Walter Martin's works, including The Christian and the
Cults (1956), The Rise of the Cults (1947) and The Kingdom of the
Cults (1965); Davies' Christian Deviations (1954) and The Challenge
of the Sects (1961); and Hoekema's The Four Major Cults (1963).

Broadly speaking, critiques of cults have contained two different kinds of messages. On the one hand, there have been doctrinal comparisons with orthodox Christianity designed to demonstrate
the inferior or heretical qualities of cult teachings. On the other
hand, there have been discussions of new religions from a tactical,
political perspective. The doctrinal criticism of cults has included at least five major points. First, there has been an affirmation of the Bible as the full and final word of God and a rejection of extrabiblical sources of spiritual authority such as the
Book of Mormon or Science and Health, with Key to the Scriptures.
For Christians to accept such new sources of authority would be to
cede spiritual supremacy to new religions. Therefore, considerable
effort was expended in questioning the revelations on which such
writings were based, denying their historical authenticity, building
a case for plagiarism and challenging new interpretations of classi-
cal texts. Second, there has been a rejection of salvation through
individual works and a corresponding insistence on salvation through
grace. Mormons, for example, contend that only obeying God's com-
mandments could insure salvation, and Christian Scientists believe
that salvation followed from cessation of sin and a belief in sin.
Christian authors condemned such beliefs since they transferred the
key to salvation from the church to the individual and from the established churches to the new religions. Third, each new religion
has possessed its own charismatic founder or leader (e.g., Joseph
Smith, Mary Baker Eddy) whose revelations supplemented the teachings
that Jesus offered God's last word and that Christ would return. It
was the messianic claims of leaders of new religions that provoked
the most angry denunciations by Christian authors. Fourth, groups
such as Jehovah's Witnesses and Mormons have proclaimed that they
alone are God's true people, and naturally Christians rejected such
claims. Finally, new religions often have claimed that the last
days of the world are at hand. Such teachings have the effect of
creating white hot intensity among members and directly clash with
Christian expectations for an ultimate, but not imminent, return of
the messiah. Christian authors carefully refuted the eschtology of
new religions and drew upon unfulfilled predictions made by their
leaders as compelling evidence of the fraudulent character of these
prophetic doctrines.

The other major thrust of Christian literature has been an assessment of the threat posed by new religions. No matter when their
books were written, Christian writers all agreed that cult
membership was growing rapidly (Braden, 1944; Lindsell, 1961:5-9).
This growth was attributed to the fact that mankind had failed to
follow the dictates of Christ, a failure which had created the host
of problems confronting the world (Van Baalen, 1938:389-391). Of
course, the ultimate source of the chaos of the time was satanic influence (Martin, 1965:13), but Christians also bore responsibility
for failing to follow the divinely mandated course. It was strongly
suggested that Christians could learn a valuable lesson in
commitment and sacrifice from cultists even though the latter had
been led astray (Braden, 1944-1945).

Christians therefore were urged to familiarize themselves with
both cult doctrines and biblical truths so that they could discern
the difference when confronted with twisted versions of Christianity. Although converts to new religions might be sincere in their
beliefs, it was stressed in this literature again and again that
they must be rejected because they represented evil (Martin, 1965:
15). Cultists engaged in deliberate deception because they themselves had been deceived or brainwashed (Martin, 1965:27-28;
Lindsell, 1961:76); they were caught up in a web of evil from which
they could not escape. Christians were entreated to spread the word
of Christ in order to stem the rising tide of cult converts, but
they were also warned of the dangers of witnessing to cultists.
Because cultists were deceived and firmly under the control of their
leaders, easy victories were not to be expected despite the fact
that Christians possessed the truth. Each book, therefore, provided
the Christian faithful with a clear delineation of the doctrinal
errors of cults and guidelines for witnessing to cult members (Van
Baalen, 1938:368-372).

In addition to compendia volumes showing the common fallacies
and heresies of cults there have, of course, been innumerable book
length condemnations of each major new religion. Such works
directed at Christian Science, for example, include Tenny's <u>Chris-
tian Science, Its Truths and Errors</u> (1888), Moore's <u>Christian Science - Its Manifold Attraction</u> (1906), Haldeman's <u>Christian Science
in the Light of Holy Scripture</u> (1909), Sheldon's <u>Christian Science
So-Called</u> (1913), Snowden's <u>The Truth About Christian Science</u>
(1920), Riley et al.'s <u>The Faith, The Falsity and the Failure of
Christian Science</u> (1925), Riddle's <u>Christian Science in Light of
Holy Scripture</u> (1931), Haushalter's <u>Mrs. Eddy Purloins from Hegel</u>
(1936), Corey's <u>Christian Science Class Instructions</u> (1945),
Studdert-Kennedy's <u>Christian Science and Organized Religion</u> (1961),
and Merritt and Corey's <u>Christian Science and Liberty</u> (1970). The
following constitute a sample of similar works on Mormonism: Howe's
<u>Mormonism Unveiled</u> (1834), Hickman's <u>Brigham's Destroying Angel</u>
(1892), Beadle's <u>Polygamy or the Mysteries and Crimes of Mormonism</u>
(1882), Lyford's <u>The Mormon Problem</u> (1886), Folk's <u>The Mormon
Monster</u> (1900), Cannon and Kapp's <u>Brigham Young and His Mormon
Empire</u> (1913), Stuart Martin's <u>The Mystery of Mormonism</u> (1920),
Snowden's <u>The Truth About Mormonism</u> (1926), Harrison's <u>Mormonism Now
and Then</u> (1961), Cowan's <u>Mormon Claims Examined</u> (1975), and Fraser's

Joseph and the Golden Plates (1978). Comparable titles concerning
Jehovah's Witnesses include Haldeman's Millennial Dawnism: The
Blasphemous Religion Which Teaches the Annihilation of Jesus Christ
(n.d.), Eaton's The Millennial Dawn Heresy (1911), Ross' Some
Facts and More Facts about the Self-Styled "Pastor" Charles T.
Russell (1912), Shadduck's The Seven Thunders of the Millennial Dawn
(1928), P.E. Hewitt's Russellism Exposed (1941), Mayer's Jehovah's
Witnesses (1943), Axup's The Jehovah's Witnesses Unmasked (1959),
Dencher's The Watchtower Heresy versus the Bible (1961), Muller's
Meet Jehovah's Witnesses: Their Confusion, Doubts and Contradictions
(1964), and Gruss' Apostles of Denial: An Examination and Expose of
the History, Doctrines and Claims of the Jehovah's Witnesses (1970).

Among the nineteenth century's new religions the two which con-
tinue to attract the greatest criticism are the Mormons and Jehovah's Witnesses; by contrast, Seventh-Day Adventists and Christian
Scientists receive less attention. In the case of the Mormons,
organizations such as the Modern Microfilm Company and the Utah
Christian Tract Society are among the most prolific publishers of
anti-Mormon material. The former organization has published a
large number of books, reports and pamphlets investigating the
history, doctrines and contemporary activities of the Mormon Church.
For example, there have been published reports accusing the Mormons
of covering up the more unsavory aspects of their doctrines and
practices, Mormonism Like Watergate? (Tanner and Tanner, 1974);
linking Joseph Smith to get-rich schemes, most notably hunts for
buried treasure ("money digging") through the use of "peepstones"
(which permitted the searcher to locate hidden treasure), Joseph
Smith and Money Digging (Tanner and Tanner, 1970); linking the
Mormon Church to covert political operations, Mormon Spies, Hughes
and the C.I.A. (Tanner and Tanner, 1976); accusing the Mormons of
racism, Joseph Smith's Curse Upon the Negro (Tanner and Tanner,
n.d.); reviewing Joseph Smith's early brushes with the law, Joseph
Smith's Bainbridge, New York Court Trials (Walters, n.d.); and chal-
lenging the authenticity of the Book of Mormon, 3,914 Changes in the
Book of Mormon (Tanner and Tanner, n.d.), Joseph Smith's Strange
Account of the First Vision (Tanner and Tanner, n.d.), and The
Mormon Papyri Question (Tanner and Tanner, 1967). The Utah Chris-
tian Tract Society has published dozens of tracts with the same
types of themes. Sample titles include Is Mormonism Based on the
Bible? (Ramson, n.d.), Changes in Mormonism (Utah Christian Tract
Society, n.d.a), Mormonism, Can It Stand Investigation? (Utah Chris-
tian Tract Society, n.d.b), and Mormonism and the Bible, Does It
Measure Up? (Davenport, n.d.).

Other organizations such as Christian Apologetics: Research and
Information Service (CARIS), Personal Freedom Outreach, and Book
Fellowship have produced a similar flow of anti-Jehovah's Witnesses
literature. Sample titles from Personal Freedom Outreach (all without author identification or publication dates) include A True
Christian Presentation to a Jehovah's Witness, Why the Name Jehovah's Witnesses?, Whom Can You Trust? Jehovah's Witnesses: The
Christian View and The World's Most Dangerous Book. Representative
titles from the Book Fellowship include From the Watchtower Society

to God (Dencher, n.d.), <u>Jehovah's Witnesses and Prophecy</u> (Van Riper, n.d.) and <u>Jehovah's Witnesses on Trial</u> (Book Fellowship, n.d.).

1. Adair, James R., and Ted Miller, eds. <u>We Found Our Way Out</u>. Grand Rapids, MI: Baker Book House, 1964. 122 pp.

2. Algermissen, Konrad. <u>Christian Sects</u>. New York: Hawthorn Books, 1962. 128 pp.

3. Atkins, Gaius G. <u>Modern Cults Religious and Movements</u>. New York: Fleming H. Revell, 1923. 359 pp.

4. Axup, Edward J. <u>The Jehovah's Witnesses Unmasked</u>. New York: Greenwick, 1959. 77 pp.

5. Bach, Marcus. <u>Strangers at the Door</u>. New York: Abingdon, 1971. 189 pp.

6. Bach, Marcus. <u>Strange Sects and Curious Cults</u>. New York: Dodd, Mead, 1961. 277 pp.

7. Bach, Marcus. <u>Report to Protestants</u>. Indianapolis: Bobbs-Merrill, 1948. 277 pp.

8. Bach, Marcus. <u>They Have Found a Faith</u>. New York: Bobbs-Merrill, 1946. 300 pp.

9. Baltzly, Oliver D. <u>The Death Pot in Christian Science</u>. Burlington, IA: Lutheran Literary Board, 1935. 24 pp.

10. Bates, Ernest S., and John V. Dittenmore. <u>Mary Baker Eddy - The Truth and the Tradition</u>. New York: Alfred A. Knopf, 1932. 476 pp.

11. Beadle, John H. <u>Polygamy or the Mysteries and Crimes of Mormonism</u>. Philadelphia: The National Publishing Co., 1882. 572 pp.

12. Beam, Maurice. <u>Cults of America</u>. New York: MacFadden Books, 1964. 127 pp.

13. Bellwald, A.M. <u>Christian Science and the Catholic Faith</u>. New York: Macmillan, 1922. 269 pp.

14. Bergesen, B.E. <u>Christian Science</u>. Decorah, IA: Lutheran Publishing House, 1912. 16 pp.

15. Billington, Ray Allen. <u>The Protestant Crusade, 1800-1860: A Study of the Origins of American Nativism</u>. Gloucester, MA: Peter Smith, 1963. 514 pp.

16. Billington, Ray Allen. "Tentative Bibliography of Anti-Catholic Propaganda in the United States (1800-1860)." <u>Catholic Historical Review</u> 18 (January 1933): 492-513.

17. Binder, Louis R. Modern Religious Cults and Society. Boston:
    The Gorham Press, 1933. 299 pp.

18. Bird, Herbert S. Theology of Seventh-Day Adventism. Grand
    Rapids, MI: Eerdmans, 1961. 137 pp.

19. Bjornstad, James. Twentieth Century Prophesy. Minneapolis:
    Dimension Books/Bethany Fellowship Press, 1969. 140 pp.

20. Book Fellowship. Jehovah's Witnesses on Trial. North
    Syracuse, NY: Book Fellowship, n.d. 4 pp.

21. Braden, Charles S. These Also Believe: A Study of Modern
    American Cults and Minority Religious Movements. New York:
    Macmillan, 1949. 491 pp.

22. Braden, Charles S. "What Can We Learn from the Cults?"
    Religion in Life 14 (Winter 1944-45): 52-64.

23. Braden, Charles S. "Why Are the Cults Growing?" The Chris-
    tian Century 16 (January-February 1944): 45-47, 78-80, 108-
    110, 137-140.

24. Brodie, Fawn (McKay). No Man Knows My History. New York:
    Alfred A. Knopf, 1946. 476 pp.

25. Brooks, D.F. St. John versus Christian Science. Chicago:
    Christian Witness Co., 1902. 83 pp.

26. Brown, John Edward. Yea, Hath God Said? Or Science and Health.
    Siloam Springs, AR: International Federation Publishing Co.,
    n.d. 241 pp.

27. Bunkley, Josephine M. The Testimony of an Escaped Novice from
    the Sisterhood of St. Joseph, Emmetsburg, Md. New York:
    Harper and Brothers, 1855. 388 pp.

28. Cabot, Tracy. Inside the Cults. Los Angeles: Holloway House,
    1970. 252 pp.

29. Cannon, Frank J., and George L. Knapp. Brigham Young and His
    Mormon Empire. New York: Fleming H. Revell, 1913. 398 pp.

30. Canright, S.M. Seventh-Day Adventism Renounced, After an
    Experience of Twenty-Eight Years by a Prominent Minister and
    Writer of that Faith. Nashville, TN: Gospel Advocate Co.,
    1978. 418 pp.

31. Canright, S.M. Seventh-Day Adventism Refuted in a Nutshell.
    Grand Rapids: Baker Book House, 1962. 83 pp.

32. Christianity and the Cults. Glendale, CA: Gospel Light
    Publications, 1963. 97 pp.

33. Clark, Elmer T. The Small Sects in America. Rev. Ed. New
    York: Abingdon Press, 1965. 256 pp.

34. Clemens, Samuel L. (Mark Twain). Christian Science, With
    Notes Containing Corrections to Date. New York: Harper
    Brothers, 1907. 362 pp.

35. Cobb, Sanford H. The Rise of Religious Liberty in America.
    New York: The Macmillan Co., 1902. 541 pp.

36. Combs, George Hamilton. Some Latter-Day Religions. New York:
    Fleming H. Revell, 1899. 261 pp.

37. Cooksey, N.B. Christian Science Under the Search Light.
    Nashville, TN: Publishing House of the Methodist Episcopal
    Church, South, 1915. 106 pp.

38. Corey, Arthur. Behind the Scenes with the Metaphysicians.
    Los Angeles: DeVorss and Co., 1969. 261 pp.

39. Corey, Arthur. Christian Science Class Instructions. San
    Francisco, CA: The Farallon Press, 1945. 301 pp.

40. Cowan, Martin W. Mormon Claims Examined. Salt Lake City: The
    Author, 1975. 107 pp.

41. Cowdrey, Wayne L., Howard A. Davis and Donald R. Scales. Who
    Really Wrote the Book of Mormon? Santa Ana, CA: Vision
    House, 1977. 257 pp.

42. Dakin, Edwin F. Mrs. Eddy, the Biography of a Virginal Mind.
    New York: Charles Scribner's Sons, 1930. 563 pp.

43. Davenport, Larry. Mormonism and the Bible, Does It Measure Up?
    LaMesa, CA: Utah Christian Tract Society, n.d.

44. Davies, Horton. The Challenge of the Sects. Philadelphia: The
    Westminister Press, 1961. 176 pp.

45. Davies, Horton. Christian Deviations. Philadelphia: The
    Westminister Press, 1954. 133 pp.

46. Davis, David B. "Some Themes of Counter-Subversion: An
    Analysis of Anti-Masonic, Anti-Catholic and Anti-Mormon
    Literature." The Mississippi Valley Historical Review 67
    (September 1960): 205-24.

47. Dencher, Ted. Why I Left Jehovah's Witnesses. Fort
    Washington, PA: Christian Literature Crusade, 1966. 238 pp.

48. Dencher, Ted. The Watchtower Heresy versus the Bible.
    Chicago: Moody Press, 1961. 160 pp.

49. Dencher, Ted. From the Watchtower Society to God. North
    Syracuse, NY: Book Fellowship, n.d. 4 pp.

50. Desmond, Humphrey J. The A.P.A. Movement. Washington: New
     Century Press, 1912. Reprint Ed. New York: Arno Press,
     1969.

51. Dohan, James H. "Our State Constitutions and Religious
     Liberty." American Catholic Quarterly Review 60 (April
     1915): 276-322.

52. Doherty, J.E. What Is a Mormon? Liguori, MO: Liguorian
     Pamphlets, 1956. 24 pp.

53. Duncan, Homer. Heart to Heart Talks with Jehovah's Witnesses.
     Lubbock, TX: Missionary Crusader, n.d. 156 pp.

54. Eaton, E.L. The Millennial Dawn Heresy. Cincinnati: Jennings
     and Graham, 1911. 153 pp.

55. Ferguson, Charles W. The Confusion of Tongues. Garden City,
     NY: Doubleday, Doran and Co., 1931. 464 pp.

56. Folk, Edgar E. The Mormon Monster. New York: Fleming H.
     Revell, 1900. 372 pp.

57. Fraser, Gordon H. Joseph and the Golden Plates. Eugene, OR:
     The Author, 1978. 124 pp.

58. Fraser, Gordon H. Is Mormonism Christian? Chicago: Moody
     Colportage Library, 1957. 192 pp.

59. Frinkell, Samri. Spirit Mediums Exposed. New York: Metro-
     politan Fiction, 1930.

60. Froiseth, Jennie Anderson, ed. The Women of Mormonism; or, the
     Story of Polygamy as Told by the Victims Themselves.
     Detroit: C.G.G. Paine, 1882. 416 pp.

61. Gauss, J.H. God's Truth versus Man's Theories. St. Louis, MO:
     Faithful Words Publishing Co., n.d. 286 pp.

62. Gerstner, John H. The Theology of the Major Sects. Grand
     Rapids, MI: Baker Book House, 1960. 206 pp.

63. Green, Nelson, ed. Fifteen Years Among the Mormons: Being the
     Narrative of Mrs. Mary Ettie V. Smith. New York: Charles
     Scribner, 1958. 388 pp.

64. Gruss, Edmond C. The Jehovah's Witnesses and Prophetic Specu-
     lation. Nutley, NJ: Presbyterian and Reformed Publishing
     House, 1972. 127 pp.

65. Gruss, Edmond C. Apostles of Denial: An Examination and
     Expose of the History, Doctrines and Claims of the Jehovah's
     Witnesses. Nutley, NJ: Presbyterian and Reformed Publishing
     Co., 1970. 324 pp.

66. Haldeman, Isaac M. Christian Science in the Light of Holy Scripture. New York: Fleming H. Revell, 1909. 441 pp.

67. Haldeman, Isaac M. Millennial Dawnism: The Blasphemous Religion Which Teaches the Annihilation of Jesus Christ. Los Angeles: Bible Institute of Los Angeles, n.d. 84 pp.

68. Hansen, Klaus. Quest for Empire. East Lansing, MI: Michigan State University Press, 1967. 237 pp.

69. Harrison, G.T. Mormonism Now and Then. Helper, UT: The Author, 1961. 368 pp.

70. Haushalter, Walter M. Mrs. Eddy Purloins from Hegel. Boston: A.A. Beauchamp, 1936. 126 pp.

71. Hewitt, Joe. I Was Raised a Jehovah's Witness. Denver, CO: Accent Books, 1979. 191 pp.

72. Hewitt, P.E. Russellism Exposed. Grand Rapids, MI: Zondervan, 1941. 59 pp.

73. Hickman, William A. Brigham's Destroying Angel. New York: G.A. Crofutt, 1892. 219 pp.

74. Higham, John. Strangers in the Land: Patterns of American Nativism 1860-1925. New Brunswick, NJ: Rutgers University Press, 1955; Reprint Ed. New York: Atheneum, 1963. 431 pp.

75. Hoekema, Anthony A. The Four Major Cults. Grand Rapids, MI: William B. Eerdmans Publishing Co., 1963. 447 pp.

76. Howe, Eber D. Mormonism Unveiled. Painesville, OH: Reprinted and published by author, 1834. 290 pp.

77. Irvine, William C. Timely Warnings. New York: Lorzeaux Brothers, 1917. 225 pp.

78. Jennings, Alvin. Traditions of Men versus the Word of God. Ft. Worth, TX: Star Bible Publications, 1973. 160 pp.

79. Kildahl, J.N. The Chief Teachings of Christian Science Compared with the Teachings of the Bible. Minneapolis, MN: Ausburg Publishing House, 1920.

80. Kinney, Bruce. Mormonism - the Islam of America. New York: Fleming H. Revell, 1912. 190 pp.

81. Kinzer, Donald L. An Episode in Anti-Catholicism: The American Protective Association. Seattle, WA: University of Washington Press, 1964. 342 pp.

82. Koch, Kurt E. The Devil's Alphabet. Grand Rapids, MI: Kregel Publications, 1971. 156 pp.

83. Krull, V.H. A Common Sense View of Christian Science.
     Collegeville, IN: St. Joseph's Printing Office, 1914. 61 pp.

84. Larsen, Egon. Strange Sects and Cults. New York: Hart Pub-
     lishing Co., 1971. 245 pp.

85. Lewis, Gordon R. Confronting the Cults. Grand Rapids, MI:
     Baker Book House, 1966. 198 pp.

86. Lindsell, Harold, et al., eds. The Challenge of the Cults.
     Grand Rapids, MI: Zondervan Publishing House, 1961. 80 pp.

87. Lyford, C. The Mormon Problem. New York: Phillips and Hunt,
     1886. 323 pp.

88. Martin, Stuart. The Mystery of Mormonism. London: Odhams
     Press, 1920. 318 pp.

89. Martin, Walter R. The Kingdom of the Cults. Minneapolis, MN:
     Bethany Fellowship Press, 1965. 443 pp.

90. Martin, Walter R. The Maze of Mormonism. Santa Ana, CA:
     Vision House, 1962. 377 pp.

91. Martin, Walter R. The Truth About Seventh-Day Adventism.
     Grand Rapids, MI: Zondervan Publishing House, 1960. 254 pp.

92. Martin, Walter R. The Rise of the Cults. Rev. and Enl. Grand
     Rapids, MI: Zondervan Publishing House, 1957. 138 pp.

93. Martin, Walter R. The Christian and the Cults. Grand Rapids,
     MI: Zondervan Publishing House, 1956. 152 pp.

94. Martin, Walter R., and Norman H. Klann. The Christian Science
     Myth. Grand Rapids, MI: Zondervan Publishing House, 1955.
     209 pp.

95. Martin, Walter R., and Norman H. Klann. Jehovah of the Watch-
     tower. Grand Rapids, MI: Zondervan Publishing House, 1953.
     221 pp.

96. Marty, Martin E. Righteous Empire: The Protestant Experience
     in America. New York: Dial Press, 1970. 295 pp.

97. Mathison, Richard R. Faiths, Cults and Sects of America.
     Indianapolis, IN: Bobbs-Merrill Co., 1960. 384 pp.

98. Maury, Rueben. The Wars of the Godly. New York: R.M. McBride
     and Co., 1928. 318 pp.

99. Mayer, Frederick E. Jehovah's Witnesses. St. Louis, MO:
     Concordia Publishing House, 1943. 52 pp.

100. McCorkle, William P. Christian Science or the False Christ of

1866. Richmond, VA: Presbyterian Committee of Publication, 1899. 321 pp.

101. McEleveen, Floyd. Will the Saints Go Marching In? Glendale, CA: Regal, 1977. 175 pp.

102. Merritt, Robert E., and Arthur Corey. Christian Science and Liberty. Los Angeles: DeVorss and Co., 1970. 224 pp.

103. Monk, Maria. Awful Disclosures of the Hotel Dieu Nunnery. New York, 1836; Reprint Ed. Hamden, CT: Archon Books, 1962.

104. Moore, Rev. A. Lincoln. Christian Science – Its Manifold Attraction. New York: Theodore E. Schulte Publishing Co., 1906. 81 pp.

105. Muller, Albert. Meet Jehovah's Witnesses: Their Confusion, Doubts and Contradictions. Pulaski, WI: Franciscan Publishers, 1964.

106. Myers, Gustavus. History of Bigotry in the United States. New York: Capricorn Books, 1960. 474 pp.

107. O'Donnell, Elliot. The Menace of Spiritualism. New York: Frederick A. Stokes, 1920.

108. O'Hair, J.C. Isms and Schisms. Chicago: J.C. O'Hair, n.d. 84 pp.

109. Orrmont, Arthur. Love Cults and Faith Healers. New York: Ballantine Books, 1961. 192 pp.

110. Personal Freedom Outreach. Jehovah's Witnesses: The Christian View. St. Louis, MO: Personal Freedom Outreach, n.d.a. 4 pp.

111. Personal Freedom Outreach. A True Christian Presentation to a Jehovah's Witness. St. Louis, MO: Personal Freedom Outreach, n.d.b. 4 pp.

112. Personal Freedom Outreach. Whom Can You Trust? St. Louis, MO: Personal Freedom Outreach, n.d.c. 4 pp.

113. Personal Freedom Outreach. Why the Name Jehovah's Witnesses? St. Louis, MO: Personal Freedom Outreach, n.d.d. 4 pp.

114. Personal Freedom Outreach. The World's Most Dangerous Book. St. Louis, MO: Personal Freedom Outreach, n.d.e. 4 pp.

115. Petersen, Lamar. Problems in Mormon Text. Salt Lake City: Modern Microfilm Co., 1957. 22 pp.

116. Petersen, William J. Those Curious New Cults. New Caanan, CT: Keats Publishing, 1973. 272 pp.

117. Ramson, Ira T. Is Mormonism Based on the Bible? LaMesa, CA:
     Utah Christian Tract Society, n.d. 16 pp.

118. Reed, Theresa, R. Six Months in a Convent. Boston: Russell,
     Odiorne and Metcalf, 1835. 192 pp.

119. Rhodes, Arnold B., ed. The Church Faces the Isms. New York:
     Abingdon Press, 1958. 304 pp.

120. Ricci, Scipio de. Female Converts: Secrets of Nunneries
     Disclosed. New York: D. Appleton and Co., 1834. 265 pp.

121. Riddle, T. Wilkinson. Christian Science in the Light of Holy
     Scripture. London: Marshall, Morgan and Scott, 1931.
     96 pp.

122. Ridenour, Fritz, ed. So What's the Difference? Glendale, CA:
     Regal Books, 1967. 168 pp.

123. Riley, Woodbridge, W. Frederick Peabody, and Charles E.
     Humiston. The Faith, the Falsity and the Failure of Chris-
     tian Science. New York: Fleming H. Revell, 1925. 408 pp.

124. Robertson, Irvine. What the Cults Believe. Chicago: Moody,
     1966. 128 pp.

125. Ropp, Harry L. The Mormon Papers. Downers Grove, IL: Inter-
     Varsity Press, 1977. 100 pp.

126. Ross, John J. Some Facts and More Facts about the Self-Styled
     "Pastor" Charles T. Russell. Philadelphia: Philadelphia
     School of the Bible, 1912. 48 pp.

127. Sanders, J. Oswald. Heresies and Cults. Rev. and Enl. Grand
     Rapids, MI: Zondervan Publishing House, 1962.

128. Schnell, William J. 30 Years a Watchtower Slave. Grand
     Rapids, MI: Baker Book House, 1971. 192 pp.

129. Seldes, Gilbert. The Stammering Century. New York: John Day
     Co., 1928. 414 pp.

130. Shadduck, B.H. The Seven Thunders of Millennial Dawn. Third
     Edition, Ashtabula, OH: Homo Publishing Co., 1928.

131. Sheldon, Henry C. Christian Science So-Called. New York:
     Eaton and Maino, 1913. 102 pp.

132. Shields, T.T. Russellism or Rutherfordism. Toronto, Canada:
     The Gospel Witness, n.d. 72 pp.

133. Shook, Charles A. The True Origin of Mormon Polygamy.
     Cincinnati, OH: Standard, 1914. 213 pp.

134. Shook, Charles A. The True Origin of the Book of Mormon.

Cincinnati, OH: Standard, 1914. 187 pp.

135. Shook, Charles A. Cumorah Revisited. Cincinnati, OH:
Standard, 1910. 589 pp.

136. Sister Agnes; or, the Captive Nun; a Picture of Convent Life.
New York: n.p., 1854.

137. Smith, Joseph J. The Impending Conflict Between Romanism and
Protestantism in the United States. New York:
E. Goodenough, 1871. 288 pp.

138. Smith, Paul B. Other Gospels. London, England: Marshall,
Morgan and Scott, 1970. 160 pp.

139. Smith, Samuel B. The Wonderful Adventures of a Lady of the
French Nobility, and the Intrigues of a Romish Priest, her
Confessor to Seduce and Murder Her. New York: Office of the
Downfall of Babylon, 1836. 108 pp.

140. Snowden, James H. The Truth About Mormonism. New York:
George H. Doran Co., 1926. 369 pp.

141. Snowden, James H. The Truth About Christian Science.
Philadelphia: Westminister Press, 1920. 313 pp.

142. Spittler, Russell P. Cults and Isms. Grand Rapids, MI: Baker
Book House, 1962. 143 pp.

143. Starkes, M. Thomas. Confronting Popular Cults. Nashville,
TN: Broadman Press, 1972. 122 pp.

144. Studdert-Kennedy, Hugh A. Christian Science and Organized
Religion. Los Gatos, CA: Farallon Foundation, 1910;
Revised Ed., 1961. 170 pp.

145. Talbot, Louis T. What's Wrong with Seventh-Day Adventism?
Findlay, OH: Dunham Publishing Co., 1956. 46 pp.

146. Tanis, Edward J. What the Sects Teach. Grand Rapids, MI:
Baker Book House, 1958. 89 pp.

147. Tanner, Jerald, and Sandra Tanner. Did Spaulding Write the
Book of Mormon? Salt Lake City, UT: Modern Microfilm Co.,
1977. 105 pp.

148. Tanner, Jerald, and Sandra Tanner. Mormon Spies, Hughes and
the C.I.A. Salt Lake City, UT: Modern Microfilm Co.,1976.
95 pp.

149. Tanner, Jerald, and Sandra Tanner. Mormonism Like Watergate?
Salt Lake City, UT: Modern Microfilm Co., 1974. 27 pp.

150. Tanner, Jerald, and Sandra Tanner. Mormonism - Shadow or
Reality? Enlarged Edition, Salt Lake City, UT: Modern

Microfilm Co., 1972. 587 pp.

151. Tanner, Jerald, and Sandra Tanner. Falsification of Joseph
      Smith's History. Salt Lake City, UT: Modern Microfilm Co.,
      1971. 23 pp.

152. Tanner, Jerald, and Sandra Tanner. Joseph Smith and Money
      Digging. Salt Lake City, UT: Modern Microfilm Co., 1970.

153. Tanner, Jerald, and Sandra Tanner. The Case Against Mormon-
      ism, I. Salt Lake City, UT: Modern Microfilm Co., 1967.
      191 pp.

154. Tanner, Jerald, and Sandra Tanner. The Case Against Mormon
      ism, II. Salt Lake City, UT: Modern Microfilm Co., 1967.
      144 pp.

155. Tanner, Jerald, and Sandra Tanner. The Mormon Papyri Ques-
      tion. Salt Lake City, UT: Modern Microfilm Co., 1967.

156. Tanner, Jerald, and Sandra Tanner. Joseph Smith's Curse upon
      the Negro. Salt Lake City, UT: Modern Microfilm Co., n.d.a.

157. Tanner, Jerald, and Sandra Tanner. Joseph Smith's Strange
      Account of the First Vision. Salt Lake City, UT: Modern
      Microfilm Co., n.d.b.

158. Tanner, Jerald, and Sandra Tanner. 3,914 Changes in the Book
      of Mormon. Salt Lake City, UT: Modern Microfilm Co., n.d.c.

159. Target, George W. Under the Christian Carpet. Brighton,
      England: Clifton Books, 1969. 207 pp.

160. Tenney, Rev. Herbert Melville. Christian Science, Its Truths
      and Errors. Cleveland, OH: The Burrows Brothers Co., 1888.
      62 pp.

161. Thomas, Stan. Jehovah's Witnesses and What They Believe.
      Grand Rapids, MI: Zondervan Publishing House, 1967. 159 pp.

162. Thurston, Herbert. The Church and Spiritualism. Milwaukee,
      WI: Bruce, 1933.

163. Tomsett, Valarie. Watchtower Chaos. London: Lakeland, 1974.
      112 pp.

164. Utah Christian Tract Society. Changes in Mormonism. LaMesa,
      CA: Utah Christian Tract Society, n.d.a. 23 pp.

165. Utah Christian Tract Society. Mormonism: Can It Stand Inves-
      tigation? LaMesa, CA: Utah Christian Tract Society, n.d.b.
      23 pp.

166. Van Baalen, Jan K. Christianity Versus the Cults. Grand

Rapids, MI: William B. Eerdman's Publishing Co., 1956.
136 pp.

167. Van Baalen, Jan K. The Gist of the Cults. Rev. and Enl.
Grand Rapids, MI: William B. Eerdman's Publishing Co., 1944.
71 pp.

168. Van Baalen, Jan K. The Chaos of Cults. Grand Rapids, MI:
Willaim B. Eerdman's Publishing Co., 1938. 414 pp.

169. Van Buren, James G. Cults Challenge the Church. Cincinnati,
OH: Standard Publishing Co., 1965. 128 pp.

170. Van Riper, Gary. Jehovah's Witnesses and Prophecy. North
Syracuse, NY: Book Fellowship, n.d. 7 pp.

171. Walters, Wesley. Joseph Smith's Bainbridge, New York Court
Trials. Salt Lake City, UT: Modern Microfilm Co., n.d.

172. Ward, Maria. Female Life Among the Mormons: A Narrative of
Many Years Personal Experience, By the Wife of a Mormon
Elder, Recently Returned from Utah. New York: Derby and
Jackson, 1857. 449 pp.

173. Whalen, William J. Minority Religion in America. Staten
Island, NY: Alba House, 1972.

174. Whalen, William J. Faiths for the Few. Milwaukee, WI: Bruce
Publishing Co., 1963. 201 pp.

175. Whalen, William J. Armageddon Around the Corner. New York:
John Day Co., 1962. 249 pp.

176. Whalen, William J. Separated Bretheren. Milwaukee, WI:
Bruce Publishing Co., 1958; Revised Ed., 1972. 287 pp.

177. Whalen, William J. Strange Gods. Huntington, IN: Our Sunday
Visitors, 1891. 130 pp.

178. Whitehead, John. The Illusions of Christian Science.
Boston: The Garden Press, 1907. 247 pp.

179. Woodbury, Josephine C. War in Heaven. Boston: S. Usher
Printer, 1897. 69 pp.

180. Woodrow, Ralph. Babylon Mystery Religion. Riverside, CA:
Ralph Woodrow Evangelistic Association, 1966. 177 pp.

181. Wright, Gerald. Perversions and Prejudices of the New World
Translation. Ft. Worth, TX: Star Bible and Tract Corpor-
ation, 1975. 80 pp.

182. Wyrick, Herbert M. Seven Religious Isms. 2nd Ed., Grand
Rapids, MI: Zondervan Publishing House, 1940. 99 pp.

183. Young, Ann Eliza. <u>Wife No. 19; or, the Story of a Life in</u>
      <u>Bondage, Being a Complete Expose of Mormonism.</u> Hartford,
      CT: Dustin, Gilman and Co., 1875. 605 pp.

CHAPTER TWO

THE AMERICAN ANTI-CULT MOVEMENT: A BRIEF HISTORICAL REVIEW

Despite its mounting vocalness and political impact during the
1970´s and into the 1980´s, there have been remarkably few materials
of a scholarly nature published—or readily available to scholars—
concerning the current North American anti-cult (or anti-"new religions") movement. Indeed, except for a handful of studies that
touch on it only tangentially (Lofland, 1977), locally (Harper,
1981a, 1981b, 1979), critically (APRL, 1977), apologetically
(Patrick and Dulack, 1977), or in relatively ahistorical terms
(Enroth, 1977), little has appeared apart from our own historical or
organizational studies on the subject (see Bromley and Shupe, 1981,
1980, 1979, forthcoming; Bromley, Busching and Shupe, 1982, 1981;
Shupe and Bromley, 1982a, 1982b, 1981, 1980a, 1980b, 1980c, 1979;
Shupe, Spielmann and Stigall, 1980, 1977). Even less is known about
anti-cult activities in Europe (Beckford n.d.; Hardin, 1981; Shupe
Hardin and Bromley, 1981).

Moreover, to the undoubted dismay of future scholars, many
early documents of the movement (such as memos, newsletters,
pamphlets, and so forth), which librarians refer to as "fugitive"
materials, were not systematically preserved. The ACM, after all,
in those early days (particularly when resources and self-identity
as a social movement were low) was totally preoccupied with its
goals of mobilizing unofficial public opinion and official bureaucratic sanctions against a coterie of marginal religious groups
loosely referred to as <u>cults</u>. Success in achieving such goals was
(from its standpoint) not far off it was hoped, and at any rate the
needs of historians and scholars of social movements were certainly
not uppermost in the minds of ACM activists. Add to this preoccupation a low motivation for systematically filing away copies of
important early documents the fact that many materials were uncopyrighted, unbound and often crudely reproduced (i.e., xeroxed or
mimeographed), and it becomes apparent why many such documents have
been lost or are in a precarious, often inaccessible, state.[1]

[1]   In recent years, a number of separate research institutes dedicated to preserving such materials have been formed. Most of our
own personal collection has been put on file with the New Religions
Research Collection of the Graduate Theological Union Library in
Berkeley, California, in the hope of making many early "fugitive"
materials more readily available to future scholars.

The brief history of the ACM which follows is therefore based
as much on our own observations, interviews, accumulated oral history and sheer anecdotal experience as it is on retrievable or ac-
cessible publications. However, we also refer readers to our recent
compilation of important representative ACM publications, many of
them "fugitive" documents, which form the basis for many of the assertions below (Shupe and Bromley, 1980a). Here we want to describe
generally the North American ACM in terms of its (1) origins, (2)
proliferation, and (3) attempts to enlist allies in its crusades.

ORIGINS

There is little question that the ACM began as a reaction
against the youthful experimentation and countercultural involvement
in the late 1960´s which spilled over into unconventional religious
participation during the 1970´s. A number of sociologists (Bellah,
1976; Cox, 1977; Doress and Porter, 1981; Foss and Larkin, 1979;
Glock, 1977; Hargrove, 1976; Hunter, 1981; Needleman, 1973; Prince,
1974) have analyzed the later redirection of the focus of much
youthful idealism and discontent away from the great secular movements of the former decade (e.g., civil rights, poverty, ecology,
anti-Vietnam War) to more introspective spiritual efforts. Downton
(1979), in his study of Divine Light Mission converts and apostates,
described a situation in which many youths became disillusioned with
the essentially shallow hedonism of the psychedelic drug subculture
but yet remained alienated from mainline "straight" culture and many
of its values. Mystical religion (often oriental or some synthesis
of East and West), which was in many ways compatible with countercultural values and perspectives, offered an acceptable way out of
the dilemma. While reliable numbers of just how many young adults
became involved in such "new" religious groups are of course unknown, it would seem that significant numbers of youths at least
came into some contact with them. Not many stayed long to pursue
careers in such movements and organizations as the Unification
Church, the International Society for Krishna Consciousness, the
Children of God and the Divine Light Mission, but enough did to
increase significantly the ranks of specific groups and provide the
general public--through the mass media--with the impression that a
new type of popular youth movement had now replaced the old.

While at first glance it might appear logical that a shift in
emphasis away from social protest and revolutionary political-
economic reform to religious idealism might have stimulated considerably less alarm on the part of parents and social observers, in
fact the opposite was the case. Many of these religious groups
constituted what we have referred to elsewhere (Bromley and Shupe,
1979) as "world-transforming movements" with rather sweeping agenda
of their own for changing values and political economies and, perhaps more importantly, communal (occasionally even monastic) lifestyles that removed youthful members from conventional career or
educational domestic trajectories. Thus, the furor which youths
enlisting in such radical groups for indefinite periods of time
caused both their families and the conventional churches that felt
explicitly challenged became the impetus for the formation of a

heterogeneous but identifiable countermovement.

This countermovement may be thought of as possessing three related but not necessarily always congenial components:

First, and most important, were the various local and regional
familial associations which coalesced, beginning in the early
1970's, as individual distraught families of youths involved in unconventional religions, through word of mouth and media-created
awareness, came to learn of others in similar predicaments. Some
former members of "new" religions, angry at what they retrospecti-
vely interpreted as their manipulation and exploitation at the hands
of various group leaders, sympathetic professionals and some friends
also constituted such associations' memberships, but immediate
family members made up the dues-paying heart of these organizations.
The fundamental goal of all such organizations (which went by such
expressive names as Love our Children, Inc., Citizens Engaged in
Reuniting Children, Inc., Citizens Organized for the Public Awareness of Cults, Inc., and Texans United for Freedom) was to restore
earlier family relations and patterns of parental influence which
had been torn asunder by youthful members giving up their college
educations, promising jobs, ordinary lifestyles and at least nominal
religious affiliations in order to join groups that were frequently
utopian, communal, ascetic and bizarre by middle-class standards.
Parents felt acute, galling frustration to see (from their perspective) their offspring squander idealism and energy on hopelessly un-
realistic cults and sects and seemingly turn over their autonomy and
the freedom to determine their own destinies to charismatic leaders
who were frequently authoritarian and foreign. Failing to appeal
successfully to their adult-age children to abandon such quixotic,
ascetic movements, and often unable to persuade governmental and law
enforcement officials to intervene for them, such persons turned
to themselves for mutual solace and to a gradually accumulating concentration of pooled resources that, after many false starts, began
to achieve some measure of political influence and public credibility by the late 1970's.

The second ACM component was one less organized than the parental anti-cult associations and more ad hoc, or vigilante-style, in
its philosophy and strategies: namely, that contingent generally
known as the deprogrammers. The definition and practice of deprogramming began in 1971 in the city of San Diego by a California
state social worker (albeit with no formal social work training)
named Theodore Roosevelt "Ted" Patrick, Jr. By his own account
(Patrick and Dulack, 1977), Patrick first became aware of the
"problem" of psychologically manipulative "cults" when his teenage
son and nephew displayed disoriented behavior following an encounter
with Children of God street missionaries. Soon after, his office
was allegedly inundated with the complaints of infuriated and distraught parents. A visitation to the group's San Diego camp, which
Patrick claimed debilitated and nearly "brainwashed" him into a
zombie-like state, convinced him of its pernicious nature. In a
short time he found that parents with offspring in other unconventional religious groups brought forth similar grievances. Concluding that these young adults had been "programmed," or coercively

and/or manipulatively indoctrinated so as to impair their rational
thought processes and free will, Patrick began to "deprogram" (i.e.,
liberate, or force psychological release of) their thinking abili-
ties in spite of their protests (i.e., coercively, including forcible abductions from their respective religious groups and prolonged
restraint as needed).

The perspective, or "deprogramming ideology," which emerged and
was soon adopted by many families, ran as follows:

> (1) that a person has experienced, through deception,
> hypnosis/drugs, or a lowering of normally resistant
> rationality by special techniques of deprivation, con-
> version to a new religious creed; (2) that after this
> conversion, the person is psychologically "enslaved"
> and is unable to act independently of a manipulator's
> directives; and (3) that a process reversal, or de-
> programming of the "programmed" victim, is necessary
> to restore free will and rational choice. Since
> these faculties are fundamental elements of the
> American values of individual pursuit of happiness
> and growth, deprogramming takes on not only presumed
> therapeutic, but also moral, legitimacy. (Shupe,
> Spielmann, and Stigall, 1974:944)

By the mid-1970's Patrick had targeted a wide variety of purported sectarian and cultic groups, including Mormons, Catholics and
agnostics, as being in need of his treatment; indeed, in essence,
his services as deprogrammer were for hire to any parent unhappy
with the direction that the latter's offspring was currently pursuing and who could afford the increasingly expensive fees. There is
now no question that this practice became immensely profitable not
only to Patrick but also to his imitators (Shupe and Bromley, 1980a:
135-41).

Deprogramming soon came to refer to a process of exit from
new religions considerably broader than Patrick originally en-
visioned. For example, any time parents, clergy, relatives and so
forth talked a younger family member into reconsidering his or her
new "total" religious commitment and eventually caused the youth to
defect, a successful deprogramming was credited. Rabbi Maurice
Davis, founder of the ACM group Citizens Engaged in Reuniting Families, termed this non-coercive procedure "reevaluation." There is no
reliable way of knowing how frequently this dialogue-creation method
met with success as Patrick himself claimed (undoubtedly for oc-
cupational reasons) publicly that his was the only feasible way of
extracting a person from a "cult." It is likely, however, that "re-
evaluation" was a successful procedure in removing many young adults
from "new" religions, second only to defections prompted by their
own disillusionment and cooling enthusiasm. Nevertheless, Patrick's
meaning for the term "deprogramming" remained as the popular definition.

Deprogrammers existed in an uneasy exchange with the anti-cult associations. The latter groups served as conduits to refer families to the deprogrammers, and the deprogrammers served to confirm the associations' worst fears and raison d'etre. Yet anti-cult associations rarely embraced or endorsed the deprogrammers openly, for the latters' fundamentally illegal actions (i.e., forcibly removing and restraining legal adults from unconventional religious groups) gave them a patently discrediting reputation. As the "cults" in question grew, as civil liberties implications of the controversy emerged and as anti-cult associations learned that quashing the activities of various controversial groups was not to be achieved overnight, sympathies for much of the deprogramming ideology remained, but more bureaucratic or lobbying--as opposed to vigilante, coercive--tactics came to accompany it.

The third ACM component consisted of religious denominations (particularly conservative Christian ones but numbering also Jewish groups) which perceived in various "new" religions a dual threat. First, groups such as the Unification Church, the Children of God and the Jews for Jesus with their respectively radical, often millenarian elitist theologies, presented the challenge of heresy. Heresy was a concept that had fallen into disuse by many religious groups, accustomed as they were to the relativist live-and-let-live climate of modern American religious pluralism. The "new" religions, however, reawakened a sense that the boundaries of acceptable religious innovation needed to be reexamined and even redefined. A second threat to the religious institutions came indirectly: given an intimate symbiosis between churches and families who constituted the formers' financial and social units, it was natural that threats to the continuity and authority of families also became threats to religious interests. The heresy most churches were well equipped to rebut. They had established theological tests, organizational barriers and the time-honored weight of respectability to prevent newcomers from automatically gaining legitimacy. Disruption of family patterns proved more troublesome. In most instances, the churches provided families with at least moral support and often donated facilities to anti-cult organizations. Some church leaders themselves even became outspoken anti-cult activists.

Their three components, then--the family based anti-cult associations, the various vigilantes and entrepreneurs who engaged in deprogramming and religious groups (particularly Jewish and evangelical Christian ones)--constituted the emerging countermovement against new religions in the 1970's.

PROLIFERATION OF THE ACM

In early 1972, when the first anti-cult group of angry parents and family members formed, membership was literally only a handful of persons. By mid-decade the total active anti-cult membership in the United States may have numbered as many as 3000 to 4000 persons in several dozen large and small associations (Shupe and Bromley, 1980a:106). Membership always fluctuated since one widespread pattern was for rank and file members to become inactive not long after

their son or daughter abandoned the unconventional religion (for
whatever reason), and turnover in such groups was high; thus our
estimate must remain tentative.

There are a number of reasons for the growth of the ACM, particularly of the anti-cult associations. Undoubtedly one basic but
often overlooked reason is the real increase in the mass of families
affected as oriental and home-grown cults and sects engaged in aggressive recruiting of young adults in urban areas and on college
campuses. Many of these youths were the sons and daughters of af-
fluent middle- or upper-middle-class parents, and their defections
from conventional career or domestic trajectories resulted in an
enormous pool of influential articulate parents suffering feelings
of relative deprivation and breached parental-child reciprocity.
These parents did not suffer these feelings in silence or silent
resignation. Such human drama is also the stuff that press and
electronic media features are made of, and there soon grew up a
natural symbiosis between the two institutions. By the mid 1970's a
media-prompted stereotype of heartbroken families, manipulative cult
leaders, blissfully naive young cult members and rapidly increasing
cult or sect growth filled press and television coverage. This
media reporting, in turn, had the effect of alerting individual families to others similarly caught in the generational dilemma, offering them the opportunity to learn of and contact one another. Formation of local groups was followed on an ad hoc basis by the creation of regional counterparts and soon led to attempts to form
national umbrella organizations aimed at combatting cults.

Another reason for the growth of the ACM can be found in the
guilt-expiating interpretation of the situation provided by perceiv-
ing "cult" recruitment as the product of a sinister brainwashing
process. It held enormous attraction for confused families of young
"cult" members. Drawing on the post-Korean War literature detail-
ing oriental communist methods of attitude change (e.g., Hunter,
1960, 1953; Lifton, 1961, 1957; Sargant, 1957; Schein, Schneider and
Backer, 1961), families discovered a ready-made explanation for
their offsprings' unconventional behavior that cast no stigma either
on them, the parents, or on their adult children. All blame could
be pinned on "exploitive, manipulative" groups that "preyed" on
idealistic young adults. The deprogramming solution, as an antidote
to the purported brainwashing process, at least held out the possibility of a relatively inexpensive, short alternative to conventional psychotherapy. Many families were faced with accounting for
their offsprings' conversions, and the ACM provided them one of the
least painful, most face-saving explanations: neither they nor their
loved ones were responsible for what otherwise might be interpreted
as bad judgment, youthful naivete and gullibility, or plain impetu-
ousness. It was an explanation readily adopted, complete with the
mantle of scientific legitimacy, which justified involvement in a
countermovement directed against unconventional religions.

A third reason for the expansion of the ACM can be traced to
the publicized activites of the unconventional religions themselves
(aside from their recruitment of middle-class youth which increased
societal suspicion and further alarmed church and parental groups).

Prominent among such activities were the Unification Church's bla-
tant attempts during the mid-1970's to lobby U.S. Congressmen for
increased military aid to the South Korean dictatorship of Park
Chung Hee and its outspoken (but futile) defense of Richard Nixon
during the Watergate investigation; the Church of Scientology's in-
filtration of certain government offices to pilfer documents and
information relevant to the latter's investigations of Scientology
during the mid-to-late 1970's; well touted events such as the Divine
Light Mission's Millennium '73 rally at the Houston Astrodome (which
ended in financial catastrophe) and the Unification Church's Bicentennial God Bless America campaign in 1976; and the seemingly
ubiquitous fundraisers of the Unification Church and the Hare
Krishna in airports, parking lots, city streets, shopping malls,
state fairs and other public places. This impression of an omni-
present growing force in religion, politics and even mundane daily
life, cultivated ironically by both a critical media and the "cults"
themselves, fed general stereotypes and prejudices, contributing to
a broad toleration for repressive solutions to the "cult problem"
and a climate of fear that led many parents to become immediately
alarmed upon learning that an offspring had joined one of these
religious groups.

ACM ATTEMPTS TO ENLIST ALLIES

The anti-cult associations, made up largely of parents and ex-
"cult" members, possessed little power to redress their grievances
directly except through occasional abductions and coercive deprogrammings or through largely ineffective lawsuits by individual families against wealthy groups such as the Unification Church or the
Hare Krishnas. Therefore, they looked to other institutions not
just for sympathy but mainly for tangible action in support of ACM
goals. The religious institution, as we noted, has always depended
heavily on the nuclear family unit for its very existence and has
had such extensive experience countering "heresies" that it fast became a natural ally. The media, while not necessarily a committed
ally, at least functioned as one for some time as it conveyed almost
exclusively the anti-cult perspective in its treatments of new religions.

Education gave some limited support. Anti-cult activists, a
good number of whom were professional educators themselves, did man-
age on a local level to make administrators and teachers more wary
of the "cult" presence in American communities and to infuse ACM
ideology into classroom lecture content when the topic of new religions came up. And they did secure policy resolutions and sometimes
even information-disseminating workshop support from some state and
national Parent Teacher Association groups. But in secondary education they ran up against the understandable inclination of intellectuals either to be more culturally relativist about new religions or
to study such groups first-hand. Academics in general did not lend
their names and efforts to the anti-cult cause so readily, though
there were of course exceptions. In fact, some of the most damaging
evidence against the arguments of the anti-cultists came from the
field research of scholars in social science and religious studies.

The most reluctant institution to aid the ACM was the polity
which did acknowledge the tragic dilemma of parents with adult
children in groups that they sincerely believed to be harmful but
which also had to deal with the long-run constitutional implications
of making policy regarding some immediate complaints and minority
religions. From the politicans´ and bureaucrats´ standpoint the
anti-cult associations (and their allies) were only one small segment of an enormous conglomeration of competing interest groups.
For years, the ACM groups petitioned federal and state legislators
to create investigatory committees, hearings, resolutions and laws
to cope with what they pictured as a nationwide crisis growing at a
menacing rate. At first government officials merely listened po-
litely to their irate constituents, "cooling them out" with resolutions that were predictably pigeonholed in committees and rarely
even voted on. But as anti-cultists learned to appreciate the dynamics of interest group politics, they became more adept at mobilizing sympathy and support from politicians. This was particularly
true after the People´s Temple massacre at Jonestown, Guyana, in
November, 1978. While actual passage, as opposed to simple sponsorship, of any anti-cult legislation still remained a rarity by the
early 1980´s (because of the enormous constitutional obstacles and
civil libertarian groups´ defense of the unconventional religions
involved), it has indisputably become more of a possibility than
ever before.

                          THE ACM IN RETROSPECT

     Even with its very modest legislative victories and the indif-
ference to the whole "cult controversy" of most Americans, there is
little question that the ACM succeeded in discrediting groups such
as the Unification Church and the Hare Krishnas to a much greater
extent than any of the latters´ actions by themselves could have
done. Some "bad press" treatment by the media and governmental
notice would likely have occurred anyway (e.g., as after Scientology
infiltrated several federal agencies during the late 1970´s and bur-
glarized an office, or during Sun Myung Moon´s brief and disastrous
dabbling in Washington politics during the Watergate and Koreagate
scandals). But the widely accepted folklore generated and tireless-
ly disseminated by anti-cult organizations that portrayed all new
religions as "cults," all their recruitment practices as "brainwashing" and all unconventional religious leaders as charlatans or worse
served to reduce dramatically the chances that these new religions
might attract substantial numbers of persons, significantly change
society´s dominant institutions or easily institutionalize themselves as they settled in the American scene. Many of the groups
wanted to devote members´ time to promulgating their utopian, opti-
mistic, change-oriented messages, but instead they were forced to
direct enormous amounts of energy and other resources away from
their primary goals in order to defend themselves. This fact illustrates the tremendous potential for repression that countermovements
(and entire social orders) can draw upon even in a time and culture
of general tolerance and political neutrality.

184. APRL (Alliance for the Preservation of Religious Liberties), Deprogramming: Documenting the Issue. New York: APRL in conjunction with the American Civil Liberties Union, (1977). 251 pp.

185. Beckford, James. "Cults, Controversy and Control: A Comparative Analysis of the Problems Posed by New Religions in the Federal Republic of Germany and France." Unpublished manuscript. Durham, England: University of Durham, n.d. 28 pp.

186. Bellah, Robert N. "New Religious Consciousness and the Crisis in Modernity." The New Religious Consciousness. Edited by Charles Y. Glock and Robert N. Bellah. Berkeley, CA: University of California Press, 1976, pp. 333-352.

187. Bromley, David G., Bruce C. Busching and Anson D. Shupe, Jr. "The Unification Church and the American Family: Strain, Conflict and Repression." Essays on Society from the Perspective of New Religious Movements. Edited by Eileen Barker. New York: The Edwin Mellen Press, 1982.

188. Bromley, David G., Bruce C. Busching and Anson D. Shupe, Jr. "Repression of Religious Cults." Research in Social Movements, Conflict and Change. Edited by Louis Kriesberg. Greenwich, CT: JAI Press, 1981, pp. 25-46.

189. Bromley, David G., and Anson D. Shupe, Jr. Strange Gods: The Great American Cult Scare. Boston: Beacon Press, 1981. 192 pp.

190. Bromley, David G., and Anson D. Shupe, Jr. "Evolving Foci in Participant Observation: Research as an Emerging Process." Fieldwork Experience: Qualitative Approaches to Social Research. Edited by William B. Shaffir, Robert A. Stebbins and Allan Turowetz. New York: St. Martin's Press, 1980, pp. 191-203.

191. Bromley, David G., and Anson D. Shupe, Jr. "Moonies" in America: Cult, Church and Crusade. Beverly Hills, CA: Sage Publications, 1979. 269 pp.

192. Bromley, David G., and Anson D. Shupe, Jr. "Repression and the Decline of Social Movements: The Case of the New Religions." Social Movements of the 1960's and the 1970's. Edited by Jo Freeman. San Francisco: Longman Publishers, forthcoming.

193. Cox, Harvey. Turning East. New York: Simon and Schuster, 1977. 192 pp.

194. Doress, Irvin, and Jack N. Porter. "Kids in Cults." In Gods We Trust: New Patterns of Religious Pluralism in America. Edited by Thomas Robbins and Dick Anthony. New Brunswick, NJ: Transaction Books, 1981, pp. 297-302.

195. Downton, James V., Jr. Sacred Journeys: The Conversion of
     Young Americans to Divine Light Mission. New York: Columbia
     University Press, 1979. 245 pp.

196. Enroth, Ronald R. "Cult/Countercult." Eternity, November
     1977, pp. 18-24, 32-25.

197. Foss, Daniel A., and R.W. Larkin. "The Roar of the Lemming:
     Youth, Postmovement Groups and the Life Construction
     Crisis." Religious Change and Continuity. Edited by Harry
     M. Johnson. San Francisco: Jossey-Bass, 1979, pp. 264-285.

198. Glock, Charles Y. "Consciousness Among Contemporary Youth."
     New York Religious Consciousness. Edited by Charles Y.
     Glock and Robert N. Bellah. Berkeley, CA: University of
     California Press, 1977, pp. 353-366.

199. Hardin, Bert. "A Comparison of Anti-Cult Movements in the
     United States and the Federal Republic of Germany." Paper
     presented at the meeting of the British Sociological Asso-
     ciation Research Group on New Religious Movements. Lincoln,
     England, 1981.

200. Hargrove, Barbara. "Church Student Ministries and the New
     Consciousness." The New Religious Consciousness. Edited by
     Charles Y. Glock and Robert N. Bellah. Berkeley, CA:
     University of California Press, 1976, pp. 205-226.

201. Harper, Charles. "The Cult Controversy: Values in Conflict."
     Proceedings of the Association for the Scientific Study of
     Religion: Southwest. Denton, TX: n.p., 1981a. 8 pp.

202. Harper, Charles. "Love Our Children: An Ethnography of Anti-
     Cult Organization." Proceedings of the Association for the
     Scientific Study of Religion: Southwest. Denton, TX: n.p.,
     1981b. 6 pp.

203. Harper, Charles. "Religious Cults and the Anti-Cult Movement
     in the Omaha Area." Report Submitted to the Nebraska Com-
     mittee for the Humanities. Omaha, NE: Creighton University,
     1979. 43 pp.

204. Hunter, Edward. Brainwashing: From Pavlov to Powers. New
     York: The Bookmailer, 1960. 329 pp.

205. Hunter, Edward. Brainwashing in Red China: The Calculated
     Destruction of Men's Minds. Enlarged Edition. New York:
     The Vanguard Press, 1953. 31 pp.

206. Hunter, James D. "The New Religions: Demodernization and the
     Protest Against Modernity." The Social Impact of New Reli-
     gious Movements. Edited by Bryan Wilson. New York: Rose of
     Sharon Press, 1981, pp. 1-19.

207. Lifton, Robert J. Thought Reform and the Psychology of Totalism. New York: W.W. Norton and Company, 1963. 510 pp.

208. Lifton, Robert J. "Thought Reform of Chinese Intellectuals: A Psychiatric Evaluation." Journal of Social Issues 13 (1957): 5-19.

209. Lofland, John. Doomsday Cult. Revised Edition. New York: Irvington Press, 1977. 362 pp.

210. Needleman, Jacob. "Winds from the East: Youth and Counter Culture." Mystery, Magic and Miracle. Edited by Edward F. Heenan. Englewood Cliffs, NJ: Prentice-Hall, 1973, pp. 78-83.

211. Patrick, Ted, and Tom Dulack. Let Our Children Go! New York: Ballantine Books, 1977. 276 pp.

212. Prince, Raymond H. "Cocoon Work: An Interpretation of the Concern of Contemporary Youth with the Mystical." Religious Movements in Contemporary America. Edited by Irving I. Zaretsky and Mark P. Leone. Princeton, NJ: Princeton University Press, 1974, pp. 251-271.

213. Sargant, William. Battle for the Mind. New York: Doubleday, 1957. 265 pp.

214. Schein, Edgar H., Inge Schneider and Curtis H. Backer. Coercive Persuasion. New York: W.W. Norton and Company, 1961. 320 pp.

215. Shupe, Anson D., Jr., and David G. Bromley. A Documentary History of the Anti-Cult Movement. New York: The Edwin Mellen Press, 1982a.

216. Shupe, Anson D., Jr., and David G. Bromley. "Shaping the Public Response to Jonestown: The People's Temple and the Anti-Cult Movement." Violence and Religious Commitment. Edited by Kenneth Levi. University Park, PA: The University of Pennsylvania Press, 1982b, pp. 105-132.

217. Shupe, Anson D., Jr., and David G. Bromley. "Apostates and Atrocity Stories: Some Parameters in the Dynamics of Deprogramming." The Social Impact of New Religious Movements. Edited by Bryan Wilson. New York: The Rose of Sharon Press, Inc., 1981, pp. 179-215.

218. Shupe, Anson D., Jr., and David G. Bromley. The New Vigilantes: Deprogrammers, Anti-Cultists, and the New Religions. Beverly Hills, CA: Sage Publications, 1980a. 267 pp.

219. Shupe, Anson D., Jr., and David G. Bromley. "Walking a Tightrope: Dilemmas of Participant Observation of Groups in Conflict." Qualitative Sociology (January 1980b): 3-21.

220. Shupe, Anson D., Jr., and David G. Bromley. "Witches, Moonies
      and Accusations of Evil." <u>In Gods We Trust: New Patterns of
      American Religious Pluralism</u>. Edited by Thomas Robbins and
      Dick Anthony. New Brunswick, NJ: Transaction Press, 1980c,
      pp. 247-262.

221. Shupe, Anson D., Jr., and David G. Bromley. "The Moonies and
      the Anti-Cultists: Movement and Counter-Movement in Con-
      flict." <u>Sociological Analysis</u> 40 (Winter 1979): 325-366.

222. Shupe, Anson D., Jr., Bert L. Hardin and David G.
      Bromley. "A Comparison of Anti-Cult Movements in the United
      States and West Germany." Unpublished manuscript.
      Arlington, TX: University of Texas at Arlington, 1981.

223. Shupe, Anson D., Jr., Roger Spielmann and Sam Stigall.
      "Cults of Anti-Cultism." <u>Society</u> 17 (March/April 1980): 43-
      47.

224. Shupe, Anson D., Jr., Roger Spielmann and Sam Stigall.
      "Deprogramming: the New Exorcism." <u>American Behavioral
      Scientist</u> 20 (July/August 1977): 941-956.

CHAPTER THREE

THE CONTEMPORARY ANTI-CULT MOVEMENT: FAMILY BASED
ASSOCIATIONS AND DEPROGRAMMERS

The single greatest problem in assessing and compiling a bibliography on the contemporary ACM is, as we intimated in Chapter Two,
that movement's poor sense of its own history. Decentralized, financially unstable as a whole and for years convinced that its goal
of repressing assorted new religious movements was not despairingly
far off, the family based ACM component, through its activists and
leaders, rarely bothered to keep anything resembling systematic
files of publications and memoranda. The deprogrammers as well,
acting on ad hoc individual bases either voluntarily or profession-
ally, were simply too busy in direct modes of action to generate or
save written materials. The few ACM accounts of the movement's history and activities that have been published tend to be very incom-
plete on organizational and historical details. They are almost exclusively apologetic and unabashedly sensationalistic. Not surprisingly, with the exception of Ted Patrick's co-authored account of
his deprogramming adventures (Patrick and Dulack, 1977), this published literature has been produced almost entirely by apostates,
most of them former members of the Unification Church (with much
less representation of other less publicized groups). Since this
body of literature has been written by individuals who have experienced (and therefore seek to legitimate) deprogramming, we will consider it separately from materials produced by the family based
anti-cult associations. We discuss this latter set of materials
first.

FAMILY BASED ASSOCIATIONS, PUBLICATIONS

Until the mid-1970's most newsletters, pamphlets and memoranda
were mailed out solely for ACM members' and sympathizers' consumption. Produced on shoestring budgets, they were cheaply reproduced
by mimeographing or xeroxing on low-grade paper stock. Grammatical
errors were frequent, artwork was nonexistent, and general sophisti-
cation of content was low. Mere reprinting of newspaper articles
and "horror story" anecdotes contributed by families constituted the
usual fare for readers. These publications were still genuine
intramovement communications of news, needs and encouragement among
persons who did not have the resources to afford better alternatives. During the first half of the decade the single exception to
this trend was the Citizens Freedom Foundation in California (later

to become a national clearinghouse organization of ACM information
called the Citizens Freedom Foundation--Information Services) which
as early as 1974 featured actual printing (not reproduced typing)
and photographs. However, CFF was uniquely aided by having a high
concentration of affected parents, or constituents, in northern and
southern California who could financially support a regional newsletter more professional in appearance. Most ACM groups had a relatively small core of active (i.e., financially contributing) members
and a larger mailing list of various noncontributing persons who
were merely sympathizers, those who had only written or queried the
given group for information or those who had become inactive when
their family members had left whatever new religion they had joined.

   Individual pamphlets prepared by family based ACM associations
were likewise of poor quality, both in their unsophisticated contents and cheap production. In the early 1970's the anti-cult ideology which drew on the Korean War brainwashing literature (see
Chapter Eight) as well as later scientific research was still being
formulated, and the exact "handle" by which anti-cultists could attack new religions had not been fully reasoned. Chalenor's 1975
pamphlet "Religion, Mind Control, Money and Power," Merritt's 1975
pamphlet, "Open Letter," Schuppin's rambling 1975 "Areas of Government Involvement in Cults and Pseudo Religious Organizations" (which
defies succinct summary), West's 1975 essay "In Defense of Deprogramming," and Crampton's 1976 pamphlet and cult inventory "Cult
Activities and Youth Involvement, Money and Power" (which in places
is almost illegible due to poor reproduction and spacing) and the
two unofficial volumes of transcript proceedings from the first
national meeting between angry parents and federal officials in
Washington, DC (CEFM, 1976) are typical of the publications of this
era. They were uncopyrighted and frequently local groups photocopied additional copies from earlier photocopied copies for speedy
dissemination.

   Toward the end of the decade, however, this general state of
declasse appearance and unsystematic ad hoc contents began to be replaced by more polished publications. A number of evangelical religious anti-cult groups, staffed by dedicated volunteers and/or
workers with missionary zeal, helped stimulate a wave of competently
researched essays and higher quality graphics (see Chapter Four).
There were still cheaply produced, homespun three-page newsletters
offset printed from typed copy, such as Love Our Children, Inc.'s
monthly announcements of relevant newspaper articles and local
announcements of cult or anti-cult activities and an almost identical parallel local publication by Trenton, Michigan's Individual
Freedom Foundation, Inc., chapter (see IFF). However, as such publications either ceded their media-monitoring efforts to larger organizations such as the Citizens Freedom Foundation--Information
Services, or became defunct (as, for example, did the Texas based
National Ad Hoc Committee Engaged in Freeing Minds one year after
its origin), a smaller number of better financed, more articulate
publications emerged.

   Of signal importance in this trend has been the American Family
Foundation, Inc.'s The Advisor. Begun in 1979 in Lexington,

Masssachusetts, it is printed in a tabloid newspaper format. The
Advisor features essays, reviews of pending state and local legislation across the nation relevant to anti-cult concerns, news of current publications on the controversy, a collegiate section that mon-
itors new religions' activities on high school and college campuses
and a letter-to-the-editor section that on occasion features a genuine exchange of views. The Advisor is distinctly anti-cult, but in
its pages the bald ethnocentrism of earlier local newsletters is ab-
sent. Occasionally, there even appear views dissenting from anti-
cult ideology (something no ACM newsletter before 1975 would have
printed). The Advisor also represents a departure in funding-base
from most struggling local ACM groups. It required in 1981 a $30
annual subscription fee (stiff by comparison with local ACM groups
elsewhere that only request several dollars per year but which send
out free copies at an indefinite and unprofitable rate) and sold reprinted transcripts on a wide variety of official and unofficial
legislative meetings' proceedings as well as other invaluable documents for an above-minimum cost "contribution."

Complete collections of these newsletters are difficult to
find. The Center for the Study of New Religions in Berkeley, California has a large number of back issues of the Citizens Freedom
Foundation Newsletter and an up-to-date collection of both the Citizens Freedom Foundation--Information Services Newsletter as well as
The Advisor. The Center also possesses a complete set of Love Our
Children, Inc., newsletters from January 1977 to February 1981 and a
number of miscellaneous copies of other newsletters and ACM pamphlets and brochures.

THE APOSTATE LITERATURE

The appearance of angry apostates from one social movement who
zealously offer their critical testimonies to the opposition, i.e.,
to an anti-movement, is a sociologically predictable phenomenon.
Anti-movements may press whatever accusations they like against a
given movement, but without first-hand experience in the group accused, they lack the authority of an "insider." Apostates, as former movement members, provide just such "smoking gun" evidence.
Their claims to have personally performed any number of actions in
question but now to have seen the error of their ways lends their
anecdotal testimonies a prima facie validity difficult to refute.
As a result, they typically enjoy a brief but well-publicized lime-
light in the media, on speaking tours and so forth, after being recruited by anti-movements. Apostates perform an indispensable function for anti-movements struggling to gain public and/or official
support for their repressive goals, so much so that, failing to produce genuine apostates, anti-movements (as in the case of the
anti-Catholic movements of the early nineteenth century discussed in
Chapter One) will fabricate them out of sheer imagination and need.

The accounts of the experiences of apostates from the new religious movements of the 1970's made dramatic reading. As a result,
toward the end of the decade a number of "exposes" of these various
groups, written by or about ex-members in the tradition of right-

eously indignant apostasy appeared for public consumption. They
found any of three distinct outlets: (1) popular newspaper and magazine articles; (2) popular books which often presented the apostates' tales in an autobiographical format; and (3) testimonies before legislative bodies holding hearings or conducting investigations concerning new religious movements. Only a handful of more
balanced introspective analyses were published (Collier, 1978;
Allen, 1982).

Newspaper and Magazine Articles

    Initially newspapers, and later popular magazines such as
Seventeen, Good Housekeeping and Reader's Digest, were the most common conduits of anti-cult claims bolstered by apostates' horrific
stories. Apostates were interviewed, and their own words were in-
terwoven with the journalist's or author's third-person narratives.
Prime examples include "The Incredible Story of Ann Gordon and Reverend Sun Myung Moon" (Crittenden, 1976) and "Why I Quit the Moon
Cult" (Remsberg and Remsberg, 1976) which blatantly suggested the
loss of psychological and moral innocences of naive youths at the
manipulative hands of malevolent "cult" leaders. Occasionally the
articles would even be written by a parent (e.g., Adler, 1978)
which added a further dramatic dimension and created further empathy
for anti-cultists among readers. There were even novels (Rodgers,
1979).

    The absolute number of newspaper articles from syndicated and
wire service sources as well as from local newspapers is of course
not known, but it is doubtlessly astronomical, particularly considering that the same wire service story was often picked up nationwide by local daily newspapers of various sizes and repeatedly published. Elsewhere we have dealt at length with the sociological
functions, or consequences, of media portrayals (particularly in the
press) of new religions in light of apostate testimonies and their
typical composition (Shupe and Bromley, 1981; Bromley, Shupe and
Ventimiglia, 1979). Suffice it to say here that this first outlet
for apostates' anti-new religions stories has unquestionably been
the largest and has been largely responsible for fixing in the
public eye the "cult" stereotype of the 1970's.

Popular Books

    The mid-to-late 1970's saw a sudden wave of apostate books,
released by reputable commercial publishing houses, that lasted only
until the end of the decade but which further discredited new religions. A variety of groups came under attack, such as the Children
of God (Hulquist, 1977; McManus and Cooper, 1980), the Divine Light
Mission (Heller, 1982), Synanon (Olsen, 1980), and the millennial
Roberts Cult (nicknamed the Garbage Eaters, after their practice of
eating only food obtained from the waste bins behind fast food res-
taurants and supermarkets—see Martin, 1979). However, the majority
of apostate books focused on the Unification Church of Sun Myung
Moon, no doubt in large part because of its own aggressively sought
public image, its political misadventures during the Watergate-
Koreagate scandals in Nixonian Washington, DC, and its large size

relative to many other rather small groups (see Underwood and
Underwood, 1979; Wood and Vitek, 1979; Edwards, 1979; Elkins, 1980;
Durham, 1981; Kemperman, 1981; Swatland and Swatland, 1982). Their
themes were basically the same: an idealistic youth with a promising
(conventional middle-class) future was duped into joining a movement
which, before his or her forced or voluntary departure, revealed its
sinister, seamy underside. After the tragic deaths of over 900
American members of the People's Temple at Jonestown, Guyana, in
1978, a flurry of books utilizing apostate testimonies or authored
by apostates of the People's Temple appeared (e.g., Thielmann and
Merrill, 1979; Kearns and Weed, 1979), but in format they were not
remarkably different from others of the genre.

   Apostates' testimonies also became important sources for
journalists and others who accepted such stories literally and used
them as the basis for making rather sweeping condemnations, if not
frequent innuendos, about the "legitimacy" (i.e., theological), law-
abiding character and overall savoryness of new religions. The most
extreme analysis probably came from Canadian journalist Josh Freed
(1980), whose own analysis has been meticulously critiqued by former
journalist Testa, (1978) and Conway and Siegelman (1978; see also
Siegelman and Conway, 1979). In particular, Conway (an interdisci-
plinary Ph.D.) and Siegelman (a journalist) concluded that conversion to new religions, as well as deconversion out of them, was ac-
complished by a sudden mental change involving massive transformation of hologrammatic image-clusters in the brain, a process they
termed "snapping." They perceived "snapping" to be a phenomenon of
modern American society in general as well as of "victims" of
"cult's" indoctrination processes and postulated that the entire
twentieth-century North American culture has been caught up in one
gigantic, collective mind-"snap." Other, less ambitious analyses
that nonetheless heavily relied on apostate testimony and case
studies with little regard for phenomenological considerations can
be found in Rudin and Rudin (1980), Rudin (1979-80), Delgado (1977)
and Stoner and Parke (1977). Stoner and Parke also illustrate another fact about family based ACM groups: the high mortality rate of
such organizations. These authors made explicit mention in the
final pages of their book of a number of ACM groups to which readers
were referred for further information. However, at least one major
national referral organization mentioned--the National Ad Hoc Committee Engaged in Freeing Minds--ironically had already become defunct by the time their book was published. Such informational ob-
solescence is not surprising. Turnover, change and various frustrated attempts at amalgamating ACM groups, often made such references (given such books' long lead-times before going to press)
somewhat out of date upon their day of publication.

   At the same time, it is possible to identify a few popular
sources, both articles and books, authored by journalists covering
the new religious phenomenon during the 1970's which made little, if
circumspect, use of such apostate evidence (e.g., Cohen, 1975;
Welles, 1976; Rasmussen, 1976) but these were relatively rare.

Testimonies Before Legislative Bodies

In February, 1976, Senator Robert Dole of Kansas held an unofficial public "information meeting" in Washington, DC, between parents and representatives of various regional family based ACM groups
and federal bureaucrats of assorted agencies as well as elected congressmen (CEFM, 1976). This was the first federal action which
acknowledged the existence of grievances of the ACM (the only prior
equivalents, on the state level, occurred in 1974 in California and
New York--see Shupe and Bromley, 1981:184). Apostates played a key
role in supporting the legitimacy of families' grievances at that
1976 meeting, as they were to do in the plethora of such hearings
held throughout the remainder of the decade and into the 1980's. As
witnesses, their testimonies helped alarm some legislators and officials, particularly at the state level, who otherwise might have
given little response to the family based ACM interest groups (e.g.,
New York, 1977, 1974; Texas, 1977; Vermont, 1977). Ex-Unification
Church members such as Chris Elkins and Allen Tate Wood made significant, damaging contributions through their testimonies before the
House Subcommittee on International Organizations's investigation
(under the chairmanship of Representative Donald Fraser) into the
role of the Unification Church in the Koreagate scandal (U.S.
Government, 1978a, 1978b) and provided ammunition for other criticisms of that particular religious group (e.g., Boettcher and
Freedman, 1980). Testimonies such as theirs also must be credited
for helping inspire the only attempt to legislate the anti-cult perspective at the federal level (U.S. Government, 1981). The fact
that until 1978 and after the tragedy at Jonestown, Guyana, had
occurred, few meaningful resolutions or legislative investigations
has been passed or conducted (meaningful in terms of directly
inhibiting the groups involved) should not obscure the apostates'
overall importance.

Their value did become more apparent as general societal and
official concern over possible destructive implications of new religions mounted following the Jonestown events in November, 1978.
Two months later several ex-Unification Church members claimed in a
New West magazine article to have received personal instruction from
Church leaders in how to slash their wrists in suicide fashion if
captured by deprogrammers (Carroll and Bauer, 1979). Others who had
made prior use of apostate testimonies, such as Conway and
Siegelman, quickly prophesied catastrophic scenarios in groups such
as the Unification Church. As a consequence Senator Robert Dole
held a second public information meeting in February, 1979 (AFF,
1979) that featured apostates and apostate information; some of the
present apostates went on to participate as "expert" witnesses in
the numerous state legislative hearings that occurred after Jonestown (e.g., Connecticut, 1981, 1980; Illinois 1979a, 1979b;
Maryland, 1981; Massachusetts, 1979; Minnesota, 1981, 1978; Oregon,
1981; Pennsylvania, 1981, 1979; Texas, 1979).

New York State undoubtedly was the scene of more ACM lobbying
efforts to press for repressive anti-cult legislation, and the scene
of more governmental response, than any other state in large part
because of the Unification Church's headquarters there and its high-

lighted presence in that state. Intense legislative pressure (itself the result of ACM lobbying) on the State's Board of Regents in
1977 and 1978 resulted in the Unification Theological Seminary at
Barrytown, New York, being denied a charter (hence accreditation --
see New York, 1978), and one state assemblyman had even submitted a
bill to make starting or promoting a "pseudo religion"--patently
aimed at communally organized utopian or "world-transforming" groups
such as the Unification Church and the Hare Krishna sect--a felony
(New York, 1977). Unificationist apostate Christopher Edwards,
author of *Crazy for God*, promoted a public hearing to examine his
charges that "cults," in particular the Unification Church, routinely practice child neglect of young members (New York State, 1979)
and, through the chairman of that hearing, Howard Lasher (who later
sponsored pro-ACM legislation), contributed to two successive attempts to relax the requirements for parents to obtain writs of temporary conservatorship or guardianship over (hence temporary and,
for the stated time, virtually unlimmited legal custody of) their
adult offspring (New York State, 1981, 1980). These attempts were
successfully supported by passage in the New York State Assembly
(both houses) and were only defeated by the governor's veto in each
instance (see, e.g., Carey, 1980), the latter in part a product of
intense civil libertarian and church-group counter lobbying.

Because apostate testimonies have as their purpose the arousal
of public ire and the mobilization of official and other sanctions,
they are typically diffused to as wide an audience as possible.
This was certainly the case with ex-new religions' apostate accounts. The official reports, resolutions, testimonies and other
sources be obtained from the archives of respective state and federal governments or, in many cases, the Center for the Study of New
Religious Movements at Berkeley, California. Popular articles and
books concerning apostates' experiences should be readily available
in libraries.

225. Adler, Warren. "Rescuing David from the Moonies." *Esquire*,
June 6, 1978.

226. *The Advisor: Journal of the American Family Foundation*.
Lexington, Massachusetts, January 1979 - present.

227. AFF (American Family Foundation). *Unofficial Transcript of
Proceedings, Information Meetings on the Cult Phenomenon in
the United States*. Lexington, MA: American Family Foundation, Inc., (1979). 161 pp.

228. Allen, Steve. *Beloved Son: A Story of the Jesus Cults*.
Indianapolis, IN: Bobbs-Merrill Co., Inc., 1982. 241 pp.

229. Bierman, James H. *In RE: Underwood*. (Original play concerned
with the conservatorship trial of Barbara Underwood, ex-
Unification Church member). Copyrighted by James H. Bierman,
Cowell College, University of California, Santa Cruz:
Original manuscript, 1979. 97 pp.

230. Boettcher, Robert, and Gordon L. Freedman. Gifts of Deceit:
      Sun Myung Moon, Tongsng Park and the Korean Scandal. New
      York: Holt, Rinehart and Winston, 1980. 402 pp.

231. Bromley, David G., Anson D. Shupe, Jr., and Joseph C.
      Ventimiglia. "Atrocity Tales, the Unification Church and
      the Social Construction of Evil." Journal of Communication
      29 (Summer 1979): 42-53.

232. California, State of. Report of the California Senate Select
      Committee on Children and Youth. Northridge, CA: California
      State University, (1974).

233. Carey, Hugh (Governor). "Return (Disapproval) Assembly Bill
      #11122-A, An Act to Amend the Mental Hygiene Law in Rela-
      tion to Temporary Conservator." Albany, NY: July 1, 1980.
      8 pp.

234. Carroll, J., and B. Bauer. "Suicide Training in the Moon
      Cult." New West, January 29, 1979, pp. 62-63.

235. CEFM (National Ad Hoc Committee Engaged in Freeing Minds). A
      Special Report. The Unification Church: Its Activities and
      Practices. Vols. I and II. Arlington, TX: National Ad Hoc
      Committee, A Day of Affirmation and Protest, (1976).
      121 pp.

236. CFF (Citizens Freedom Foundation). News. Chula Vista, CA:
      January 1974 - January 1980.

237. CFF-IS (Citizens Freedom Foundation--Information Services).
      News. Chula Vista, CA: January 1980 - present.

238. Chalenor, Robert E. Religion, Mind Control, Money and Power.
      Chula Vista, CA: Citizens Freedom Foundation, (1975). 3 pp.

239. Cohen, Daniel. The New Believers. New York: Ballantine
      Books, 1975. 171 pp.

240. Collier, Sophia. Soul Rush: The Odyssey of a Young Woman of
      the Seventies. New York: William Morrow and Co., Inc.,
      1978. 240 pp.

241. Connecticut, State of. "An Act Concerning Conservatorship
      (Temporary Guardians)." (Substitute Senate Bill 1429 File
      #649, Committee on Judiciary.) Hartford: Connecticut
      General Assembly. January 1981. 6 pp.

242. Connecticut, State of. "An Act Concerning Establishment of a
      Commission to Investigate Activities in Connecticut of the
      Rev. Sun Myung Moon and the Unification Church of America."
      (Proposed Bill No. 7337, Referred to the Committee on Gen-
      eral Law.) Hartford: Connecticut General Assembly. January
      1980. 1 pp.

243. Conner, Robert. Walled In: The True Story of a Cult. New York: New American Library, 1979. 308 pp.

244. Conway, Flo, and Jim Siegelman. Snapping: America's Epidemic of Sudden Personality Change. New York: Lippincott, 1978. 254 pp.

245. Crampton, Henrietta. Cult Activities and Youth Involvement, Money and Power. Redondo Beach, CA: Volunteer Parents Chapter, Citizens Freedom Foundation, (1976). 11 pp.

246. Crittenden, Ann. "The Incredible Story of Ann Gordon and Reverend Sun Myung Moon." Good Housekeeping, October 1976, p. 86 ff.

247. Delgado, Richard. "Religious Totalism: Gentle and Ungentle Persuasion Under the First Amendment. Southern California Law Review 51 (November 1977): 1–98.

248. Durham, Deanna. Life Among the Moonies: Three Years in the Unification Church. Plainfield, NJ: Logos International, 1981.

249. Edwards, Christopher. Crazy for God. Englewood Cliffs, NJ: Prentice-Hall, Inc., 1979. 233 pp.

250. Elkins, Chris. Heavenly Deception. Wheaton, IL: Tyndale House, 1980. 142 pp.

251. Freed, Josh. Moonwebs: Journey Into the Mind of a Cult. Toronto: Dorset Publishing, Inc., 1980. 216 pp.

252. Heller, R.K. Deprogramming for Do-It-Yourselfers: A Cure for the Common Cult. Medina, OH: The Gentle Press, 1982.

253. Hultquist, Lee. They Followed the Piper. Plainfield, NJ: Logos International, 1977. 162 pp.

254. IFF (Individual Freedom Foundation, Inc.). Newsletter, 1978–1980.

255. Illinois, State of. Transcript of Hearings to Consider Cult Activities in the State of Illinois. Conducted by State Representative Betty Hoxsey. Springfield, IL: Illinois House of Representatives, (August 1979a). 135 pp.

256. Illinois, State of. House Resolution 121. Springfield, IL: Illinois House of Representatives, (1979b). 2 pp.

257. Jaggs, Kenneth W. A Survey of the Development of New Religious Movements with Particular Reference to the Movement Known as Scientology. Toronto, Canada: Addiction Research Foundation, 1976.

258. Kemperman, Steve. <u>Lord of the Second Advent</u>. Ventura, CA: Ventura Books, 1981. 178 pp.

259. Kerns, Phil, with Doug Weed. <u>People's Temple, People's Tomb</u>. Plainfield, NJ: Logos International, 1979. 288 pp.

260. Levitt, Ken, with Ceil Rosen. <u>Kidnapped for My Faith</u>. Van Nuys, CA: Bible Voice, Inc., 1978. 126 pp.

261. LOCI (Love Our Children, Inc.). <u>Newsletter</u>. Omaha, NE: January 1977 - February 1981.

262. Martin, Rachel. <u>Escape</u>. Denver, CO: Accent Books, 1979. 191 pp.

263. Maryland, State of. <u>A House Joint Resolution Concerning Cults in Maryland</u>. (House Joint Resolution No. 67.) Annapolis, MD: February 13, 1981. 2 pp.

264. Massachusetts, State of. <u>Transcript of Commonwealth of Massachusetts Public Hearing</u>, Senator John G. King, Chair, Committee on Commerce and Labor. Reprinted by American Family Foundation, Lexington, Massachusetts. Boston, MA: (March 21, 1979). 83 pp.

265. McManus, Una, and John C. Cooper. <u>Not for a Million Dollars</u>. Nashville, TN; Impact Books, 1980. 182 pp.

266. Merritt, Jean. "Open Letter." Lincoln, NE: Return to Personal Choice, Inc., (1975). 6 pp.

267. Minnesota, State of. "A Bill for an Act Relating to Civil Actions; Authorizing Converts to Organizations Promising Religious or Philosophical Self-Fulfillment to Maintain Actions for Damages: Authorizing Family Members of Converts to Organizations Promising Religious or Philosophical Self-Fulfillment to Maintain Actions for Damages, Proposing New Law Coded as Minnesota Statutes, Chapter 608. St. Paul: Legislature of the State of Minnesota, February, 1981. 2 pp.

268. Minnesota, State of. "Charitable Funds--Regulation of Solicitation." (Section 209-50, Subdivision 10 of Minnesota Statutes 1976. Amendment of Chapter 601 [H.F. No. 1248]) St. Paul: 70 Minnesota Legislature, 1978. 12 pp.

269. New York, State of. "An Act to Amend the Mental Hygiene Law, in Relation to the Appointment of Temporary Guardians." (Article 80.) Albany: New York State Assembly, April 1981. 13 pp.

270. New York, State of. "An Act to Amend the Mental Hygiene Law, in Relation to temporary Conservator." (Proposed Article #11122-A.) Albany: New York State Assembly, March 25, 1980. 4 pp.

271. New York, State of. <u>Transcript of Public Hearing on Treatment of Children by Cults</u>. Albany: The State Assembly of New York. Reprinted by American Family Foundation, Lexington, Massachusetts, (August 9-10, 1979). 678 pp.

272. New York, State of. <u>Recommendation of the New York State Regents' Committee to Review Application of Unification Theological Seminary for State Chapter</u>. Albany: New York State Board of Regents, (February 22, 1978). 6 pp.

273. New York, State of. "Promoting a Pseudo-Religious Cult." (Proposed Bill AB 9566-A, Section 240.46.) Albany: New York State Assembly. October 5, 1977. 1 p.

274. New York, State of. <u>Final Report on the Activities of the Children of God to Hon. Louis J. Lefkowitz, Attorney General of the State of New York</u>. Albany: New York State Charity Fraud's Bureau, (1974). 65 pp.

275. Olin, Williams, <u>Escape from Utopia: My Ten Years in Synanon</u>. Santa Cruz, CA: Unity Press, 1980. 288 pp.

276. Oregon, State of. "A Bill for an Act Relating to Guardianship." (Senate Bill 5248, Committee on Justice.) Portland, Oregon: Oregon Legislative Assembly, 1981. 1 p.

277. Patrick, Ted, and Tom Dulack. <u>Let Our Children Go!</u> New York: Ballantine Books, 1977. 276 pp.

278. Pennsylvania, State of. "Creating a Temporary Study Commission to Study Groups Which Seek to Unduly Exert Control Over Children and Youth." (House Bill No. 406.) Harrisburg: General Assembly of Pennsylvania, February 1981. 4 pp.

279. Pennsylvania, State of. <u>House Resolution No. 20</u>. Harrisburg: General Assembly of Pennsylvania, 1979. 2 pp.

280. Rasmussen, Marc. "How Sun Myung Moon Lures America's Children." <u>McCall's</u>, September 1976, p. 102 ff.

281. Remsberg, Charles, and Bonnie Remsberg. "Why I Quit the Moon Cult." <u>Seventeen</u>, July 1976, pp. 107, 117, 127.

282. <u>Report of the Board of Inquiry into Scientology, 1965</u>. Melbourne, Australia: Government Printer, 1965.

283. <u>Report of the Commission of Enquiry into Scientology</u>. Capetown, South Africa, 1972.

284. Rogers, William D. <u>Cult Sunday</u>. Denver, CO: Accent Books, 1979. 318 pp.

285. Rudin, A. James, and Marcia R. Rudin. <u>Prison or Paradise? The New Religious Cults</u>. Philadelphia, PA: Fortress Press, 1980. 164 pp.

286. Rudin, Marcia R. "The Cult Phenomenon: Fad or Fact?" New York University Review of Law and Social Change 19 (1979-1980): 17-32.

287. Schuppin, Eric A. Areas of Government Involvement in Cults and Pseudo Religious Organizations. Arlington, TX: National Ad Hoc Committee, Citizens Engaged in Freeing Minds, (1975). 3 pp.

288. Scott, R.D. Transcendental Misconceptions. San Diego, CA: Beta Books, 1978. 227 pp.

289. Shupe, Anson D., Jr., and David G. Bromley. "Apostates and Atrocity Stories: Some Parameters in the Dynamics of Deprogramming." The Social Impact of New Religious Movements. Edited by Bryan M. Wilson. New York: The Rose of Sharon Press, Inc., 1981, pp. 179-215.

290. Shupe, Anson D., Jr., and David G. Bromley. The New Vigilantes: Anti-Cultists, Deprogrammers and the New Religions. Beverly Hills, CA: Sage Publications, Inc., 1980. 267 pp.

291. Siegelman, Jim, and Flo Conway. "Playboy Interview: Ted Patrick." Playboy, March 1979, p. 53 ff.

292. Sklar, Dusty. Gods and Beasts: The Nazis and the Occult. New York: Thomas Y. Crowell, 1977.

293. Stoner, Carrol, and Jo Anne Parke. All Gods Children. Radnor, PA: Chilton, 1977. 324 pp.

294. Swatland, Susan, and Anne Swatland. Escape from the Moonies. London, England: New English Library, 1982. 159 pp.

295. Testa, Bart. "Making Crime Seem Natural: News and Deprogramming." A Time for Consideration: A Scholarly Appraisal of the Unification Church. Edited by M. Darrol Bryant and Herbert W. Richardson. New York: The Edwin Mellen Press, 1978, pp. 41-81.

296. Texas, State of. Senate Resolution No. 485. Austin, TX: Senate Committee on State Affairs, 1979. 2 pp.

297. Texas, State of. House Resolution No. 35. Austin, TX: House of Representatives Committee on Criminal Jurisprudence. May 10, 1977. 3 pp.

298. Thielmann, Bonnie, with Dean Merrill. The Broken God. Elgin, IL: David C. Cook Publishing Co., 1979. 154 pp.

299. Underwood, Barbara, and Betty Underwood. Hostage to Heaven. New York: Clarkson N. Potter, Inc., 1979. 304 pp.

300. U.S. Government. Discussion Draft of a Bill to Amend Title 18, United States Code, To Provide Penalties for Certain

Deceptive and Coercive Practices Used by Certain Organizations in Recruiting Members for Other Purposes. Submitted by Representative Richard Ottinger. U.S. House of Representatives, 97th Congress, First Session. Washington, DC: June 24, 1981. 6 pp.

301. U.S. Government. Investigation of Korean-American Relations. (Report of the Subcommittee on International Organizations of the Committee on International relations, U.S. House of Representatives.) Washington, DC: U.S. Government Printing Office, (1978a). 447 pp.

302. U.S. Government. Appendices I and II to Investigation of Korean-American Relations. (Report of the Subcommittee on International Organizations of the Committee on International Relations, U.S. House of Representatives.) Washington, DC: U.S. Government Printing Office, (1978b). 1523 pp.

303. Vermont, State of. Report of the Senate Committee for the Investigation of Alleged Deceptive, Fraudulent and Criminal Practices of Various Organizations in the State. Montpelier: Senate, (January 1977).

304. Welles, Chris. "The Eclipse of Sun Myung Moon." New York Magazine, September 27, 1976, pp. 33-38.

305. West, William. In Defense of Deprogramming. Arlington, TX: International Foundation for Individual Freedom, (1975). 4 pp.

306. Whittier, Charles H. The Cultic Phenomena. Washington, DC: Congressional Research Service, Library of Congress, 1979.

307. Wood, Allen Tate, with J. Vitek. Moonstruck: A Memoir of My Life in a Cult. New York: William Morrow, 1979. 189 pp.

CHAPTER FOUR

THE CONTEMPORARY ANTI-CULT MOVEMENT: CHURCHES

In contrast to the family based anti-cult associations the religiously based opposition to new religions formed more quickly and
easily. As Chapter One demonstrated, resistance to new religious
forms is as old as American religious history itself. Earlier waves
of new religions aroused the ire of their contemporaries and received an equally hostile response. It was precisely because there
had been such recurrent clashes between new and established religious groups that the latter were so well prepared for this latest
challenge. Church congregations provided ready made constituencies
and previously established criteria for theological orthodoxy or
legitimacy and provided a readily available means for evaluating and
rejecting new religions.

The interests of family and religious opponents of new religions varied considerably. Parents (and other family members) who
formed the nucleus of the anti-cult associations had as their primary objective the extrication of their offspring from the new religious group with which they had become affiliated. Indeed, once
parents had succeeded in recovering their offspring they often with-
drew from anti-cult associations. The conflict between new religions and established churches centered on theological differences.
None of the new religions achieved a large enough number of conversions to erode the membership base of any of the major denominations. Still, conversions to the new religions were a major source
of concern to the established church for two reasons. First, mainline denominations were experiencing significant losses of membership and young adults were prominent among the ranks of the disenchanted. Conversions to the new religions only served to dramatize
this problem. Second, the new religions offered alternative lifestyles with their own distinctive theological legitimation. To the
extent that new religions were successful they constituted visible
evidence of equally or even more rewarding avenues to spiritual fulfillment. In the final analysis, however, it was the theological
disputes which were paramount. Several new religions openly challenged the precepts of orthodox Christianity and asserted the supe-
riority of their own doctrines. Established Christian churches felt
compelled to refute such claims since their spiritual authority was
at issue. Only if the Bible did constitute God's full and final
word were the established churches secure. If new revelations and
scriptures supplanted the Bible, then new religions possessed supreme spiritual authority. It is not surprising, therefore, that

51

Christian opponents of the new religions concentrated their fire on
the heretical doctrines promulgated by the new religions. Although
refutations of such doctrines were in one sense aimed at the new religions, they were in a more important way directed at practicing
Christians. Theological refutations were designed to reassert the
supremacy of Christian theology and thereby keep intact the spiritual authority of Christian churches and clergy and retain the confidence and commitment of individual Christian parishioners. It was,
then, not merely a battle over ideas per se; at stake were the stability of the churches and the loyalty and security of their members.

Since the interests of families and churches diverged, the ACM
as a whole was a loose coalition. There were some areas of obvious
disagreement. Anti-cult associations were willing to support deprogramming while most churches stopped short of open advocacy of deprogramming or even opposed it. Church leaders were understandably
uncomfortable with complicity in forcible abductions, and legalizing
deprogramming would have opened the door to governmental control
over churches. For their part, the churches were interested in a
broad range of religious groups which challenged Christian theology
whereas the anti-cult associations (their rhetoric notwithstanding)
were concerned predominantly with communally organized new religions
that recruited young adults. Despite such differences there were
also important joint interests. Many members of the anti-cult associations also were churchgoers who shared their churches' repudi-
ation of heretical doctrines. Reciprocally, church leaders felt
compelled to support members of their congregations whose children
had fallen prey to cults. Thus, the natural alliance between church
and family constituted a strong bond in the ACM coalition.

Religious opposition to the new religions was concentrated in
the fundamentalist or evangelical groups although mainline denominations also rejected the new religions. Fundamentalist groups were
particularly threatened by attacks on biblical literalism. Evangelicals saw in the new religions a threat to their own efforts to win
converts to Christ. Much of the literature reviewed in the pages
which follow, therefore, was written and distributed by fundamentalist or evangelical groups. We shall review a number of issues
raised in such literature: the definition of "cult," the groups
designated as "cults," Christian explanations for the success of
new religions and strategies for coping with the challenge of new
religions. Following this discussion we shall review the Jewish
response to new religions shaped by the unique history and concerns
of Jewish Americans. Finally, we shall consider the organized opposition to new religions from the Christian and Jewish communities.

DEFINING "CULT"

Religious opponents of cults have tended to define the term
"cult" in theological rather than lifestyle terms although social
characteristics sometimes are included in these definitions. There
is no consensus on what constitutes a cult, but the most common
standards by which new religions are judged are the doctrines of

orthodox Christianity. The most important characteristic of cults,
then, is that they are un-Christian or non-Christian. Breese (1975:
14), for example, defined a cult as follows:

> ... a religious perversion. It is a belief and
> practice in the world of religion which calls
> for devotion to a religious view or leader
> centered in false doctrine. It is an organized
> heresy. A cult may take many forms but it is
> basically a religious movement which distorts
> or warps orthodox faith to the point where
> truth becomes perverted into a lie. A cult is
> impossible to define except against the abso-
> lute standard of the teaching of Holy Scripture.
> When contrasted to biblical truth, a cult is
> seen to have distinguishing marks by which it
> can be labeled as being fatally sub-Christian.

Definitions of a cult based upon conformity to orthodox Christian
theology have led to laundry lists of attributes which characterize
cults. Breese (1975) listed twelve "marks" of cults: (1) extra
biblical revelation (i.e., rejection of the Bible as the full and
final revelation of God), (2) a false basis of salvation (i.e., assertion that salvation comes through works rather than faith), (3)
uncertain hope (i.e., rejection of the certainty of salvation), (4)
presumptuous messianic leadership (i.e., elevation of a human leader
to messianic status), (5) doctrinal ambiguity (i.e., continual
changes in doctrine, emphasis on emotion rather than reason and posing questions rather than providing answers), (6) claims of special
discoveries (i.e., purported, unauthenticated revelations), (7) de-
fective Christology (i.e., rejection of Jesus as humanity and deity
and rejection of the trinity), (8) segmented biblical attention
(i.e., taking biblical passages out of context), (9) enslaving organizational structure (i.e., demands for total commitment from converts), (10) financial exploitation (i.e., exploitation of followers
to satisfy leaders' greed), (11) denunciation of others (i.e., rejection of all other groups and doctrines as satanic and corrupt)
and (12) syncretism (i.e., attempting to meld the best qualities of
various religions). Williams in Identifying and Dealing with Cults
(n.d.:22-32) offered a similar list of traits: (1) deviation from
biblical truth, (2) rejection of Jesus as the unique Son of God,
(3) antitrinitarianism, (4) an extra-biblical figurehead, (5) insistence on being regarded as Christian, (6) martyr-like attitudes, (7)
apocalyptic preoccupation, (8) separation from the world, (9) practice of self-salvation, (10) emphasis on self-sacrifice, (11) opposition to the institutional church as truly divine in origin and
(12) syncretism.

Other definitions have centered on one or a few characteristics. Beck (1977:29) distinguished cults in terms of improper use
of scripture. Nederhood (1979) concentrated on false leadership,
citing greed, boldness, arrogance and sexual immorality as characteristic traits. Enroth (1979:14) emphasized deception ("the attempt to package, conceal, mollify and modify their message") and
counterfeit nature ("they represent 'other gospels' that the New

Testament warns against"). Peterson (1973:266) argued that "revelation of the secret purposes of God and the end of the world" constituted the common threat among cults.

Since these definitions and sets of characteristics were designed to allow faithful Christians to identify counterfeits, they
frequently were juxtaposed with characteristics of true Christianity. Sparks (1977:22-24), for example, reasserted these central
tenets: (1) unconditional acceptance of all parts of the Scripture,
(2) acceptance of Christ as fully man and God simultaneously, (3)
doctrine of the Trinity, (4) salvation through and (5) practices
consistent with biblical injunctions. In all of these treatments,
then, the central objective was to distinguish true and counterfeit
religion and to reassert the former over the latter. The problem
that Christian writers faced was that no group fit the polar-type
characteristics in common and no one of them rejected all of the
central tenets of Christianity, still all of them failed on at least
a few dimensions to measure up to the qualifications of true religion.

WHAT ARE THE CULTS?

The new religions which appear on lists of cults are extremely
diverse in terms of doctrines, practices and organizational styles.
A partial list of cults defined by Christian authors would include
the following: Eckankar, The Farm, Transcendental Meditation, Sun-
burst Communities, The Church Universal and Triumphant, Scientology,
Erhard Seminars Training, Synanon, the Local Church, The Way Inter-
national, the Walk, the Glory Barn, Love Family, The Church of Bible
Understanding, the Alamo Christian Foundation, Self Realization
Fellowship, the International Society of Krishna Consciousness,
Meher Baba, The Children of God, the Divine Light Mission, Happy
Healthy Holy, Ananda Marga, the Unification Church and Soka Gahkai.

While refutations of the doctrines and practices of many of the
above groups were written by Christian authors (e.g., Alexander,
1979; Carruth, 1980; Spiritual Counterfeits Project, 1978a; Spiritual Counterfeits Project, 1979; Spiritual Counterfeits Project,
1977b), it was the largest and most visible groups which received
the greatest attention. These included the Unification Church, Hare
Krishna, Children of God, Divine Light Mission, The Way International and Transcendental Meditation.

Transcendental Meditation

Opposition to Transcendental Meditation reveals the difference
in interest between anti-cult parent and religious groups. Parent
groups were not overly concerned with Transcendental Meditation
since, in most cases, no major lifestyle change was involved in the
practice of meditation. By contrast, Christian writers poured out a
torrent of literature against Transcendental Meditation (Miller,
1977; Bjornstad, 1976b; Haddon and Hamilton, 1976; Maloney, 1976;
Haddon, 1975; Lewis, 1975; Lightener, 1975; Christian Apologetics
and Research Service, n.d.).

Christians opposing Transcendental Meditation argued that it was a religion in disguise. As Clements (1975:32) put it:

> ... the Hindu roots are not far below the surface and in the TM ceremony a disciple must pay homage to the Maharishi's own Spiritual Master. There is great danger that an agnostic who learns the TM technique will get subtly and almost unconsciously sucked into monistic philosophy.

Christian authors pointed out that Transcendental Meditation denied a personal God, the creator, the fall of man, the unique divinity of Christ and the necessity of Christ's and mankind's suffering (Haddon and Hamilton, 1976:135-170). Furthermore, Christians saw in Transcendental Meditation pure escapism, an attempt to convince followers that perfection was easily attainable and that a spiritual life demanded no self-sacrifice. As Gerberding (1977:23) put it:

> TM offers everything and keeps on stressing how easy it is. TM gives the illusion that one can have spiritual development nearly free, something for nothing. Christ promises everything, but He also asks for everything.... The central symbol of Christianity is the cross....

The Way International

Christian opposition to The Way has centered on its rejection of the Trinity, its denial of Jesus Christ as simultaneously human and divine and its practice of speaking in tongues. The movement's founder, Victor Paul Wierwille, contended that the doctrine of the Trinity was a pagan intrusion into Christianity. According to Wierwille, Jesus was the Son of God but not God, and the holy spirit is a gift (which has a number of manifestations such as speaking in tongues) from God and not a component of the Trinity. The implication of these doctrines was that while Jesus' sacrifice on the cross won legal redemption for man, true salvation depended upon personal transformation, a renewal of one's mind. It was this mental renewal which The Way offered, and speaking in tongues was regarded as the only pure, true form of worship, the way of communing directly with God.

Christians of course rejected such doctrines, for they implied new, special, extra-biblical sources of spiritual knowledge, and they elevated The Way to a superior spiritual position since it was the only source through which the knowledge necessary for salvation could be obtained. In evaluating Wierwille's biblical reinterpretations one Christian author (Sparks, 1977:191) labeled Wierwille's scholarship "irresponsible, slipshod and false." The Way's interpretation of the Trinity was firmly rejected (Williams, 1979:59):

> Wierwille's Christ is a Christ who cannot save, because He is not fully God and fully man. For Christ to be a bridge between man and God, He must, like a physical bridge, be firmly established on both shores.

Similarly, Christians rejected speaking in tongues as the only true form of worship. As MacCollam (1978:27) put it:

> Speaking in tongues, like other gifts, is given
> to some and not to others, according to the will
> of the Holy Spirit. It is not a necessary condi-
> tion or sign of true worship or conversion.

Sparks (1977:198-199) went even further, warning that: "There are tongues that are true and biblical, and there are tongues that are false. The tongues of The Way are false."

Divine Light Mission

Denunciations of the Divine Light Mission have emphasized its rejection of Jesus as the only Lord and Savior of mankind and its insistence that the goal of individuals should be to discover divinity within themselves rather than to enter the kingdom of God. According to the Guru Maharaj Ji, leader of the Divine Light Mission, Jesus was only one of many incarnations of God. The Guru is viewed as a contemporary manifestation of God in a human body. Naturally, Christians have rejected the elevation of Maharaj Ji to a Christ-like status since such contentions would undermine Jesus' unique position. As Sparks (1977:84) asserted:

> Jesus Christ, the ONE, the only begotten Son of God
> is alone the Savior of mankind.... Can it be clearer?
> There is no other name--certainly not Guru Maharaj
> Ji! Only Jesus is the acceptable Savior....

Maharaj Ji's insistence that the goal of human life is to achieve oneness with God by expressing the divinity within also has been rejected, for a kingdom of God on earth rather than a Kingdom of God in heaven is implied. Sparks (1977:87) made this clear:

> Historically, the Church sought to live under the
> reign of Christ, guiding the people as He commands
> in this age so they are protected and prepared for
> that kingdom which will last forever. This modern
> day anti-christ, Guru Maharaj Ji, wants to set up an
> earthly kingdom, with him at its head. He stands
> condemned by God and His church for this blasphemy!

Hare Krishna

Hare Krishna has confronted Christians with a perplexing challenge similar in some respects to those presented by Transcendental Meditation and Divine Light Mission. As Clements (1975:27) noted: "They claim (as do DLM and TM) to have no desire to change any man's religion, but only to make him 'a better Christian' or a better Muslim, since Krishna-consciousness is the underlying experiential truth in all religions." It is hardly surprising that Christians had little confidence in such claims or that they rejected Krishna claims to possessing "underlying truth." There was a more basic conflict, however, since Krishnas rejected the Christian

conception of sin and the goal of entering the kingdom of God. From
a Krishna perspective sin is merely ignorance. Mankind has lost
touch with Krishna consciousness; once this relationship has been
re-established, mankind will achieve oneness with God. Christians
repudiated such views. As Petersen (1973:172) put it:

> The key problems are not solved but dissolved....
> Everything that you need to be saved from is de-
> clared to be an illusion.... The chief problem of
> living today is what we call sin. To the Hindu,
> sin is caused by ignorance; once ignorance is re-
> moved, man is restored to one-ness with God! But
> Christianity says that sin is caused by man's own
> willfulness. Krishna says that man can save him-
> self; Christianity says that man needs outside
> help.... Krishna Consciousness twists reality into
> unreality and asks you to accept temporary states
> of ecstasy as reality.

Children of God

The children of God have been attacked on a number of counts
including the pretensions of the group's founder (Moses David Berg)
to be a prophet, predictions of an imminent destruction of America
by God, rejection of Christian churches as corrupt and satanic, and
various organizational practices deemed immoral. Precisely because
the Children of God accept so much of orthodox Christian theology
and yet reject the Christian church as corrupt the group has come in
for harsh condemnation. Sparks (1977:181) warned that it would be
difficult for outsiders to recognize that the Children of God were
in fact heretical with the result that "They identify the Children
of God with the true Church of God and reject the latter because of
the bizarre excesses of the former." Sparks went on to condemn the
Children of God even more bluntly (1977:177):

> The blunt truth of the matter is that the Children
> of God is a bastard orphan heresy. It is bastard
> because it admits its mother to be a whore; an orphan
> because it pronounces its whore-mother dead; and a
> heresy because it has departed from the true teach-
> ings of the Scriptures as those teachings have been
> passed down through the historic Church.

In addition to theological disputes, the lifestyle within the
Children of God has been a source of conflict. The group has been
condemned for high pressure recruitment and socialization tactics
and deliberate disruption of family ties. The heaviest criticism,
however, has been directed against the group's sexual practices.
Like many communal groups which seek equalitarianism and attempt to
prevent the formation of interpersonal alliances within the group,
the Children of God closely controlled members' sexual relationships. Over time, Moses David Berg began advocating a variety of
unconventional sexual practices. As McBeth (1977:60-61) described
it:

... Berg advocates polygamy, concubinage, group sex,
incest and even sex between small children, volun-
teering that his own first intercourse was at the
age of seven. Sex, he said, should be performed publicly like other acts of worship, and he puts this
into practice by requiring his wife to witness his
relations with a young girl who became his "con-
cubine."

The most widely publicized of these aberrant sexual practices was
what he termed "flirty fishing," a practice in which female members
of the group became "hookers for Jesus." Love, Berg taught, meant
sharing not only possessions with others but whatever else (including physical love) was needed (Enroth, 1979:84-85). What enraged
Christians about such practices was that Berg insisted that only the
Children of God were true Christians and justified such practices on
the basis of biblical passages. In the case of flirty fishing, for
example, Berg legitimated the practice by claiming that Jesus had
had sexual encounters with some of the women he lived with.

Unification Church

Of all the new religions the Unification Church has been the
most consistently condemned. In addition to the numerous apostate
accounts discussed in Chapter Three, there have been several book
length attacks on the Unification Church including Yamamoto's The
Puppet Master (1977b), Bjornstad's The Moon Is Not the Son (1976)
and Levitt's The Spirit of Sun Myung Moon (1976). The Unification
Church, like the Children of God, claimed to be a legitimate Christian group, and naturally this created an intensely hostile response
from Christians who sought to clearly distinguish the Unification
Church from legitimate Christianity.

Three major doctrinal points were at issue. First, Sun Myung
Moon asserted that Jesus had failed to complete his divine mission.
Because Jesus had not completed the process of restoring man to God,
a new messianic figure was to be sent, and the new messiah's bio-
graphical characteristics were strikingly similar to Moon's own.
Christians reacted angrily to Moon's messianic pretensions.
Yamamoto (1977b:115) stated:

If Reverend Moon is to succeed in selling himself
as the Lord of the Second Advent, he must severely
discredit Jesus as the first messiah.... He must
embrace Jesus, praise him and even witness in his
name, but simultaneously he must teach that Jesus
is not the only Savior and Lord, nor is he God.

Second, Moon elevated the product of his own spiritual revelations,
the Divine Principle, to a position superior to the Bible. According to Moon, the Bible was a cryptogram which could be deciphered
by means of the Divine Principle. Finally, Moon stressed the necessity of paying indemnity for sin as a condition for achieving full
and final restoration to God (Yamamoto, 1977b:106). This doctrine
meant that an affirmation of faith in the Christian churches would

not be sufficient for salvation. In each case, then, the Christian
churches reacted to what they correctly perceived was an assault
upon their spiritual authority.

THE SUCCESS OF CULTS

Up to a point Christian authors analyzing the reasons for the
growth of new religions agreed with secular analysts. For example,
Enroth (1979:47-54) argued that youths have been drawn to new religions as a result of problems of adolescence, a spiritual vacuum in
America, a lack of personal identity, youthful idealism, a need for
a sense of family, a desire for absolutist leadership and a need for
a sense of community. MacCollam (1979:47-54) listed factors such as
geographic mobility, disintegration of the extended family and problems of adolescence. McBeth (1977:27-32) cited disillusionment of
youth, fear of the future, family disintegration, drug usage and
failure of traditional churches to meet spiritual needs and demonstrate the way to live a spiritual life as causes for the rise of
cults. Finally, Beck (1977:11-20) argued that dominance of feelings
over intellect, a shift from a sense of certainty to one of relatively, the breakdown of community, an increase in leisure time and
a tension between the need for authority and the need for freedom
have been contributing factors.

In addition, however, evangelical and fundamentalist authors
stressed spiritual causes. Beck (1977:16-20) contended that a lack
of serious, deep knowledge of the Bible left Christians unable to
stand up to cultists. Furthermore, he insisted that the churches
have failed to boldly proclaim the true meaning of life and the need
for personal involvement based upon one´s belief system. Sparks
(1977:261) made a similar point in the course of defending Christian
churches.

> In saying all this, there is something that must
> honestly be admitted before we consider these
> truths. That is, much of what we call the Church
> has failed--often miserably--in carrying out its
> role before God, itself and the world. Though it
> is still loved and even protected by the Lord, it
> has moved an embarrassingly great distance from
> its original foundations.

Beyond such social ills and Christian shortcomings lurked the
ultimate source of cultic success, Satan. Hunt (1980:240) asserted
that: "There is a cult explosion that is unprecedented in human
history. In light of biblical prophecies, this seems to indicate an
approaching climax in the battle between God and Satan for the minds
and eternal destiny of mankind and the future of planet earth."
Enroth (1977:202) was even more explicit:

> From the Christian perspective, the so-called new-
> age cults represent the most recent manifestation
> of an age old struggle--the battle between good and
> evil, between God and God´s adversary, Satan. The

phenomena described in this book are neither random
nor accidental: they are profoundly patterned. As
simplistic as it may sound to some, they indicate a
demonic conspiracy to subvert the true gospel of
Jesus Christ through human agents whose minds have
been blinded by the evil one.

Other Christian authors were quick to proclaim that cult leaders
were so deceived. Breese (1975:124) put it this way: "Clever individuals with a smattering of religious knowledge are emboldened by
their own pride and motivated by Satan to press for their own piece
of influence in today's religious scene." Yamamoto (1977b:128-129)
specifically linked Sun Myung Moon, founder and leader of the Unification Church, to such a satanic plot:

Moon may have a strong hold on his followers, but
the strings do not begin with him. Moon himself is
more deceived than those whom he deceives. Moon
is not the puppet master. Moon is the master puppet.
Satan is the puppet master.

REACTING TO THE CULT CHALLENGE

In contrast to anti-cult parents' groups, Christian authors
generally downplayed deprogramming as a solution to the problem of
young adults joining new religions although they expressed great
sympathy for the plight of parents. Yamamoto (1977:100), for example, insisted that even though deprogramming might produce the
desired results it is not an appropriate tactic:

Some psychologists say that deprogramming is simply
a reverse pattern of brainwashing. The Unification
church may be brainwashing its converts, but whether
they are or not, deprogramming cannot be condoned,
for although the content is different, the method
is the same. Thus, if one is wrong, so is the
other.

Lochhaas (1979b:30) also recommended that professional deprogrammers
be avoided since "some operate outside the law and have been over-
ruled by the courts." In rejecting deprogramming, however, Christian authors had few substantive alternatives to offer parents.
Enroth (1977b:98) advised that "patience and prayer combined with a
hopeful and sustained love--despite the desperately trying circum-
stances--is an appropriate Christian response." Lochhaas (1979b:30)
urged families to pray, "exchange ministry" with others, be loving,
be informed, keep lines of communication open, avoid taking a martyr
role and refrain from self-deprecation.

If evangelical and fundamentalist Christian authors had little
solace to offer distraught parents, they sought a long-term solution
to the cult problem through the strengthening of Christian churches.
Readers were urged not simply to dismiss the new religions out of
hand. Enroth (1977:119-124) observed that "it is evident that the

cults are meeting very real needs and that they effect very real changes in the lives of members," citing the attractiveness of such groups to youths who are disenchanted with a "technological materialistic way of life." There was unanimous agreement that many problems would disappear if Christians demonstrated greater unity, dedication, assertion and commitment to a life based on Christian principles. As Yamamoto (1977b:105) put it: "As long as there are divisions within the Christian church and a lack of total fidelity to the Bridegroom, Satan will always conjure false pictures of Christ to confuse the world and disturb the body."

Christians were exhorted to contend for their faith and not to regard personal assertiveness as unspiritual or undignified. Breese (1975:128) reminded Christians that the world is a battlefield and that "the essential struggle on that field of conquest is the struggle between truth and untruth. In addition, Christians were encouraged to live exemplary moral lives (exhibiting love, kindness, patience, self control, justice and integrity) rather than relying on "Madison Avenue evangelistic techniques" (Sparks, 1977:270) as a means of regaining the moral initiative from cults. Enroth (1977: 121) concurred, noting that it has been non-Christians who have been addressing the issues of justice and equality and the creation of a new social order. Youths have simply been moving to "where the action is." And while he decried such reliance on personal experience rather than scriptural truths, he warned Christians that they must demonstrate Christian principles in a more visible and meaningful way.

In seizing the initiative Christians were warned not to make the battle against cults the focus of attention. Yamamoto (1977b: 106) warned that it might be part of Satan's strategy to decoy Christians into a skirmish against cults rather than pursuing the Kingdom of God. Too, there was some disagreement about whether or not Christians should familiarize themselves with cult doctrines. Some authors suggested that familiarity with cult doctrines would help Christians to spot counterfeits; others felt this unnecessary. As Breese (1975:126) so colorfully put it, "One has only to eat a good steak to realize that the contents of a thousand garbage cans are simply beneath his standards." Naturally all of these writers prescribed greater reading and understanding of the Bible as a way of sustaining Christian faith and preventing cultic incursions.

A sizeable literature developed on witnessing to cultists and fending off cult missionaries. This literature advised Christians to be polite and loving but firm in dealing with cult members. After all, whether wittingly or unwittingly, such individuals were agents of the anti-Christ. The sincerity and elaborate preparation of these missionaries was not to be doubted, however. The Lutheran Church-Missouri Synod, for example, published a series of booklets instructing Christians on how to respond to various cults. Each booklet was entitled "How to Respond to" followed by the name of one or a set of cults (Lochhaas, 1979a, 1979b; Beck, 1977; Gerberding, 1977; Hoover, 1977; Rongstad, 1977). In a general booklet, How to Respond to the Cults (Beck, 1977:37-38), the author listed a series of typical admonitions to Christians: (1) Don't be hostile, (2)

Don't slam the door in their face, (3) Don't argue heatedly, (4)
Don't show anxiety and (5) Don't rely on yourself alone. Beck
further counseled against expecting quick, easy victories. He observed, "Any lack of success, as one may repeatedly experience, is
not a sign of an absence of the spirit."

JEWISH OPPOSITION TO CULTS

The Jewish response to the new religions was just as negative
as the evangelical Christian response. From a Jewish perspective
the new religions were only the latest in a series of groups which
sought to convert Jews. Christian witnessing to Jews had long been
a problem for the Jewish community, and many Jewish authors have
addressed the question of how to deal with this challenge (Jacobs,
1977, 1975). Actually Jews were perhaps more vexed by the Jews for
Jesus (Cohen, 1979, 1978; Gillelsohn, 1979; Rudin and Rudin, 1977;
Eichhorn, 1976), which they regarded as a cult, than the new religions.

The central issue for Jews was recruitment of Jewish youth.
The literature by Jewish authors contains familiar tales of children
lost to cults (Yanoff, 1981; Solender, 1978; Wax, 1977) and accounts
by former members of cults (Sweet, 1977). Jewish writers expressed
concern that Jewish youths were disproportionately represented among
the ranks of converts to new religions and were aggressively recruited. Andron (1979) estimated that between twelve and fifteen
percent of the membership of cults was Jewish; Jewish Week (1981)
reported that over one thousand Jewish youths in the New York area
were involved in cults; and Pearlstein (1977) asserted that one-
third of the members of the Unification Church were Jewish. Jewish
spokespersons were worried not only about the sheer number of Jewish
youths being recruited by new religions (although these estimates
were grossly inflated) but also that it was the "cream" of Jewish
youth who were the targets of cult recruiters (Andron, 1979). Various explanations were offered by Jewish writers (Kollin, 1980;
Spero, 1977) for the attractiveness of new religions to young Jews,
and these lists of reasons (youthful innocence, identity seeking,
affluence, permissiveness, spiritual poverty of Judaism, idealism)
closely resembled those produced by Christian authors.

A related source of concern to Jewish leaders was the promi-
nence of Jews in leadership positions within various new religions.
Such figures might serve to attract Jewish youth to these movements.
Porter (1978), for example, reported on the number of Jewish intel-
lectuals who attended Unification Church sponsored International
Conferences on the Unity of Science. The number of Jewish leaders
in the Unification Church (such as Dr. Mose Durst, President of the
Unification Church of America, Dr. William Bergman and Dan
Fefferman) was also a concern although all three were excommunicated
by the Supreme Rabbinic Court of America. Furthermore, apostate
Jews founded a number of the more controversial new religions
including the Children of God (Moses David Berg), the Tony and Susan
Alamo Foundation and The Way International (Victor Paul Wierwille).

A number of Jews joined the ACM as a result of their concerns about proselytization of Jewish youth. The Rabbi Maurice Davis was certainly the most visible and flamboyant of these figures. Davis founded the Citizens Engaged in Reuniting Families, an anti-cult group committed to non-coercive techniques (i.e., "re-evaluation"), to extricate converts to new religions. Davis was frequently given to verbal hyperbole. In the wake of the tragic events at Jonestown, for example, he testified at an informal congressional hearing on cults (American Family Foundation, 1979:77).

> How many more Jonestowns must there be before we
> begin to do something? Gentlemen of the Congress:
> I am not here to protest against religion or reli-
> gions. I am here to protest against child molesters,
> for as surely as there are those who lure children
> with lollypops in order to rape their bodies, so
> too, are there those who lure children with candy-
> coated lies in order to rape their minds.

Steve Hassan founded Ex-Moon Inc., an anti-cult group which specifically targeted the Unification Church. James and Marcia Rudin wrote and lectured widely on the dangers and abuses of cults (1980; 1978; 1977). James Rudin also served as the Assistant National Director of Interreligious Affairs of the American Jewish Committee. Journalists Joshua Freed (1980) and Berkeley Rice (1976) produced a string of popular articles critical of the Unification Church. Edward Levine, a Jewish sociologist, produced more scholarly but critical articles on the new religions and defended deprogramming (Levine, 1980). Despite the active participation of a number of Jews in the ACM it would be inaccurate to characterize the Jewish community as solidly anti-cult. There was, for example, a lively debate between supporters and opponents of deprogramming (Zakim, 1979; Goldberg, 1977; Haramgaal, 1977), and some Jews dismissed the whole cult controversy as a fabricated problem (Israel, 1980). Too, as our review of legal issues surrounding new religions will demonstrate, a number of Jews were in the front ranks of civil libertarians who defended freedom of religion.

THE ORGANIZATION OF RELIGIOUS OPPOSITION

Two major types of religious organizations were in the forefront of the struggle against cults, groups associated with established denominations and evangelical groups. In the first category were denominational organizations, councils and interfaith groups. In the second category were groups which either had been opposing the preceding wave of new religions (e.g., Mormons, Jehovah's Witnesses) or arose specifically in response to the contemporary cults. In general, these groups simply issued informational or educational literature, but there were a few cases in which action was taken against new religions.

Some denominations, such as the Presbyterians (Langford, 1977) and Lutherans (Lutheran Church-Missouri Synod, 1978; Lutheran Council in the USA, 1978) issued reports and critiques on various new

religions as did local and regional interfaith groups (University
Religious Council, 1979; Pennsylvania Conference on Interchurch Cooperation, n.d.). These documents contained a mixture of religious
refutations and warnings of mental manipulation, advice on what individual congregations could do to counter cults, and even the names
of anti-cult groups to which to turn for help. In addition, the
National Council of the Churches of Christ's Commission on Faith and
Order conducted a thorough review specifically of the Unification
Church's theology, concluding that it was not Christian (Cunningham
et al., 1978):

> ... we conclude that the Unification Church is not
> a Christian church because its doctrine of the
> nature of the true God is erroneous; its Christo-
> logy is incompatible with Christian teaching and
> belief; and its teaching on salvation and the means
> of grace is inadequate and faulty. We further con-
> clude that the claims of the Unification Church to
> Christian identity cannot be recognized because the
> role and authority of Scripture are compromised in
> the teachings of the Unification Church; revela-
> tions invoked as divine and normative in Divine
> Principle contradict basic elements of Christian
> faith; and a "new, ultimate, final trust" is pre-
> sented to supplant all previously recognized reli-
> gious teachings, including those of Christianity.

A similar series of reports were issued by local Jewish organizations in a number of states (Task Force on Missionary Activity,
1980; New York Jewish Community Relations Council, 1979; Philadelphia Jewish Community Relations Council, 1978; Board of Jewish Education, 1978; Fishman, 1977). There also were specific reports
offering suggestions for means of preventing recruitment of Jewish
youths (Morgan, 1979) and legal strategies that might be employed
against cults (Stern, 1978). Some of these reports received considerable play in Jewish periodicals (Edelstein, 1981). In addition, the American Jewish Committee issued an analysis and critique of the theology of the Unification Church (Tanenbaum, 1978;
Rudin, 1976). This report was significant for it reflected another
major Jewish concern, a resurgence of anti-Semitism. In his report
to the American Jewish Committee, Rudin (1976) reported over 125
examples of anti-Semitic statements and teachings in the Divine
Principle. These included references to the faithlessness of the
Israelites, to the Jews, culpability in the crucifixion of Jesus and
to Jewish persecution through history as punishment for their sins.
Rudin emphasized that while mainline denominations had openly repudiated such doctrines, the Unification Church was moving in
precisely the opposite direction. Stung by this criticism, Moon
himself issued a statement repudiating anti-Semitism. While the
report's framers welcomed this statement, they called for a
follow-up with concrete actions to demonstrate good faith
(Tanenbaum, 1978).

The evangelical organizations issued stinging critiques of the
theologies of the major and a number of minor new religions. Some

of these organizations, such as Walter Martin´s Christian Research
Institute, had opposed earlier new religions and simply added the
contemporary groups to their list. The Christian Research Institute
distributes Martin´s own works on cults as well as publications of
other evangelical groups. Like many other such groups the Christian
Research Institute has begun to emphasize the distribution of
cassette tapes since they can be produced inexpensively and have
audience appeal. Certainly the best known and most active of the
evangelical groups is the Spiritual Counterfeits Project of
Berkeley, California. As Saliba (1981:452) put it:

> The Spiritual Counterfeits Project (SCP) of
> Berkeley, California, understands itself to be
> a ministry of rebuttal and rejoinder to the new
> movements. The principle work of its full-time
> staff is to gather and disseminate information,
> chiefly through an extensive publication program
> of books, leaflets and pamphlets.

The Spiritual Counterfeits Project is a branch of the Berkeley
Christian Coalition which traces its history to the Jesus People
movement of the late 1960´s. The Project´s monthly newsletter has
produced the most sophisticated theological analyses of what it
regards as satanically inspired cults. Research reports issued on
specific groups defined as cults and testimonies of former cult
members have formed the basis for broadcasting warnings to Christians and evangelizing cult members. Spiritual Counterfeits Project, for example, has issued reports such as "A Critical Analysis
of Eckankar" (1979), The God Men: Witness Lee and the Local Church
(1978a), "Church Universal and Triumphant" (1977a), The Children of
God: Disciples of Deception (1977b), Bubba Free John: An American
Guru (n.d.a), Christ and Guru Maharaj Ji: The Savior´s Second Coming
or the Sages Eternal Return? (n.d.b), Moon Survey (n.d.d) and Uniting All Faiths: The Holy Order of Mans (n.d.g). A number of these
reports were reprinted or distributed by other evangelical groups,
and so Spiritual Counterfeits Project assumed considerable
prominence and influence in the Christian crusade against cults.

There were relatively few instances of direct action against
new religions beyond such educational and evangelical campaigns.
Churches did rebuff attempts by new religions to gain membership in
interfaith groups and in a few cases called for governmental investigations of new religions. The only clear instance of a direct initiative against a new religion involved the Spiritual Counterfeits
Project´s central role in a suit against Transcendental Meditation.
Evangelicals were disturbed that meditation techniques were being
taught in schools, prisons, alcoholism centers and other govern-
mentally funded programs, and elected officials were openly embrac-
ing meditation as a therapeutic technique (Williams, n.d.:28-30).
The suit to enjoin the teaching of Transcendental Meditation in the
New Jersey public schools was successful. As the presiding judge
concluded (Spiritual Counterfeits Project, 1978b:72):

> Although defendants have submitted well over 1500
> pages of briefs, affidavits and deposition testi-

mony on opposing plantiff´s motion for summary
judgment, defendents have failed to raise the
slightest doubt as to the facts or as to the
religious nature of the teachings of the Science
of Creative Intelligence and the puja. The teachings of the SCI/TM course in New Jersey public
high schools violates the establishment clause of
the first amendment, and its teaching must be
enjoined.

This represented one of the few clear-cut legal victories achieved
against new religions, and it is ironic that it involved a contention by the evangelicals that Transcendental Meditation should be
a legitimate religious organization for legal purposes.

308. Alexander, Brooks. "Eckankar versus Everybody." Spiritual
      Counterfeits Project Journal 3 (September 1979): 26-28.

309. American Family Foundation. Information Meeting on the Cult
      Phenomenon in the United States (Transcript of Proceedings).
      Lexington, MA: American Family Foundation (1979).

310. Andron, Sandy. "Our Gifted Teens and the Cults." Pedagogic
      Reporter 31 (Fall 1979): 37-38.

311. Anthony, C. "In Moon´s Church: One Woman´s Story." Our
      Sunday Visitor, April 7, 1977, pp. 3-4.

312. Appell, Michael. "Cult Encounters." Moment 4 (November
      1978): 19-24.

313. Avon, Gene. My Search. Seattle, WA: Life Messengers, 1974.
      15 pp.

314. Baldwin, Frank. "Korea Lobby." Christianity and Crisis.
      July 19, 1976, pp. 162-168.

315. Baltagar, Eulalio R. "TM and the Religion-in-School Issue."
      Christian Century, August 18-25, 1976, pp. 708-709.

316. Beck, Hubert F. How to Respond to the Cults. St. Louis, MO:
      Concordia Publishing House, 1977. 40 pp.

317. Beisner, Cal, Robert Passantino and Gretchen Passantino. The
      Teachings of Witness Lee and the Local Church. San Juan
      Capistrano, CA: Christian Research Institute, 1978. 21 pp.

318. Bergfalk, Lynn, and others. "TM Opponents: Which Battle to
      Fight (Reader´s Response)." Christian Century, February 16,
      1977, pp. 150-154.

319. Berry, Harold J. Witnessing to the Cults. Lincoln, NE: Back
      to the Bible, 1974. 14 pp.

320. Berry, W.J. A Brief Survey of the Present-Day Cults/False
     Teachings/Satanic Deceptions/with a Warning to God's People.
     Elon College, NC: Primitive Publications, 1970. 78 pp.

321. Bjornstad, James. The Moon Is Not the Son. Minneapolis:
     Dimension Books/Bethany Fellowship Press, 1976a. 126 pp.

322. Bjornstad, James. The Transcendental Mirage. Minneapolis:
     Dimension Books/Bethany Fellowship Press, 1976b. 93 pp.

323. Board of Jewish Education. The Cult Phenomenon. Baltimore:
     Board of Jewish Education, 1978.

324. Breese, Dave. Know the Marks of Cults: The Twelve Basic
     Errors of False Religion. Wheaton, IL: Victor Books, 1975.
     128 pp.

325. Brow, Robert. "Religion, Comparatively Speaking." HIS Maga-
     zine, March 1973, pp. 12-14.

326. Burrell, Maurice, and H. Stafford Wright. Whom Then Can We
     Believe? Chicago, IL: Moody Press, 1976. 128 pp.

327. Bush, Larry. "The Challenge of the Cults." Jewish Currents,
     December 1980, pp. 9-13.

328. Campbell, Colin. "Who Really Owned Eden?" Psychology Today,
     December 1975, pp. 72, 74, 104.

329. Campbell, Joseph. "Seven Levels of Consciousness."
     Psychology Today, December 1975, pp. 77-78.

330. Carruth, Joseph. Children of God: (aka Family of Love).
     Berkeley, CA: Spiritual Counterfeits Project, 1981. 6 pp.

331. Carruth, Joseph. "The Farm." Spiritual Counterfeits Project
     Journal, April 4, 1980, pp. 19-20.

332. Chandler, Russell. "Fighting Cults: The Tucson Tactic."
     Christianity Today, February 4, 1977, pp. 57-61.

333. Chandler, Russell. "By the Light of the Saviourly Moon
     (Rev. Sun Myung Moon, a Korean Evangelist, Head of the
     Unification Church, Staging Pro-Nixon Rallies)."
     Christianity Today, March 1, 1974, pp. 101-102.

334. Chang, Lit-sen. Transcendental Meditation. Nutley, NJ:
     Presbyterian and Reformed Publishing Co., 1978. 92 pp.

335. "Children of God: Disciples of Deception." Christian Century,
     February 18, 1977, pp. 20-21.

336. Christian Apologetics and Research Service. TM: Penetrating
     the Veil of Deception. Santa Ana, CA: Christian Apologetics
     Research and Information Service, n.d. 8 pp.

337. Christian Research Institute. Today Could Be Your Re-
      Birthday. San Juan Capistrano, CA: Christian Research
      Institute, n.d. 5 pp.

338. Clements, R.D. God and the Gurus. Downers Grove, IL: Inter-
      Varsity Press, 1975. 64 pp.

339. Cohen, Daniel. The New Believers: Young Religion in America.
      New York: Ballantine, 1975.

340. Cohen, Mark. "Missionaries in Our Midst: The Appeal of Alter-
      natives." Analysis, March 1978, p. 8.

341. Cohen, Robert A. "Infiltrating the Jews for Jesus." Jewish
      Digest, February 1979, pp. 8-12.

342. "Confronting the Moonies." United Synagogue Review Quarterly
      30 (Summer 1977): 3.

343. Cox, Harvey G. "Eastern Cults and Western Culture: Why Young
      Americans are Buying Oriental Religions." Psychology Today,
      July 1977a, pp. 36-42.

344. Cox, Harvey G. "Real Threat of the Moonies." Christianity
      and Crisis, November 14, 1977b, pp. 258-263.

345. Cult Exodus for Christ. A Second Exodus Has Begun. Covina,
      CA: Cult Exodus for Christ, n.d.a. 2 pp.

346. Cult Exodus for Christ. The Maze of Cults. Covina, CA: Cult
      Exodus for Christ, n.d.b. 2 pp.

347. Cult Exodus for Christ. The Three Steps. Covina, CA: Cult
      Exodus for Christ, n.d.c. 2 pp.

348. "Cults Pose Challenge to Parents, Jewish Community." Women's
      World, February/March 1981, p. 6.

349. "Cults Said to Have Entrapped 1,000 Jewish Kids in this Area."
      Jewish Week, April 12, 1981, p. 32.

350. Cunningham, Agnes, et al. "Critique of the Theology of the
      Unification Church as Set Forth in Divine Principle."
      Science, Sin and Scholarship: The Politics of Reverend Moon
      and the Unification Church. Edited by Irving Louis
      Horowitz. Cambridge, MA: MIT Press, 1978. 290 pp.

351. Daum, Annette. Missionary and Cult Movements. New York:
      Department of Interreligious Affairs, Union of American
      Hebrew Congregations, 1977. 80 pp.

352. Davis, Rabbi Maurice. "Update on Moon." Brotherhood, March/
      April 1977.

353. Davis, Rabbi Maurice. "Moon for the Misbegotten." Reform Judaism, November 1974.

354. Dilley, John R. "TM Comes to the Heartland of the Midwest." Christian Century, December 10, 1975, pp. 1129-1132.

355. Dnavamony, M. "Transcendental Meditation." Clergy Review, November 1978, pp. 418-425.

356. Donohue, J. "New Jersey Mantra: Transcendental Meditation (TM) and the Science of Creative Intelligence (SCI) in High School." America, November 19, 1977, p. 360.

357. Drener, J. "Can a Christian Practice TM: Reprint from The Providence Visitor." Our Sunday Visitor, August 13, 1978, p. 8.

358. Duddy, Neil T. The God-Men: An Inquiry Into Witness Lee and the Local Church. Downers Grove, IL: Inter-Varsity Press, 1981. 156 pp.

359. Duncan, Homer. An Expose of The Way International, Inc. Lubbock, TX: Missionary Crusader, n.d. 2 pp.

360. Dunfey, C. "An Encounter with the Children of God." Sisters, May 1977, pp. 592-597.

361. Edelstein, Andrew. "Cults are Rising as Social Peril." Jewish Week, April 12, 1981, p. 52.

362. Eichhorn, D.M. "Hebrew Christianity." Jewish Spectator 41 (Fall 1976): 33-35.

363. Enroth, Ronald M. "Any Preventive for the Cults?" Christian Herald, March 1979, pp. 13-15.

364. Enroth, Ronald M. Youth, Brainwashing and the Extremist Cults. Kentwood, MI: Zondervan Publishing House, 1977. 221 pp.

365. Ericson, E.E., and P. Macherson. "Deceptions of the Children of God." Christianity Today, July 20, 1973, pp. 14-20.

366. Evans, Christopher. Cults of Unreason. New York: Farrar, Straus and Giroux, 1973. 258 pp.

367. Fackre, Gabriel. "Going East: Neomysticism and Christian Faith." Christian Century, April 14, 1971, pp. 457-461.

368. Fishman, Samuel Z. Comments on the Campus: The Moonies and the Response of the Jewish Community. Washington, DC: B'nai Brith/Hillel Foundations, 1977.

369. Flanagan, F. "Alternatives to Transcendental Meditation." Clergy Review, July 1979a, pp. 247-252.

370. Flanagan, F. "TM: Self-transcendence or Self-deception."
     Clergy Review, May 1979b, pp. 167-172.

371. Freed, Joshua. Moonwebs: Journey Into the Mind of a Cult.
     Toronto: Dorset Publishing, Inc., 1980. 216 pp.

372. Freedman, Theodore. "Religious Cults: How Serious a Danger?"
     ADL Bulletin, April 1977, pp. 1-2.

373. Garvey, John. "Are the Cults a Judgement on the Churches?"
     Katallagete (Fall 1977): 21-26.

374. Gerberding, Keith A. How to Respond to Transcendental
     Meditation. St. Louis, MO: Concordia Publishing House, 1977.
     31 pp.

375. Gibbons, G. "Transcendental Meditation and Christian Prayer:
     How Different Are They?" Liquorian, June 1976, pp. 13-15.

376. Gittelsohn, Roland B. "Jews for Jesus: Are They Real?"
     Midstream, May 1979, pp. 41-45.

377. Goldberg, W., et al. "Deprogramming: An Exchange." American
     Zionist, October 1977, pp. 34-38.

378. Gruss, Edmond C. Cults and the Occult. Phillipsburg, NJ:
     Presbyterian and Reformed Publishing Co., 1980. 150 pp.

379. Gruss, Edmond C. Cults and the Occult in the Age of Aquarius.
     Grand Rapids, MI: Baker Book House, 1974. 132 pp.

380. Guinness, Oswald. "The Eastern Look of the Modern West."
     Today, January 27, 1974, pp. 2-4.

381. Haddon, David. "Transcendental Meditation Challenges the
     Church." Christianity Today, March 27, 1976, pp. 15-18.

382. Haddon, David. Transcendental Meditation: A Christian View.
     Downers Grove, IL: Inter-Varsity Press, 1975. 30 pp.
     tianity Today, December 21, 1973, pp. 9-12.

383. Haddon, David. "New Plant thrives in a Spiritual Desert."
     Christianity Today, December 21, 1973, pp. 9-12.

384. Haddon, David, and Vail Hamilton. T.M. Wants You. Grand
     Rapids, MI: Baker Book House, 1976. 204 pp.

385. Haines, Aubrey B. "Taking a Flier with TM." Christian
     Century, August 16, 1978, pp. 770-771.

386. Haramgaal, Y. "Deprogramming: A Critical View." American
     Zionist, May/June 1977, pp. 16-19.

387. Hefley, James C. The Youthnappers. Wheaton, IL: Victor
     Books, 1977. 208 pp.

388. Herm, S. Mark. "Divine Principle and the Second Advent." Christian Century, May 11, 1977, pp. 448-453.

389. Holck, Frederick, and Eleanor Cate. "Ex Oriente Lux." Christian Century, March 5, 1969, pp. 315-318.

390. Hoover, David W. How to Respond to the Occult. St. Louis, MO: Concordia Publishing House, 1977. 31 pp.

391. Hopkins, Joseph M. "Are Moonies in New Phase: Raiders and Koreanization." Christianity Today, June 27, 1980, p. 60.

392. Hopkins, Joseph M. "Is Forum Integrity Eclipsed by Moon?" Christianity Today, January 19, 1979, pp. 38-39.

393. Hopkins, Joseph M. "Children of God: New Revelations." Christianity Today, February 24, 1978a, p. 44.

394. Hopkins, Joseph M. "Meeting the Moonies on Their Territory." Christianity Today, August 18, 1978b, p. 41.

395. Hopkins, Joseph M. "How to Spot a Cult." Moody Monthly, July/August 1977, pp. 6-7.

396. Hopkins, Joseph M. "Baiting the Hook." Christianity Today, December 30, 1977, pp. 436-437.

397. Hunt, Dave. The Cult Explosion: An Expose of Today's Cults and Why They Prosper. Eugene, OR: Harvest House Publishers, 1980. 270 pp.

398. Israel, Richard J. "The Cult Problem Is a Fake!" The National Jewish Monthly, January 1980.

399. Jacobs, Steven. "Are Your Children Immune from Missionaries?" Jewish Digest, December 1977, pp. 10-12.

400. Jacobs, Steven. "How to Answer the Christian Missionary." Jewish Digest, September 1975, pp. 14-17.

401. Jaeger, Harry J. "By the Light of a Masterly Moon." Christianity Today, December 19, 1975, pp. 13-16.

402. Jahnke, Art. "They Call Him the Negative Messiah." Real Paper (Boston), August 28, 1980, p. 7.

403. Kang, Wi Jo. "Influence of the Unification Church in the United States of America." Missiology, July 1975, pp. 357-368.

404. Kemperman, Stephen. "My 3 1/2 Years with the Moonies." Sign, December 1979/January 1980, pp. 44-51.

405. Kenkelen, B. "Law Enrages Cult Opponents." National Catholic Reporter, November 18, 1980, p. 5.

406. Kim, Rev. Hyun Chil. "Sun Myung Moon and His Unification
      Church." Capital Baptist, September 9, 1976, pp. 3-6.

407. Koch, Kurt. Christian Counseling and Occultism. Grand
      Rapids, MI: Kregel Publications, 1972. 338 pp.

408. Koch, Kurt. Occult Bondage and Deliverance. Grand Rapids,
      MI: Kregel Publications, 1970. 198 pp.

409. Kolbe, Edward H. "Cults and the Christian Faith (Eph. 4:
      11-16)." Christian Ministry, November 1979, pp. 24-25.

410. Kollin, Gilbert. "The Call of the Strange Cults." Jewish
      Digest, October 1980, pp. 25-35.

411. Krishna, Paul M. Journey from the East. Downers Grove, IL:
      Inter-Varsity Press, 1972. 48 pp.

412. Kroll, U.M. "Doctor's View of TM." Frontier, Spring 1974,
      pp. 31-33.

413. Kulanday, V. "Transcendental Meditation and the Great Night
      Festival of Shiva, March 11, 1975." Social Justice Review,
      February 1976, pp. 345-346.

414. Kulanday, V. "The Trap: Transcendental Meditation." Social
      Justice Review, December 1975, pp. 249-252.

415. LaMore, George E. "Secular Selling of a Religion." Christian
      Century, December 10, 1975, pp. 1133-1137.

416. Langford, Harris. Traps: A Probe of Those Strange New Cults.
      Montgomery, AL: Committee for Christian Education and Publi-
      cations, Presbyterian Church in America, 1977. 191 pp.

417. Lester, Elenore. "Cultists Focusing on Young Jews as Prime
      Prospects." Jewish Week, December 28, 1980.

418. Levin, S. "Battered People Syndrome?" Judaism, Spring 1977,
      pp. 217-221.

419. Levine, Edward M. "The Case for Deprogramming Religious Cult
      Members." Society, March/April 1980.

420. Levine, Faye. The Strange World of the Hare Krishnas. New
      York: Fawcett Publications, 1974. 189 pp.

421. Levitt, Zola. The Spirit of Sun Myung Moon. Irvine, CA:
      Harvest House Publishers, 1976. 127 pp.

422. Lewis, Gordon. What Everyone Should Know About Transcendental
      Meditation. Glendale, CA: Regal Books, 1975. 92 pp.

423. Lightner, Robert P. Meditation That Transcends. Denver, CO:
      Accent Books, 1975. 64 pp.

424. Lochhaas, Philip H. How to Respond to the Eastern Religions.
     St. Louis, MO: Concordia Publishing House, 1979a. 32 pp.

425. Lochhaas, Philip H. How to Respond to the New Christian
     Religions. St. Louis, MO: Concordia Publishing House,
     1979b. 31 pp.

426. Lutheran Church-Missouri Synod. Packet on "New Religions.
     St. Louis, MO: The Lutheran Church - Missouri Synod, Commis-
     sion on Organizations, 1978.

427. Lutheran Council in the USA. The Cults: A Resource Packet.
     Chicago, IL: The Lutheran Council in the USA, Division of
     Campus Ministry and Education Services, 1979.

428. Luxenberg, Stan. "The Soul Snatchers of Long Island."
     Moment, May 1977, pp. 7-10.

429. MacCollam, Joel A. Carnival of Souls: Religious Cults and
     Young People. New York: Seabury Press, 1979. 188 pp.

430. MacCollam, Joel A. The Way of Victor Paul Wierwille. Downers
     Grove, IL: Inter-Varsity Press, 1978. 30 pp.

431. MacCollam, Joel A. "The Way Seemed Right But the End
     Thereof ...." Eternity, November 1977, pp. 23-26.

432. MacCollam, Joel A. The Weekend That Never Ends. New York:
     Youth and College Ministries Office of the Executive Council
     of the Episcopal Church, (1977). 37 pp.

433. MacCollam, Joel A. "The Unification Church." The Living
     Church, December 12, 1976, pp. 8-9.

434. Maharaj, Rabindranath R., with Dave Hunt. Death of a Guru.
     Philadelphia, PA: A.J. Holman Co., 1977. 224 pp.

435. Malamed, Gad. "How to Answer Street Missionaries." Jewish
     Digest, February 1977, pp. 49-51.

436. Malko, George. Scientology: The Now Religion. New York:
     Delta Books, 1971. 205 pp.

437. Maloney, George A. T.M. and Christian Meditation. Pecos, NM:
     Dove Publications, 1976.

438. Marchand, R. "Mr. Moon and the Unification Church."
     Liquorian (June 1978): 34-39.

439. Marchand, R. "New Light on T.M." Liquorian (September 1978):
     38-43.

440. Marty, Martin E. "Religious Cause, Religious Cure." Chris-
     tian Century, February 28, 1979, p. 212.

441. Matthews, Arthur H. "Meeting Moon at the Monument." <u>Chris-</u>
      <u>tianity Today</u>, October 8, 1976, pp. 59-62.

442. Maust, John. "The Moonies Cross Wits with Cult-watching
      Critics." <u>Christianity Today</u>, July 20, 1979, pp. 38-40.

443. Mazzarella, P. "The Maharishi's Spiritual Novocaine." <u>Sign</u>,
      April 1977, pp. 12-13.

444. McBeth, Leon. <u>Strange New Religions</u>. Nashville, TN: Broadman
      Press, 1977. 154 pp.

445. McGowan, T. "The Unification Church." <u>The Ecumenist</u> 17
      (January/February 1978): 21-25.

446. Means, Pat. <u>The Mystical Maze</u>. San Bernardino, CA: Campus
      Crusade for Christ, 1976. 275 pp.

447. Melton, Gordon J. "What is Moon Up To?" <u>Christianity Today</u>,
      April 7, 1978, p. 47.

448. Miller, Calvin. <u>Transcendental Hesitation: A Biblical</u>
      <u>Appraisal of TM and Eastern Mysticism</u>. Kentwood, MI:
      Zondervan Publishing House, 1977. 185 pp.

449. Mook, Jane Day. "New Growth on Burnt-Over Ground." <u>A.D.</u>,
      May 1974, pp. 30-36.

450. "Moon's Credibility Game." <u>Christian Century</u>, September 24,
      1975, pp. 812-813.

451. Morgan, Hesh. <u>Is This the End of the Battle?</u> New York: Anti-
      Missionary Institute, 1979.

452. Moriconi, John. <u>Children of God, Family of Love</u>. Downers
      Grove, IL: Inter-Varsity Fellowship, 1980. 39 pp.

453. Nederhood, Joel. <u>Cult Insurance</u>. Palos Heights, IL:
      Christian Reformed Church, The Back to God Hour, 1979.
      12 pp.

454. New York. Jewish Community Relations Council. <u>Resource Kit</u>
      <u>on Missionaries and Cults</u>. New York: Jewish Community Rela-
      tions Council, 1979.

455. Nichols, Woodrow, and Brooks Alexander. "Paul Twitchell and
      the Evolution of Eckankar." <u>Spiritual Counterfeits Project</u>
      <u>Journal</u> 3 (September 1979): 6-23.

456. Noorbergen, Rene. <u>The Soul Hustlers</u>. Kentwood, MI: Zondervan
      Publishing House, 1976. 190 pp.

457. O'Connor, L. "The Moonies: An Exercise in Manipulation."
      <u>St. Anthony Messenger</u> (May 1977): 28-34.

458. Patton, John E. <u>Religion Maharishi Style: The Camouflage</u> <u>Technique</u>. n.p.: The Author, 1976a. 57 pp.

459. Patton, John E. <u>The Case Against T.M. in the Schools</u>. Grand Rapids, MI: Baker Book House, 1976b. 100 pp.

460. Pearlstein, Ira. "Jews and Reverend Moon." <u>Women's American</u> <u>Ort Reporter</u> (March/April 1977): 3.

461. Pearlstein, Ira. <u>The Reverend Moon Phenomenon</u>. Jewish Student Press Service, 1976.

462. Peerman, Dean. "Korean Moonshine." <u>Christian Century</u>, December 4, 1974, pp. 1139-1141.

463. Pennsylvania Conference on Interchurch Cooperation. <u>The</u> <u>Dangers of Pseudo-Religious Cults</u>. Harrisburg, PA: Pennsylvania Conference on Inter-Church Cooperation, n.d.

464. Perrin, Ann. <u>Cults: What Are They and Is Government Inter-</u><u>vention Warranted</u>. New York: National Conference of Christians and Jews, March 1979. 6 pp.

465. Peterson, William J. <u>TM: Ado About Nothing</u>. New Canaan, CT: Keats Publishing Co., 1976. 106 pp.

466. Peterson, William J. <u>Those Curious New Cults</u>. New Canaan, CT: Keats Publishing Co., 1973. 272 pp.

467. Philadelphia Jewish Community Relations Council. <u>The</u> <u>Challenge of the Cults</u>. Philadelphia: Jewish Community Relations Council, 1978. 70 pp.

468. Plowman, Edward E. "Help Us Get Our Children Back." <u>Chris-</u><u>tianity Today</u>, March 12, 1976, pp. 45-46.

469. Plowman, Edward E. "Deprogramming: A Right to Rescue?" <u>Christianity Today</u>, May 7, 1976, pp. 38-39.

470. Plowman, Edward E. "Where Are All the Children Now?" <u>Chris-</u><u>tianity Today</u>, April 27, 1973, pp. 35-36.

471. Poppinga, Julius B. "Transcendental Meditation: How Long Can Its PR Transcend Its Realities." <u>The Christian Lawyer</u> 3 (Spring 1978): 38-47.

472. Porter, Jack N. "Many Jewish Professors at Moon's Conference in Boston." <u>The Jewish Advocate</u> (December 1978).

473. Raab, Earl. "Reverend Moon and the Jews: The San Francisco Experience." <u>Congress Monthly</u> 43 (December 1976): 8-12.

474. Rice, Berkeley. "Honor Thy Father Moon." <u>Psychology Today</u> January 1976, pp. 36-47.

475. Richardson, H. "The Psychiatric State: Attacks on the Unifi-
      cation Church of Sun Myung Moon." The Ecumenist (November/
      December 1978): 11-13.

476. Roberts, Dana. Understanding Watchman Nee. Plainfield, NJ:
      Haven Books, n.d. 194 pp.

477. Robertson, Irvine. "The Eastern Mystics Are Out to Take You
      In." Moody Monthly (July/August 1973): 24-28.

478. Rongstad, L. James. How to Respond to the Lodge. St. Louis,
      MO: Concordia Publishing House, 1977. 32 pp.

479. Ross, B. "Despite Korea Clouds, the Moon Also Rises."
      National Catholic Reporter, September 9, 1977, p. 16.

480. Rudin, A. James. "The Peril of Reverend Moon." Jewish
      Digest, June 1977, pp. 74-78.

481. Rudin, A. James. Jews and Judaism in Reverend Moon's Divine
      Principle: A Report. New York: American Jewish Committee,
      1976.

482. Rudin, Marcia R. "The New Religious Cults and the Jewish
      Community." Religious Education, May/June 1978, pp. 350-
      360.

483. Rudin, A. James, and Marcia R. Rudin. Prison or Paradise: The
      New Religious Cults. Philadelphia, PA: Fortress Press,
      1980.

484. Rudin, A. James, and Marcia R. Rudin. "Onward (Hebrew) Chris-
      tian Soldiers." Present Tense 4 (Summer 1977): 17-26.

485. Saliba, John A. "The Christian Response to the New Religions:
      A Critical Look at the Spiritual Counterfeits Project."
      Journal of Ecumenical Studies 18 (Summer 1981): 451-473.

486. Saliba, John A. "The Guru: Perceptions of American Devotees
      of the Divine Light Mission." Horizons 7 (Spring 1980):
      69-71.

487. Sandon, Leo, Jr. "Korean Moon: Waxing or Waning?" Theology
      Today (July 1978a): 159-167.

488. Sandon, Leo Jr. "Moonie Family: We All Have a Stake in Being
      Fair to the Far-Out." Worldview (October 1978b): 7-11.

489. Sandon, Leo Jr. True Family: Korean Communitarianism and Ameri-
      can Loneliness. New York: United Ministries to Higher Edu-
      cation Communication Office, (1978c). 13 pp.

490. Sawatsky, Rodney. "Dialogue with the Moonies." Theology
      Today (April 1978): 88-91.

491. Schaeffer, Edith. "Testing TM." Christianity Today,
     March 26, 1976, pp. 29-30.

492. Schwartz, Lita L., and Florence Kaslow. "Cults, The
     Individual and the Family." Journal of Marital and Family
     Counseling (April 1979).

493. Schwartz, Lita L., and Florence Kaslow. "Cults and the Vul-
     nerability of Jewish Youth." Jewish Education (Summer
     1978): 23-26.

494. "Scientology: What Do the Records Reveal?" Christianity
     Today, May 19, 1978, pp. 60-62.

495. Shah, Douglas. The Meditators. Plainfield, NJ: Logos Inter-
     national, 1975. 147 pp.

496. "(Shaky) Federal Case Against Scientology." Christianity
     Today, August 12, 1977, pp. 32-33.

497. Short, Shirl. "The Menace of the New Cults." Moody Monthly
     (July/August 1977): 1-5.

498. Silver, Marc, and Barbara Pash. "Cults." Baltimore Jewish
     Times, 3 June, 1977.

499. Silverberg, David. "Heavenly Deception: Rev. Moon's Hard
     Sell." Present Tense 4 (Autumn 1976): 49-56.

500. Solender, Elsa. "The Making and Unmaking of a Jewish Moonie."
     National Jewish Monthly 93 (December 1978).

501. Smith, A. "Transcendental Meditation." African Ecclesiasti-
     cal Review 20 (June 1978): 189-192.

502. Sparks, Jack. The Mind Benders. Nashville, TN: Thomas
     Nelson, Inc., Publishers, 1977. 283 pp.

503. Spero, Moshe H. "Cults: Some Theoretical and Practical Per-
     spectives." Journal of Jewish Communal Service 53 (Summer
     1977): 330-338.

504. Spiritual Counterfeits Project. "A Critical Analysis of
     Eckankar." Spiritual Counterfeits Project Journal 3
     (September 1979): 34-41.

505. Spiritual Counterfeits Project. The God Men: Witness Lee and
     the Local Church. Berkeley, CA: Spiritual Counterfeits
     Project, 1978a. 80 pp.

506. Spiritual Counterfeits Project. TM in Court. Berkeley, CA:
     Spiritual Counterfeits Project, 1978b. 75 pp.

507. Spiritual Counterfiets Project. "Church Universal and Trium-
     phant (Summit Lighthouse)." Spiritual Counterfeits News-

letter (December/January 1977a).

508. Spiritual Counterfeits Project. The Children of God: Dis-
      ciples of Deception. Berkeley, CA: Spiritual Counterfeits
      Project, 1977b. 5 pp.

509. Spiritual Counterfeits Project. Who Is This Man and What Does
      He Want? Berkeley, CA: Spiritual Counterfeits Project,

510. Spiritual Counterfeits Project. Bubba Free John: An American
      Guru. Berkeley, CA: Spiritual Counterfeits Project, n.d.a.
      2 pp.

511. Spiritual Counterfeits Project. Christ and Guru Maharaj Ji:
      The Savior´s Second Coming or the Sage´s Eternal Return?
      Berkeley, CA: Spiritual Counterfeits Project, n.d.b. 3 pp.

512. Spiritual Counterfeits Project. Cutting Through Spiritual
      Cop-Outs. Berkeley, CA: Spiritual Counterfeits Project,
      n.d.c. 3 pp.

513. Spiritual Counterfeits Project. Moon Survey. Berkeley, CA:
      Spiritual Counterfeits Project, n.d.d. 3 pp.

514. Spiritual Counterfeits Project. The Path and the Crossroads.
      Berkeley, CA: Spiritual Counterfeits Project, n.d.e. 3 pp.

515. Spiritual Counterfeits Project. The Politics of Experience.
      Berkeley, CA: Spiritual Counterfeits Project, n.d.f. 7 pp.

516. Spiritual Counterfeits Project. Uniting All Faiths: The Holy
      Order of Mans. Berkeley, CA: Spiritual Counterfeits Proj-
      ect, n.d.g. 2 pp.

517. Stern, Marc D. The Cults and the Law, CLSA/UA Reports. New
      York: American Jewish Congress (February 1978).

518. Stentzel, James. "Rev. Moon and His Bicentennial Blitz."
      Christianity and Crisis, July 19, 1976, pp. 173-175.

519. Sweet, Larry. "Why I Left the Moonies." Jewish Digest 23
      (September 1977): 67-70.

520. Tanenbaum, Marc H. "Addendum to Jews and Judaism in Reverend
      Moon´s Divine Principle: A Report." Science, Sin, and
      Scholarship: The Politics of Reverend Moon and the
      Unification Church. Edited by Irving Louis Horowitz.
      Cambridge, MA: MIT Press, 1978, pp. 84-85.

521. Task Force on Missionary Activity. Selected Bibliography on
      Cults. New York: Jewish Community Relations Council of New
      York, Inc., (1980).

522. University Religious Council. Understanding Cult Involvement:
      For Counselors, Clergy, and Group Workers. Berkeley, CA:

University Religious Council at the University of California (1979).

523. Vieg, E.L. "Lure of Novel Religious Forms: Three Autiobiographical Sketches." Soundings 57 (Winter 1974): 403-419.

524. Wallerstedt, Alan. Victor Paul Wierwille and The Way. Berkeley, CA: Spiritual Counterfeits Project, 1976. 32 pp.

525. Walter, Robert G. The False Teachings of the R.B. Theme Jr. Collinwood, NJ: The Bible for Today, 1972. 102 pp.

526. Wax, Judith. "Sharing a Son with Hare Krishna." The New York Times Magazine, May 1, 1977, p. 40.

527. Weldon, John F. "Sampling of the New Religions: Four Groups Described." International Review of Mission 67 (October 1978): 407-426.

528. Whalen, W. "TM: Expensive Meditation." U.S. Catholic (January 1977): 32-36.

529. Whalen W. "The Rev. Sun Myung Moon: Pied Piper of Tarrytown." U.S. Catholic (October 1976): 29-33.

530. Whalen W. "Scientology: Making Everybody Perfectly Clear." U.S. Catholic (November 1975): 35-39.

531. Williams, J.L. Victor Paul Wierwille and The Way International. Chicago, IL: Moody Press, 1979. 159 pp.

532. Williams, J.L. Identifying and Dealing with Cults. Burlington, NC: The New Directions Evangelistic Association, n.d.a. 55 pp.

533. Williams, J.L. Transcendental Meditation. Burlington, NC: The New Directions Evangelistic Association, n.d.b. 107 pp.

534. Willoughby, W.F. "Deprogramming Jesus Freaks and Others: Can America Tolerate Private Inquisitions?" Christian Century, May 2, 1973, pp. 510-511.

535. Wilson, Clifford. The Occult Explosion. San Diego, CA: Master Books, 1976.

536. Yamamoto, J. Isamu. The Moon Doctrine. Downers Grove, IL: Inter-Varsity Press, 1977a. 41 pp.

537. Yamamoto, J. Isamu. The Puppet Master. Downers Grove, IL: Inter-Varsity Press, 1977b. 136 pp.

538. Yamamoto, J. Isamu. Hare Krishna Hare Krishna. Downers Grove, IL: Inter-Varsity Press, 1975. 28 pp.

539. Yanoff, Morris. Where is Joey? Lost Among the Hare Krishnas.

Athens, OH: Ohio University Press and Swallow Press, 1981.

540. Zakim, Leonard P. "Cults: A Calm Perspective." The Jewish
      Advocate, July 5, 1979, p. 19.

541. Zeldner, Max. "Are We Losing Our Children?" Jewish Frontier
      44 (May 1977): 8-11.

CHAPTER FIVE

THE ANTI-CULT MOVEMENT AND SOCIAL SCIENCES

In the 1970´s and into the 1980´s there existed a popular
stereotype, promulgated aggressively by a minority of writers, that
the "cult" phenomenon was beyond ordinary understanding by psychologists, psychiatrists, sociologists and other scientists (as well
as legal experts) who worked within conventional theories and perspectives. For example, Siegelman (a journalist) and Conway (a behavioral scientist) blanketly proclaimed (1979:59):

> The cult experience and its accompanying state of
> mind defies all legal precedents. It has also
> taken the mental-health profession by surprise:
> The conceptual models and diagnostic tools of psy-
> chiatry and psychology have proved inadequate to
> explain or treat the condition.

A review of the (readily) available professional literature
demonstrates otherwise. While it is true that scientists both among
and within disciplines did not reach unanimity on the meaning, degree of threat and long-range implications of new religious movements, much less on whether or not such movements could appropriately or without bias be labeled "cults," they most certainly did not
lack conceptual tools by which to understand the various phenomena
associated with such groups. A substantial literature on group dynamics and attitude-belief change in psychology, conversion in religious studies and religious movements in sociology and anthropology had been accumulating since the beginning of the twentieth century. Serious students of religions, whatever their orientations,
were hardly caught unaware. There was, in short, no paucity of
research on new religions and the issues accompanying them either
before or during the modern "new religions" controversy (though
unquestionably the latter uproar did stimulate further field studies
as well as both conceptualization and theorization). While we do
not have the space to cite the multitude of field studies on various
new religions (nor is that our goal in this bibliographic history of
the ACM), we do refer to exemplary or often-publicized sources which
demonstrate social science awareness of new religions.

In this chapter we review that body of social scientific research in terms of four dimensions. First, we examine the pre-
1970´s (or pre-ACM) research on radical attitude-belief change,
particularly as it contained themes of "brainwashing" and "mind con-

trol" following the Korean War. Second, we consider psychological
and psychiatric sources; third, anthropological and sociological
sources; and fourth, religious studies sources. Not as a partisan
or apologetic interpretation but rather as an independent, objective
summary of the research literature, we conclude in advance that the
vast bulk of scientific findings--whatever clinical, field observation or survey methodologies used--never supported the ACM perspective that most "cult" members were duped or psychologically shang-
haied into membership, coercively maintained in subservience as
slaves or impaired in any meaningful way through their membership.
The fact that much of these research findings remained in relative
obscurity outside their professional audiences can be explained by
several factors. Foremost was their mostly non-sensationalistic and
circumspect nature, in keeping with the ultimate tentativeness of
all scientific findings but not conducive to widespread dissemination particularly among partisans or by the sensationally entre-
preneurial media. In the early to mid-1970's, such research findings simply did not make "good press." Moderate and qualified conclusions were often ignored by the mass media while the grossest ex-
aggerations were uncritically printed and reported nationwide.
Furthermore, anti-cultists remained ignorant of such research or
deliberately skirted the scientific literature's implications, increasing the chances that such reports (typically written by non-
crusading individuals) would receive little notice. It was not to
be until the early 1980's that the true parameters of social scientific research on new religions began to attract media attention as
a correction to the earlier excesses of the 1970's.

THE POST-KOREAN WAR "BRAINWASHING" LITERATURE

One of the most shocking revelations to Americans during the
1950's was the alleged instances of "brainwashing" or psychological
manipulation of captured U.S. servicemen by North Korean and communist Chinese captors. The latter idealogues had supposedly mastered
sinister powers of behavioral conditioning that permitted them to
erase the previous values, allegiances and attitudes of American
POW's (just as they purportedly had done to millions of their own
citizens in Asian countries). A number of psychiatric books and
articles, most aimed at the general public (e.g., Hunter, 1962,
1953; Mereloo, 1956; Sargant, 1957), as well as more scholarly
works (e.g., Lifton, 1963; 1957; Schein, Schneier and Backer, 1961;
Schein, 1958) appeared (on the surface at least) to lend credence to
this impression. Such works had a powerful impact on the public of
the pre-Vietnam era. This literature survived into the early 1970's
to be revived by anti-cult groups searching for some key with which
they could interpret their sons' and daughters' sudden abandonment
of domestic and career plans to join millenarian, utopian communal
and culturally bizarre religious groups labeled (pejoratively) as
"cults," and at least one of the original authors later took an
active revitalized role in turning his analytical model of manipulative "thought reform" to the activities of new religions (see
Lifton, 1979).

There were several ironies in this ACM revival of psychological

studies of purported "mind control." The first was that a poor
choice of metaphor to describe the attitude changes instituted by
Asian communists on both POW's and citizens in communist countries
resulted in a superficial reification of the change process. That
is, the term "brainwashing," actually a misnomer produced by a simplistic translation of the Chinese term "to cleanse thoughts" (i.e.,
to correct political philosophy) by Hunter (1953), quickly became a
popular "buzzword" that implied virtual annihilation of one's
thought and will and subsequent psychological enslavement to manipulative destructive forces. Lifton (1963:4), who preferred his term
"thought reform" to refer to this systematic process of realigning
political loyalties, explicitly cautioned that the term "brainwashing" might be seized upon by partisans in some future conflict and
indiscriminately applied because its

> loose usage makes the word a rallying point for
> fear, resentment, urges toward submission, justi-
> fication for failure, irresponsible accusation,
> and for a wide gamut of emotional extremism.

Some would argue that this abuse of the term was precisely what occurred in the 1970's.

A second irony lay in the fact that the "brainwashing" conditioning process, as described by various authors, was neither mys-
terious nor a recent innovation of Asian communists. The attitude
change in doctrination "workshops" (called revolutionary colleges")
which POW's and refugees from communist China described in detail
resembled a familiar setting of peer support and pressure well
known to western psychologists, psychotherapists, sociologists
(e.g., Lieberman, 1956) and the armed forces (Dornbusch, 1955).
Kurt Lewin, the famous German social psychologist, regularly performed such "feats" of attitude change in his experiments during
World War II simply by varying the conditions of the group in which
subjects were exposed to new information. These conditions were
remarkably similar to the "revolutionary college" indoctrination
workshops in Maoist China. Lewin (1958:204-9) noted:

> Experience in leadership training and in many areas
> of re-education, such as re-education regarding
> alcoholism or delinquency, indicates that it is
> easier to change the ideology and social practice of
> a small group handled together than of single indivi-
> duals. One of the reasons why "group carried changes"
> are more readily brought about seems to be unwilling-
> ness of the individual to depart too far from group
> standards; he is likely to change only if the group
> changes.... It is possible that the success of group
> decision and particularly the permanency of the effect
> is, in part, due to the attempts to bring about a
> favorable decision by removing counterforces within
> the individuals rather than by applying outside pres-
> sure.

A third irony lay in the relative inefficiency and overall dis-
mal results of the much-touted "brainwashing" procedures. Psychologist Edgar Schein (1958:221), who examined returning POW´s, concluded from his study of the subject:

> The extent to which the Chinese succeeded in con-
> verting prisoners of war to the Communist ideology
> is difficult to evaluate because of the previously
> mentioned hazards in measuring ideological change
> and because of the impossibility of determining
> the latent effects of the indoctrination. In
> terms of overt criteria of conversion or ideo-
> logical change, one can only conclude that, con-
> sidering the effort devoted to it, the Chinese
> program was a failure (1958:332).

More recent authors, Scheflin and Opton (1978:89) concurred in noting that out of approximately 3,500 American servicemen taken pris-
oner during the Korean War, only about 50 (or one percent) ever made
pro-communist or anti-American statements and only about 25 POW´s
refused repatriation when the war ended. In Scheflin and Opton´s
estimation:

> These numbers do not add up to a persuasive case
> that the Communists developed a method to control
> the mind.... In the civil war ... about two per-
> cent of the Union soldiers captured by the South
> enlisted in Confederacy.

Thus, there is this final irony that ACM supporters, who were quick
to refer to the post-war scientific literature on "brainwashing" and
"thought reform" when pressed to defend the legitimacy of their
claims, apparently never read these cited sources very carefully.
They avoided many of the ultimate conclusions on the limited effi-
cacy of attempts to produce profound attitudinal change over a relatively short period of time and virtually ignored Lifton´s warning
to moderate any application of such a persuasion model beyond POW´s.

THE MODERN PSYCHIATRIC AND PSYCHOLOGICAL LITERATURE

The modern psychiatric and psychological literature was split
between studies which found that persons in new religious movements
manifested dramatically evident impairment (however much such group
members denied it) and contrary research that uncovered no serious
or noteworthy negative effects among such individuals. The research
findings of these two respective groups of scholars, not surprisingly, were taken up and touted loudly by the antagonists in the "cult-
anti-cult" controversy (i.e., the ACM versus the new religions plus
their civil libertarian sympathizers). A survey of the first group
of studies illustrates a prevalent tendency among many psychiatrists
to assume emotional pathology from mere social deviance and to
transfer this "medical model" (i.e., to "medicalize" social deviance
and try to treat it as a physician might the biological fact of a
virus) to their analyses of followers of new religions. For ex-

ample, Binder (1933:132) half a century ago, clearly expressed this
perspective that people would only join bizarre or unconventional
movements out of abnormal motives:

> One of the most amazing things that arrests our
> attention is the fact that the cults number among
> their constituency so many apparently intelligent
> and progressive spirits. It is more than likely,
> however, that not infrequently even the reported
> enlightenment of these adherents is offset by some
> particular psychological deficiency of emotional
> complex.

Casey (1941) likewise arrived at a similar conclusion about the converts to the unconventional "transient cults" of his day, and it is
safe to say that this fundamentally ethnocentric component of the
psychiatric perspective played a role in many later studies of
"cult" groups.

Another basic assumption frequently embedded in this psychiatric perspective was that religion, as a fundamental dimension of (an
often reified concept of) personality, could only change when accompanied by parallel profound psychological changes in the individual (Parrucci, 1968). Such an assumption meshed well with the
claims that profound "mind control" (i.e., personality change) techniques had been developed in the Orient by persons with malevolent
motives. Clinical psychologists, psychiatrists and other health
professionals thus lent considerable prestige to a revitalized post-
Korean War coercive socialization or thought reform or brainwashing
model when it was applied to modern religious groups. Clark (1979a,
1979b, 1978, 1976), Clark et al. (1981), Dellinger, (1979), Galanter
et al. (1979), Miller (1979), Schwartz and Kaslow (1979), Shapiro
(1977), Singer (1979a, 1978) and Verdier (1977) made specific
charges that participation in "cults" (a category defined only in
the most general terms but whose boundaries can be inferred by the
ad hoc examples used by these writers to support their accusations)
led to disintegration of members' physical health (including allegedly stress-related cessation of menstruation in women and of facial
hair growth in men), ego regression, destruction of capabilities to
reason autonomously and erosion of positive self-image. At a number
of local and regional professional meetings as well as at national
conventions, research papers on new religions' indoctrination and
recruitment methods, lifestyles and counseling treatment for ex-
members were disseminated (e.g., Miller, 1979; Galper, 1977a, 1977b,
1976; Grossman, 1978; Marks, 1978). Many were heavily anecdotal
and/or highly qualitative and subjective. Furthermore, due to their
prevalence across the country, and to the fact that the majority of
such papers were never published, the total size of this body of
research remains unknown.

Several of the authors in this group whose findings supported
the mind control model loosely patterned after the post-Korean War
psychiatric literature, in particular Clark and Singer, frequently
spoke at ACM-sponsored meetings and regularly appeared as expert
witnesses at national (federal) hearings and before state legisla-

tors and at trials when official action against new religions was
contemplated. Their model of analysis was uniformly clinical, and
though over time each could claim a relatively large (by clinical
standards) number of patients studied and observed, the dangers of
subjectivity and clinician-induced direction in reconstructing
patients' "cult" experiences (however unintended) became serious
grounds for their critics to challenge their findings.

In contrast to this group of scholars was a set of psychiatrists and clinical psychologists, some of whom integrated their
clinical interviews with questionnaires, standardized paper-and-
pencil personality inventory tests and field observation, that found
little or no pathology in new religions' members. Their studies
included DeMaria (1978), Levine and Salter (1976), various research
reports reviewed by Richardson (1980), Solomon (1981), Ungerleider
(1979a, 1979b), Ungerleider and Wellisch (1979a, 1979b) and Weisman
(1980). Reaction to the "medical model" approach of psychiatry and
clinical psychology had been growing for some time in the social
psychology of social movements (e.g., Zygmunt, 1972; Neal, 1970).
It was explicitly criticized in a series of articles by Robbins
(1979b), Robbins and Anthony (1980a, 1980b, 1979), Anthony and
Robbins (1981, 1974), Anthony, Robbins and McCarthy (1980) and
Anthony et al. (1977). Indeed, Robbins and Anthony (1981) even suggested how one new religion, the Meher Baba sect, could function
positively as drug rehabilitation and as a means of reintegrating
former addicts and "dropouts" into less destructive lifestyles as
did Galanter and Buckley (1978) with a similar group that meditated.
Chorover (1980) illustrated what he considered to be the ultimate
relativity and temperocentrism of the "medical model" in his discussion of "drapetomania" (i.e., "the insane desire to wander away from
home"), a presumed mental disorder which had reached epidemic pro-
portions among black slaves in ante-bellum Louisiana, prompting the
Louisiana State Medical Society in 1850 to investigate why this particular subpopulation was so mysteriously afflicted.

The general public, the press and electronic media, and many
professionals remained generally ignorant of this corpus of research
findings that contradicted the "brainwashing" explanation of "cult"
membership. Only at the close of the decade and during the early
1980's did the media, in its persistent search for novel scientific
findings and conclusions, discover that there were in fact two
competing views of the "brainwashing" controversy and that the
available research did not lead to any consensus of opinion among
mental health specialists. ACM activists certainly saw little of it
and probably most had no idea of its existence. An examination of
the references and bibliographies in professional publications of
the "pro-brainwashing explanation" group of psychiatric and psychological writers reveals that they made virtually no citations of
work by their colleagues in the opposite "anti-brainwashing explanation" camp (West and Singer, 1980). Conversely, the second group of
writers would customarily refer to authors such as Singer and Clark,
if at all, only as departure points for setting up their own research. In all, there were few specific acknowledgements by psychiatrists and psychologists in their respective writings of other
research findings that disagreed with their own. Moreover, it can

only be concluded that those pro-ACM authors who found in the recruitment and indoctrination tactics of communal groups such as the
Unification Church a radical, dangerous new mode of "ensnaring"
young adults seemed surprisingly blind to the wealth of social psychological findings (existing many decades prior to the modern
"cult" controversy) on group dynamics, small groups' sensitivity
training techniques and attitude change.

THE ANTHROPOLOGICAL AND SOCIOLOGICAL LITERATURE

In this section we discuss the anthropological and sociological
literature pertaining to the American ACM rather than sources concerned with anti-cult movements in other countries (though readers
are referred to Beckford, 1979a, 1979b, 1978a, 1978b, n.d.a.,
n.d.b., for an introduction to such sources). It is important to
note at the outset that such research did not begin with, or emerge
merely in response to, the claims of either the ACM or the psychiatric and psychological literature cited above. Research on most of
the major groups embroiled in the new religions controversy had been
conducted prior to the formation of the ACM and/or was going on during the controversy without any explicit mention of the ACM. For
instance, Lofland (1966) and Lofland and Stark (1965) studied the
Unification Church's earliest missionary outposts in the United
States during the late 1950's and early 1960's, Daner (1976) researched the Hare Krishna sect, Balch (1980) and Balch and Taylor
(1976) did extensive participant observation of the Bo and Peep UFO
cult, Downton (1979) conducted in-depth interviews and case histories of followers of Guru Maharaj Ji's Divine Light Mission,
Wallis (1981, 1979, 1977) analyzed the organizational history of
Scientology, and Richardson, Stewart and Simmonds (1979) studied a
Jesus movement communal sect over an extended period. All investi-
gated various substantive issues such as conversion, faith maintenance, and movement history and organization, yet they devoted
virtually no attention to the ACM's impact on the new religions and
deprogramming controversies. (Of course, the ACM had not yet come
into existence when the studies by Lofland and Lofland and Stark
were written.) Indeed, in the two major anthologies of social
science research on new religions during the 1970's (Glock and
Bellah, 1976; Zaretsky and Leone, 1974) as well as in other often-
cited sources (e.g., Wuthnow, 1978; Heenan, 1973) not one article--
or even a section of an article--mentioned the ACM.

One reason for this general lack of theoretical interest in the
psychologically problematic reasons people joined and remained in
new religions may be the rejection of deprivation and social pathology theories of social movements which, as we remarked in the previous section, had grown in popularity within sociology. This rejection, in turn, can in part be attributed to the general cultural
relativist orientation of many sociologists (a methodological bor-
rowing from sister discipline anthropology) who engaged in direct
contact with new religions' members during their fieldwork and found
the pathology model a poor set of assumptions on which to base in-
teraction and realistic conclusions. Hine (1974) commented, in
failing to uncover significant alienation (among other psycholog-

ical problems) in one study, that many past studies seemed to go
out of their way to make an argument for pathology. Similar observations were made by Bromley and Shupe (1979c) in their field study
of a Unification Church evangelistic team and Heirich's (1974)
research on Catholic charismatics. Indeed, Yinger (1946:88), almost
thirty years before the modern new religions deprogramming
controversy had developed full-blown, dismissed the
deprivation-pathology model entirely:

> Scholars generally assume that sects and cults
> produce more emotionally unstable and mentally
> ill persons than denominations and churches.
> Many mentally ill persons indeed are found in
> sects, but there may be proportionately as many
> in churches. What appears to be a causal rela-
> tionship may result only from variation in the
> self-selection that operates in religious bodies
> with voluntary membership. Although socially
> isolated persons may find fellowship and security
> in a sect and sect preachers occasionally precip-
> itate a psychosis in persons under severe emotional
> stress, there is no evidence that sect membership
> is an indication of poor mental health.

A body of largely sociological literature addressing many of
the issues raised by the ACM and the psychiatric and psychological
research reports—particularly the question of whether or not new
religions (as an assumed homogeneous type) used coercive mental
techniques to recruit and control members—did emerge by the mid-
1970's. Some of it was clearly polemical, such as the many articles
by psychologist Dick Anthony, sociologist Thomas Robbins and their
collaborating colleagues cited in the previous section (see also
Robbins, 1979a, 1977a, 1977b), though Anthony and Robbins also
conducted fieldwork with more conceptual goals (Anthony and Robbins,
1977, 1974; Robbins and Anthony, 1981; Robbins et al., 1976). But
within a short time a burgeoning corpus of research and research-
grounded essays appeared that took ACM claims very seriously as
subjects for investigation. The bulk of this literature produced
findings that boded ill for both ACM allegations and supporters of
the psychological pathology approach. The primary reason would
seem to be that, given most sociologists' theoretical predisposition
to suspect the older deprivational "medical model" approach to
understanding social movements and their recruits and accumulating
fieldwork perceived as reinforcing this predisposition, the civil
liberties implications of ACM activities became more evident.
Gradually the research focus began a shift away from simple investigation of ACM claims to more theoretical (and constitutionally
related) topics. Rather than remaining at the descriptive level of
dealing exclusively with the truth or falsity of ACM claims, many
sociologists took these claims themselves as contemporary examples
of more perennial themes in the sociology of social movements, deviance and religious conflict (Bromley and Shupe, 1979; Hargrove,
1980; Kim, 1979; Richardson, 1980, 1977; Richardson and Stewart,
1977; Robbins, 1979c; Shupe and Bromley, 1981a, 1981b, 1981c, 1981d,
1980a, 1980c; Simmonds, 1977).

Moreover, a number of sociologists took notice of the ACM itself as a countermovement locked in conflict with various new religions and analyzed its origins, interests, membership composition,
structural and organizational problems, and relations to other institutions (Bromley, Busching and Shupe, 1982, 1981; Bromley and
Shupe, 1982, 1981, 1979a; Harper, 1981a, 1981b, 1979; Lofland, 1977;
Shupe and Bromley, 1982, 1980a, 1979a; Shupe, Spielmann and Stigall,
1980, 1977). In fact, the difficulties involved in the fieldwork of
researching the ACM became a subject by itself for reporting in the
qualitative methodological literature (see Bromley and Shupe, 1980;
Shupe and Bromley, 1980b). By the beginning of the 1980´s, unlike
the research anthologies of the 1970´s, reports on the ACM were
varied and noticeable in edited collections (e.g., Robbins and
Anthony, 1981; Wilson, 1981).

Most of the anthropological and sociological research, as we
mentioned, presented findings and/or viewpoints unsympathetic to the
ACM ideology and was inconsistent with at least a part of the psy-
chiatric-psychological literature. However, there were exceptions.
Enroth (1979a, 1979b, 1977a, 1977b), an outspoken evangelical Christian sociologist and consultant to the Berkeley based ACM group
Spiritual Counterfeits Project (see Chapter Four on religious institutional sources), accepted ACM claims of brainwashing, coercion and
psychophysical injury to "cult" members, as did Levine (1980, 1979).
Levine in fact became an active participant rather than simply an
observer at ACM functions. Likewise, Horowitz (1981, 1978, 1977), a
political sociologist, criticized both the Unification Church and
his sociological colleagues who participated in the well-publicized
annual International Conferences on the Unity of Science lavishly
staged by the Church´s controversial founder, Rev. Sun Myung Moon,
on the grounds that the social scientists, by attending, lent
legitimacy and credibility to the Unification Church. Horowitz was
sued at one point by the Church over alleged copyright infringement
(he included in his 1978 anthology of articles on the Unification
Church a speech of Rev. Moon that had been passed out publicly on
handbills without obtaining their permission), but the suit was later dropped. Suffice it to say that these three authors accepted
ACM claims and media accounts of the same at face value as crimino-
logically significant facts, unburdened by the more abstract and
historical-phenomenological-analytical viewpoints of their colleagues. This smaller number of writers drew upon psychiatric-
psychological sources to support their arguments and formed a vocal,
if minority, segment of sociological researchers and writers on the
new religions and deprogramming controversies.

THE RELIGIOUS STUDIES LITERATURE

The response of theologians and scholars of religious studies
(as opposed to that of denominational and sectarian groups expressed
by the literature reviewed in Chapter Four) resembled the strictly
social science literature in that opinions were divided. Since religion is by its very nature non-empirical in that it has no criteria for determining validity other than subjective means, perhaps
this division was to be expected. However, an interesting feature

of essays and articles that addressed anti-cult concerns and activities was their reliance on the psychiatric/psychological and an-
thropological/sociological literatures as well as on historical
studies. In addition, because of the uneven awareness of these
scholarly sources (and perhaps because of an unknown amount of
defensiveness about their own faiths), this reliance was highly
selective. For example, the following excerpt by Haack
(1978:442-443) is typical of theological writers who were hostile
toward the new religions, uncritical about the media-promulgated
"cult" stereotypes and reliant only on psychiatrists and
psychologists supportive of those sentiments. Haack argues that
"cults" are distinguishable from wholesome and legitimate religions
in that the former practice "psychomutation":

> In contrast to the process in a normal shift of
> consciousness, a complete spiritual reorientation
> may lead very quickly to an almost total change of
> personality. This has been called the "phenomenon
> of forced and lasting conversion." The concept of
> "conversion" does not, however, seem quite appro-
> priate to describe the following results:
>
> > --Complete reorientation of life according to
> > hitherto unknown or unapplied principles.
> > --Total alteration of behavior towards the
> > world around them. No longer viewed as the
> > context of their own existence, the world is
> > dealt with and thought of exclusively as a
> > hostile element that has to be changed.
> > --Radicalization in all areas of life.
> > --Total subordination of the power of judgement
> > and critical faculty to the authority of an-
> > other (person or system).
> > --A kind of siege mentality which expresses it-
> > self in staying as close as possible to like-
> > minded companies (commune, ashram, "family,"
> > etc.).
> > --Close ties, amounting in some cases to total
> > dependence, binding one to a leader, head or
> > guru, or his deputy, and the adoption of his
> > world-view and example.
> > --The short duration of the process.
>
> As a result of psychomutation, the converts develop
> the ability, in a relatively short time, to infect
> others with their exclusive conviction. The word
> "conversion" cannot properly be applied here.

Likewise, Weldon (1978) and Streiker (1978) reviewed the belief
systems of various new religions in surprisingly superficial, openly
critical terms. Such sources also often included allegedly scanda-
lous or unsavory intimations about groups' founders, organizations
and lifestyles in rather patent attempts to impugn leaders' motives
(hence their doctrines' validity) or to cause discrediting by infer-
ence. Not infrequently, like Sovik (1978:474), they referred read-

ers for additional information to anti-cult associations. Religious scholars' involvement as partisans in countermovements is, of course, not new and even represents something of a tradition within that branch of academia (e.g., Shupe, 1981; Martin, 1977). The author who rejected the new religions without resorting to ACM ideology and who could still be introspective about personal prejudice and ethnocentric biases, such as Amirthan (1978), was an anomaly.

At the opposite pole were liberal theologians who held varying amounts of sympathy for the minority plight of new religions (usually expressed in civil libertarian terms) while still rejecting much of their doctrines and who criticized the ACM for its basically parochial, self-serving ideology. Their usual method of attack was to point out similar countermovements in American history and note how, from a contemporary vantage point, misguided were these hysterias and anti-Catholic, anti-Quaker, anti-Mormon, anti-Jehovah's Witnesses and anti-Mason movements (Sawatsky, 1978; Cox, 1978a, 1978b; Judah, 1978; Needleman and Baker, 1978). Harvard theologian Harvey Cox, author of Turning East (1977) which took the sympathetic position toward new religions that western Christianity could actually benefit from learning about them, argued (1982:1):

> Despite all the elegant rhetoric about the Pilgrim
> father and the smiling exchanges of interfaith
> banquets, America has not set an exemplary record
> in the area of religious freedom.... Mormons, Jews,
> Masons, Jesuits, and ordinary Roman Catholics felt
> the hard edge of harassment and discrimination be-
> cause of their convictions. A couple of generations
> ago, Jehovah's Witnesses were the main target of
> prejudice. Now we have the "cults." It seems
> Americans are never really happy unless there is
> some unfamiliar religious group to abuse. The
> spirit of theocracy lingers on.... The hanging of
> the Quakers and the hounding of the Mormons is over,
> but the fear and suspicion that built the gallows
> and fired the hatred are still there. We have
> learned, it seems, very little. And that is dis-
> appointing.

Others concerned themselves with specific legal issues (e.g., Richardson, 1980), the dynamics of hostility expressed toward specific groups (e.g., Rausch, 1980) or the phenomenological implications of accepting ACM "social reality" (Rubenstein, 1980).

In almost all writings both pro and con the ACM or the new religions, however, various social science findings were used to defend particular points of view and lend at least the appearance of scientific (i.e., empirical) validity to arguments.

542. Amirthan, Samuel. "The Challenge of New Religions to Christian Theological Thought." International Review of Mission
62 (October 1978):399-406.

543. Anthony, Dick, and Thomas Robbins. "New Religions, Families, and Brainwashing." In Gods We Trust: New Patterns of Religious Pluralism in America. Edited by Thomas Robbins and Dick Anthony. New Brunswick, NJ: Transaction Press, 1981, pp. 263-274.

544. Anthony, Dick, and Thomas Robbins. "The Meher Baba Movement: Its Effect on Post-Adolescent Social Alienation." Religious Movements in Contemporary America. Edited by Irving Zaretsky and Mark Leone. Princeton, NJ: Princeton University Press, 1974, pp. 479-511.

545. Anthony, Dick, Thomas Robbins, and Jim McCarthy. "Legitimating Repression." Society 17 (March/April 1980):39-42.

546. Anthony, Dick, Madeline Doucas and Thomas G. Curtis. "Patients and Pilgrims: Changing Attitudes Toward Psychotherapy of Converts to Eastern Mysticism." American Behavioral Scientist 20 (July/August 1977): 861-886.

547. Babbie, Earl, and Donald Stone. "An Evaluation of the est Experience by a National Sample of Graduates." Biosciences Communications 3 (1977): 123-140.

548. Bainbridge, William S. "The Rise and Decline of Transcendental Meditation." The Social Impact of New Religious Movements. Edited by Bryan Wilson. New York: Rose of Sharon Press, 1981, pp. 135-158.

549. Bainbridge, William, and Rodney Stark. "Client and Audience Cults in America." Sociological Analysis 41 (1980a): 199-214.

550. Bainbridge, William, and Rodney Stark. "Sectarian Tension." Review of Religious Research 22 (1980b): 105-124.

551. Bainbridge, William, and Rodney Stark. "Scientology: To Be Perfectly Clear." Sociological Analysis 41 (1980c): 128-136.

552. Bainbridge, William, and Rodney Stark. "Cult Formation: Three Compatible Models." Sociological Analysis 40 (1979): 283-295.

553. Balch, Robert. "Looking Behind the Scene in a Religious Cult: Implications for the Study of Conversion." Sociological Analysis 41 (Summer 1980): 137-143.

554. Balch, Robert, and David Taylor. "Seekers and Saucers: The Role of the Cultic Milieu in Joining a UFO Cult." American Behavioral Scientist 20 (July/August 1976): 839-960.

555. Barker, Eileen. "With Enemies Like That: Some Functions of Deprogramming as an Aid to Sectarian Membership." The Brainwashing/Deprogramming Controversy: Sociological, Psy-

chological, Legal and Historical Perspectives. Edited by
James T. Richardson and David G. Bromley. New York: Edwin
Mellen Press, forthcoming.

556. Barker, Eileen. "Who´d Be a Moonie? A Comparative Study of
      Those Who Join the Unification Church in Britain." The
      Social Impact of New Religious Movements. Edited by Bryan
      Wilson. New York: Rose of Sharon Press, 1981, pp. 59-96.

557. Barker, Eileen. "Whose Service Is Perfect Freedom: The Con-
      cept of Spiritual Well-Being in Relation to Rev. Sun Myung
      Moon´s Unification Church in Britain." Spiritual Well-
      Being. Edited by D.O. Moberg. Washington, DC: University
      Press of America, 1979.

558. Barker, Eileen. "Living the Divine Principle: Inside the
      Reverend Sun Myung Moon´s Unification Church in Britain."
      Archives de Sciences Sociales des Religions 45 (1978):71-
      83.

559. Barker, Eileen. "Conversion into the Rev. Moon´s Unification
      Church in Britain." Paper presented at the meeting of the
      British Sociological Association´s Sociology of Religion
      Group, London School of Economics, London, England, 1977a.

560. Barker, Eileen. "Inside the Unification Church: Followers of
      the Reverend Sun Myung Moon." Paper presented at the 14th
      International Conferences for the Sociology of Religion,
      Strasbourg, France, 1977b.

561. Barker, Eileen, ed. New Religious Movements: A Perspective
      for Understanding Society. New York: Edwin Mellen Press,
      1982.

562. Barnhart, Joseph. "Deprogramming, Free Will, and Brainwash-
      ing." Denton, TX, n.d.

563. Bateson, Daniel. "Moon Madness: Greed or Creed?" American
      Psychological Association Monitor 1 (1976): 32-35.

564. Beckford, James A. "Beyond the Pale: Cults, Culture and Con-
      flict." New Religious Movements: A Perspective for Under-
      standing Society. Edited by Eileen Barker. New York: The
      Edwin Mellen Press, forthcoming.

565. Beckford, James A. "Brainwashing and Deprogramming in
      Britain: The Social Sources of Anti-Cult Sentiment."
      Durham, England, The University of Durham, 1979a.

566. Beckford, James A. "Politics and the Anti-Cult Movement."
      Annual Review of the Social Sciences of Religion 3 (1979b):
      169-190.

567. Beckford, James A. "Accounting for Conversion." British
      Journal of Sociology 29 (1978a): 249-262.

568. Beckford, James A. "Cults and Cures." Japanese Journal of
      Religious Studies 5 (December 1978b): 225-257.

569. Beckford, James A. "Through the Looking-Glass and Out the
      Other Side: Withdrawal from the Rev. Moon's Unification
      Church." Les Archives de Sciences Sociales des Religions
      45 (1978c): 95-116.

570. Beckford, James A. "Happy Families and Deprogramming in
      Britain." Durham, England, University of Durham, October,
      1977.

571. Beckford, James A. "Cults, Controversy and Control: A Com-
      parative Analysis of the Problems Posed by New Religious
      Movements in the Federal Republic of Germany and France."
      Durham, England, University of Durham, n.d.a.

572. Beckford, James A. "Anti-Cultism and Anti-Witchcraft."
      Durham, England, University of Durham, n.d.b.

573. Binder, Louis Richard. Modern Religious Cults and Society.
      New York: AMS Press, 1933. 325 pp.

574. Bird, Frederick. "The Pursuit of Innocence: New Religious
      Movements and Moral Accountability." Sociological Analysis
      40 (Winter 1979): 335-346.

575. Bird, Frederick. "A Comparative Analysis of the Rituals
      Used by Some Contemporary New Religious and Para-Religious
      Movements." Paper presented to the Society for the Sci-
      entific Study of Religion, 1974.

576. Bromley, David G., Bruce C. Busching and Anson D. Shupe, Jr.
      "The Unification Church and the American Family: Strain,
      Conflict, and Repression." New Religious Movements: A Per-
      spective for Understanding Society. Edited by Eileen
      Barker. New York: The Edwin Mellen Press, forthcoming.

577. Bromley, David G., Bruce C. Busching and Anson D. Shupe, Jr.
      "Repression of Religious Cults." Research in Social Move-
      ments, Conflicts and Change. Edited by Louis Kriesberg.
      Greenwich, CT: JAI Press, 1981, pp. 25-46.

578. Bromley, David G., and Anson D. Shupe, Jr. "Repression and
      the Decline of Social Movements: The Case of the New Reli-
      gions." Social Movements of the 1960's and the 1970's.
      Edited by Jo Freeman. San Francisco: Longman Publishers,
      forthcoming.

579. Bromley, David G., and Anson D. Shupe, Jr. Strange Gods: The
      Great American Cult Scare. Boston: Beacon Press, 1981.
      192 pp.

580. Bromley, David G., and Anson D. Shupe, Jr. "Evolving Foci in
      Participant Observation: Research as an Emerging Process."

Fieldwork Experience: Qualitative Approaches to Social Research. Edited by William B. Shaffer, Robert A. Stebbins and Allan Turowitz. New York: St. Martin's Press, 1980, pp. 191-203.

581. Bromley, David G., and Anson D. Shupe, Jr. "Moonies" in America: Cult, Church and Crusade. Beverly Hills, CA: Sage Publications, 1979a. 269 pp.

582. Bromley, David G., and Anson D. Shupe, Jr. "The Tnevnoc Cult." Sociological Analysis 40 (Winter 1979b): 361-366.

583. Bromley, David G., and Anson D. Shupe, Jr. "Just a Few Years Seem Like a Lifetime: A Role Theory Approach to Participation in Religious Movements." Research in Social Movements, Conflicts and Change. Edited by Louis Kriesberg. Greenwich, CT: JAI Press, 1979c, pp. 159-185.

584. Campbell, Colin. "The New Religious Movements, the New Spirituality and Post-Industrial Society." New Religious Movements: A Perspective for Understanding Society. Edited by Eileen Barker. New York: The Edwin Mellen Press, forthcoming.

585. Casey, Robert D. "Transient Cults." Psychiatry 4 (November 1941): 525-534.

586. Chorover, Stephen. "Mental Health as a Social Weapon." New Religions and Mental Health: Understanding the Issues. Edited by Herbert Richardson. New York: The Edwin Mellen Press, 1980, pp. 14-18.

587. Clark, John C., Jr. "Cults." Journal of the American Medical Association 242 (1979a): 179-181.

588. Clark, John C., Jr. "Sudden Personality Change and the Maintenance of Critical Governmental Institutions." Paper presented to the International Society of Political Psychology, Washington, DC, 1979b.

589. Clark, John C., Jr. "Problems in Referral of Cult Members." Journal of the National Association of Private Psychiatric Hospitals 9 (1978): 27-29.

590. Clark, John C., Jr. "Testimony to the Special Investigating Committee of the Vermont Senate Investigating the Effects of Some Religious Cults on the Health and Welfare of Their Converts." Arlington, TX: Reprinted by the National Ad Hoc Committee, Citizens Engaged in Freeing Minds, 1976. 11 pp.

591. Clark, John C., Jr., Michael D. Langone, Robert E. Schecter and Roger C.B. Daly. Destructive Cult Conversion: Theory, Research, and Treatment. Boston, MA: American Family Foundation, Center on Destructive Cultism, (1981). 34 pp.

592. Cox, Harvey. "Introduction." In David G. Bromley and Anson
     D. Shupe, Jr. *Strange Gods: The Great American Cult Scare*.
     Boston: Beacon Press, 1982.

593. Cox, Harvey. "Deep Structures in the Study of New Reli-
     gions." *Understanding the New Religions*. Edited by Jacob
     Needleman and George Baker. New York: The Seabury Press,
     1978a, pp. 122-130.

594. Cox, Harvey. "Myths Sanctioning Religious Persecution." *A
     Time for Consideration: A Scholarly Appraisal of the Unifi-
     cation Church*. Edited by M. Darrol Bryant and Herbert W.
     Richardson. New York: The Edwin Mellen Press, 1978b, pp.
     3-19.

595. Cox, Harvey. *Turning East*. New York: Simon and Schuster,
     1977. 192 pp.

596. Dallinger, Robert W. *Cults and Kids: A Study of Coercion*.
     Boys Town, NE: The Boys Town Center, n.d. 21 pp.

597. Daner, Francine Jeanne. *The American Children of KRSNA*.
     New York: Holt, Rinehart and Winston, 1976. 127 pp.

598. Davis, Rex, and James T. Richardson. "The Organization and
     Functioning of the Children of God." *Sociological Analysis*
     37 (1975): 321-340.

599. DeMaria, Richard. "A Psycho-Social Analysis of Conversion."
     *A Time for Consideration: A Scholarly Appraisal of the
     Unification Church*. Edited by M. Darrol Bryant and Herbert
     W. Richardson. New York: The Edwin Mellen Press, 1978, pp.
     82-130.

600. Derks, Frans. "Differences in Social Isolation Between Mem-
     bers of Two New Religious Movements (Ananda Marga and
     Divine Light Mission)." *Proceedings of the Colloquy of
     European Psychologists of Religion at Nymegen*. Department
     of Psychology of Culture and Religion, Catholic University,
     Mymegan, The Netherlands, 1981.

601. Derks, Frans, and Jan van der Lans. "Subgroups in Divine
     Light Mission Membership." Paper presented at the British
     Sociological Association Conference on the New Religions,
     Lincoln, England, 1981.

602. Deutsch, A. "Observations on a Sidewalk Ashram." *Archives
     of General Psychiatry* 32 (1975): 116-175.

603. Domino, G. "Transcendental Meditation and Creativity: An
     Empirical Investigation." *Journal of Applied Psychology* 62
     (1977): 358.

604. Dornbusch, Sanford N. "The Military Academy as an Assimilat-
     ing Institution." *Social Forces* 33 (May 1955): 315-321.

605. Downton, James V., Jr. "An Evolutionary Theory of Spiritual Conversion and Commitment: The Case of Divine Light Mission." *Journal for the Scientific Study of Religion* 19 (1980): 381-396.

606. Downton, James V., Jr. *Sacred Journeys: The Conversion of Young Americans to Divine Light Mission*. New York: Columbia University Press, 1979. 245 pp.

607. Eister, Allan W. "Culture Crises and New Religious Movements: A Paradigmatic Statement of a Theory of Cults." *Religious Movements in Contemporary America*. Edited by Irving Zaretsky and Mark Leone. Princeton, NJ: Princeton University Press, 1974, pp. 612-627.

608. Eister, Allan W. "An Outline of a Structural Theory of Cults." *Journal for the Scientific Study of Religion* 11 (1972): 319-334.

609. Enroth, Ronald M. *The Lure of the Cults*. Chappaqua, NY: Christian Herald Books, 1979a. 139 pp.

610. Enroth, Ronald M. "The Power Abusers." *Eternity*, October 1979b, pp. 23-27.

611. Enroth, Ronald M. *Youth, Brainwashing, and the Extremist Cults*. Kentwood, MI: Zondervan, 1977a. 218 pp.

612. Enroth, Ronald M. "Cult/Countercult." *Eternity*, November 1977b, pp. 18-22, 32-35.

613. Etamed, B. "Extrication from Cultism." *Current Psychiatric Therapy* 18 (1978): 217-223.

614. Fenwick, P.B., et al. "Metabolic and EEG Changes During Transcendental Meditation: An Explanation." *Biological Psychology* 5 (1977): 101.

615. Festinger, Leon, Henry W. Riecken and Stanley Schachter. *When Prophecy Fails*. New York: Harper Torchbooks, 1974. 253 pp.

616. Fichter, Joseph. "Youth in Search of the Sacred." *The Social Impact of New Religious Movements*. Edited by Bryan Wilson. New York: Rose of Sharon Press, 1981, pp. 21-42.

617. Foss, Daniel, and Ralph W. Larkin. "Worshipping the Absurd: The Negation of Social Causality Among the Followers of Guru Maharaj Ji." *Sociological Analysis* 39 (Fall 1978): 156-164.

618. Freund, Peter. "Documenting Experiences: Telling and Retelling as Meditation." Paper presented at the annual meeting of the American Sociological Association, 1976.

619. Galanter, Marc. "Psychological Induction into the Large-
      Group: Findings from a Modern Religious Sect." American
      Journal of Psychiatry 137 (1980): 1574-1579.

620. Galanter, Marc. "The 'Relief Effect': A Sociobiological
      Model for Neurotic Distress and Large-Group Therapy."
      American Journal of Psychiatry 135 (1978): 588-591.

621. Galanter, Marc, Richard Rabkin, Judith Rabkin and Alexander
      Deutsch. "The Moonies: A Psychological Study of Conver-
      sion and Membership in a Contemporary Religious Sect."
      American Journal of Psychiatry 136 (1979): 165-169.

622. Galanter, Marc, and Peter Buckley. "Evangelical Religion and
      Meditation: Psychotherapeutic Effects." Journal of Nervous
      and Mental Disease 166 (October 1978): 685-691.

623. Galper, Marvin F. "Indoctrination Methods of the Unification
      Church." Paper presented at the annual meeting of the
      California Psychological Association, Los Angeles, 1977a.

624. Galper, Marvin F. "Adolescent Identity Diffusion and the Ex-
      tremist Religious Cult." Paper presented at the annual
      meeting of the Western Psychological Association, Seattle,
      WA, 1977b.

625. Galper, Marvin F. "The Cult Indoctrinee: A New Clinical Syn-
      drome." Paper presented to the Tampa-St. Petersburg Psy-
      chiatric Society, Tampa-St. Petersburg, FL, 1976.

626. Glass, L., M. Kirsch and F. Parris. "Psychiatric Disturb-
      ances Associated with Erhard Seminars Training: A Report of
      Cases." American Journal of Psychiatry 134 (March 1977):
      245-247.

627. Glock, Charles Y., and Robert N. Bellah, eds. The New Reli-
      gious Consciousness. Berkeley: University of California
      Press, 1976.

628. Gordon, David. "The Jesus People: An Identity Synthesis In-
      terpretation." Urban Life 3 (1974): 159-179.

629. Grossman, Jan C. "The Cult Victim: A Forensic Case of Com-
      petency." Paper presented at the annual meeting of the
      Philadelphia Society of Clinical Psychologists, Phila-
      delphia, PA, 1978.

630. Haack, Friedrich W. "New Youth Religions, Psychomutation,
      and Technological Civilization." International Review of
      Mission 62 (October 1978): 436-447.

631. Harder, Mary W., and James T. Richardson. "The Jesus Move-
      ment: Some Preliminary Empirical Evidence." Paper pre-
      sented at the annual meeting of the Society for the Sci-
      entific Study of Religion, Chicago, October 1971.

632. Hargrove, Barbara. "Social Sources and Consequences of the
      Brainwashing Controversy." The Brainwashing/Deprogramming
      Controversy: Sociological, Psychological, Legal and Histor-
      ical Perspectives. Edited by James T. Richardson and David
      G. Bromley. New York: Edwin Mellen Press, forthcoming.

633. Hargrove, Barbara. "Evil Eyes and Religious Choices."
      Society 17 (March/April 1980): 20-24.

634. Hargrove, Barbara. "Some Thoughts About the Unification Move-
      ment and the Churches." Science, Sin and Scholarship: The
      Politics of Reverend Moon and the Unification Church.
      Edited by Irving Louis Horowitz. Cambridge, MA: The MIT
      Press, 1978, pp. 86-101.

635. Harper, Charles. "Love Our Children: An Ethnography of Anti-
      Cult Organization." Proceedings of the Association for the
      Scientific Study of Religion: Southwest. Denton, TX:
      1981a. 6 pp.

636. Harper, Charles. "The Cult Controversy: Values in Conflict."
      Proceedings of the Association for the Scientific Study of
      Religion: Southwest. Denton, TX, 1981b.

637. Harper, Charles. Religious Cults and the Anti-Cult Movement
      in the Omaha Area. Report Monograph Submitted to the
      Nebraska Committee for the Humanities. Omaha, NE:
      Creighton University, 1979. 43 pp.

638. Heenan, Edward F., ed. Mystery, Magic and Miracle: Religion
      in a Post-Aquarian Age. Englewood Cliffs, NJ: Prentice-
      Hall, 1973. 180 pp.

639. Heirich, Max. "Change of Heart: A Test of Some Widely Held
      Theories About Religious Conversion." American Journal of
      Sociology 83 (November 1977): 653-680.

640. Hine, Virginia H. "The Deprivation and Disorganization
      Theories of Social Movements." Religious Movements in Con-
      temporary America. Edited by Irving I. Zaretsky and Mark
      P. Leone. Princeton, NJ: Princeton University Press, 1974,
      pp. 646-661.

641. Holloman, Regina E. "Ritual Opening and Individual Transfor-
      mation: Rites of Passage at Esalen." American Anthropol-
      ogist 76 (1974): 265-280.

642. Horowitz, Irving Louis. "The Politics of New Cults: Non-
      Prophetic Observations on Science, Sin and Scholarship."
      In Gods We Trust: New Patterns of Religious Pluralism in
      America. Edited by Thomas Robbins and Dick Anthony. New
      Brunswick, NJ: Transaction Press, 1981, pp. 161-170.

643. Horowitz, Irving Louis. "Science, Sin and Sponsorship." The
      Atlantic Monthly, March 1977, pp. 98-102.

644. Horowitz, Irving Louis, ed. <u>Science, Sin and Scholarship:</u>
     <u>The Politics of Reverend Moon and the Unification Church</u>.
     Cambridge, MA: MIT Press, 1978. 312 pp.

645. Horton, P.C. "The Mystical Experience as a Suicide Preven-
     tive." <u>American Journal of Psychiatry</u> 130 (1973): 294-296.

646. Hunter, Edward. <u>Brainwashing: From Pavlov to Powers</u>. New
     York: The Bookmailer, 1962. 329 pp.

647. Hunter, Edward. <u>Brainwashing in Red China: The Calculated</u>
     <u>Destruction of Men's Minds</u>. New York: Vanguard, 1953.
     311 pp.

648. Hunter, James D. "The New Religions: Demodernization and the
     Protest Against Modernity." <u>The Social Impact of New Reli-</u>
     <u>gious Movements</u>. Edited by Bryan Wilson. New York: Rose
     of Sharon Press, 1981, pp. 1-20.

649. Johnson, Benton. "A Sociological Perspective on the New Re-
     ligions." <u>In Gods We Trust: New Patterns of Religious</u>
     <u>Pluralism in America</u>. Edited by Thomas Robbins and Dick
     Anthony. New Brunswick, NJ: Transaction Press, 1981, pp.
     51-66.

650. Johnson, Gregory. "The Hare Krishna in San Francisco." <u>The</u>
     <u>New Religious Consciousness</u>. Edited by Charles Glock and
     Robert Bellah. Berkeley, CA: University of California
     Press, 1976, pp. 31-51.

651. Johnston, Hank. "The Marketed Social Movement: A Case Study
     of the Rapid Growth of TM." <u>Pacific Sociological Review</u> 23
     (1980): 333-354.

652. Judah, J. Stillson. "New Religions and Religious Liberty."
     <u>Understanding the New Religions</u>. Edited by Jacob Needleman
     and George Baker. New York: The Seabury Press, 1978, pp.
     201-208.

653. Judah, J. Stillson. "Programming and Deprogramming." Paper
     presented at the Conference on Religion, Toronto, School of
     Theology, University of Toronto, April, 1977.

654. Judah J. Stillson. <u>Hare Krishna and the Counterculture</u>. New
     York: Wiley, 1974. 301 pp.

655. Kim, Byong-Suh. "Religious Deprogramming and Subjective
     Reality." <u>Sociological Analysis</u> 40 (Fall 1979): 197-207.

656. Kim, Byong-Suh. "Indoctrination in the Unification Church."
     Paper presented to the Society for the Scientific Study of
     Religion, 1976.

657. Kirsch, M., and L. Glass. "Psychiatric Disturbances Asso-
     ciated with Erhard Seminars Training, II: Additional Cases

and Theoretical Considerations." American Journal of Psychiatry 134 (1977): 1254.

658. Kuner, Wolfgang. "New Religious Movements and Mental Health: Empirical Research into Three New Religious Movements in the Federal Republic of Germany." Paper presented at the Lincoln Conference on New Religious Movements of the British Sociological Association, April, 1981.

659. Levine, Edward M. "Deprogramming Without Tears." Society 17 (March/April 1980a): 34-38.

660. Levine, Edward M. "Rural Communes and Religious Cults." Adolescent Psychiatry, Vol. 8. Edited by Sherman C. Feinstein et al. Chicago: University of Chicago Press, 1980b, pp. 138-153.

661. Levine, Saul V., and Nancy E. Salter. "Youth and Contemporary Religious Movements: Psychosocial Findings." Canadian Psychiatric Association Journal 21 (1976): 411-420.

662. Lewin, Kurt. "Group Decision and Social Change." Readings in Social Psychology. Third Edition. Edited by Eleanor E. Maccoby, Theodore M. Newcomb and Eugene L. Hartley. New York: Holt, Rinehart and Winston, 1958, pp. 197-211.

663. Lewis, Warren. "Coming-Again: How Society Functions Through Its New Religions." New Religious Movements: A Perspective for Understanding Society. Edited by Eileen Barker. New York: Edwin Mellen Press, forthcoming.

664. Lieberman, Seymour. "The Effects of Changes in Role on the Attitudes of Role Occupants." Human Relations 9 (1956): 385-402.

665. Lifton, Robert J. "The Appeal of the Death Trip." The New York Times Magazine, 7 January 1979, pp. 26-31.

666. Lifton, Robert J. Thought Reform and the Psychology of Totalism. New York: W.W. Norton, 1963. 510 pp.

667. Lifton, Robert J. "Thought Reform of Chinese Intellectuals: A Psychiatric Evaluation." Journal of Social Issues 13 (1957): 5-20.

668. Lofland, John. Doomsday Cult. Revised Edition. New York: Irvington Press, 1977. 362 pp.

669. Lofland, John, and Rodney Stark. "Becoming a World-Saver: A Theory of Conversion to a Deviant Perspective." American Sociological Review 30 (December 1965): 862-874.

670. Marks, Edward S. "Religious Cults Use Brainwashing." Paper presented at the annual meeting of the Philadelphia Society of Clinical Psychologists, Philadelphia, PA, 1978. 3 pp.

671. Martin, Walter. The Kingdom of the Cults. Minneapolis:
      Bethany Fellowship, 1977. 443 pp.

672. McBride, James, and Paul A. Schwartz. "On the Application of
      Religious Totalism and Authoritarian Personality Models to
      the New Religious Movements." Paper presented to the
      Western Psychological Association, April, 1982.

673. McGee, Michael. "Meher Baba - The Sociology of Religious
      Conversion." Graduate Journal 9 (1974): 43-71.

674. Meerloo, J. The Rape of the Mind. New York: World Publish-
      ing, 1956. 320 pp.

675. Melton, J. Gordon. "Deprogramming: A Response to the Rise of
      Cults." Paper presented at the annual meeting of the
      Society for the Scientific Study of Religion, Philadelphia,
      October, 1980.

676. Messer, Jeanne. "Guru Maharaj-Ji and the Divine Light Mis-
      sion." The New Religious Consciousness. Edited by Charles
      Glock and Robert Bellah. Berkeley, CA: University of Cali-
      fornia Press, 1976, pp. 52-72.

677. Miller, Donald E. "Deprogramming in Historical Perspective."
      The Brainwashing/Deprogramming Controversy: Sociological,
      Psychological, Legal and Historical Perspectives. Edited
      by James T. Richardson and David G. Bromley. New York:
      Edwin Mellen Press, forthcoming.

678. Miller, Jesse. "The Utilization of Hypnotic Techniques by
      Religious and Therapy Cults." Paper presented to the
      International Society of Political Psychology, Washington,
      DC, 1979.

679. Neal, Arthur A. "Conflict and the Functional Equivalence of
      Social Movements." Sociological Focus 3 (Spring 1970): 3-
      12.

680. Needleman, Jacob, and George Baker, eds. Understanding the
      New Religions. New York: Seabury Press, 1978. 314 pp.

681. Nelson, Geoffrey K. "The Concept of Cult." The Sociological
      Review 16 (1968a): 351-362.

682. Nelson, Geoffrey K. "The Analysis of a Cult." Social
      Compass 15 (1968b): 649-681.

683. Nicholi, Armand. "A New Dimension of the Youth Culture."
      American Journal of Psychiatry 131 (April 1974): 396-401.

684. Nordquist, Ted A. "New Religious Movements in Sweden." New
      Religious Movements: A Perspective for Society. Edited by
      Eileen Barker. New York: The Edwin Mellen Press, forth-
      coming.

685. Nordquist, Ted A. <u>Ananda Cooperative Village</u>. Uppsala, Sweden: Religionhistoriska Institunionen, 1978.

686. Pagano, R.R., and L.R. Frumpkin. "The Effect of Transcendental Meditation on Right Memesphoric Functioning." <u>Biofeedback Self-Regulation</u> 2 (1977): 407.

687. Pagano, R.R., et al. "Sleep During Transcendental Meditation." <u>Science</u> 191 (1976): 308.

688. Parrucci, Dennis J. "Religious Conversion: A Theory of Deviant Behavior." <u>Sociological Analysis</u> 29 (Fall 1968): 144-154.

689. Plarzyk, Thomas. "Conversion and Alternation Processes in the Youth Culture: A Comparative Analysis of Religious Transformations." <u>Pacific Sociological Review</u> 21 (October 1978a): 379-405.

690. Plarzyk, Thomas. "The Origin, Development and Decline of a Youth Culture Religion: An Application of Sectarianization Theory." <u>Review of Religious Research</u> 20 (1978b): 23-43.

691. Plarzyk, Thomas, and L. Bharaduaj. "What Is Real? Problems with the Phenomenological Approach in a Field Study of Divine Light Mission." <u>Humanity and Society</u> 3 (1979): 14-34.

692. Plarzyk, Thomas, and C. Jacobson. "Christians and the Youth Culture: A Life History of an Urban Commune." <u>Wisconsin Sociologist</u> 14 (1977): 136-151.

693. Pollack, A.A., et al. "Limits of Transcendental Meditation in the Treatment of Essential Hypertension." <u>Lancet</u> 1 (1977): 73.

694. Rausch, David. "Jews Against Messianic Jews." <u>New Religions and Mental Health: Understanding the Issues</u>. Edited by Herbert W. Richardson. New York: The Edwin Mellen Press, 1980, pp. 39-47.

695. Richardson, Herbert W. "Mental Health, Conversion, and the Law." <u>New Religions and Mental Health: Understanding the Issues</u>. Edited by Herbert W. Richardson. New York: The Edwin Mellen Press, 1980a, pp. ix-lv.

696. Richardson, Herbert W. "Critique of the Goelters Report." <u>Juegendliche in destructiven religiosen Gruppen</u> (Youth in Destructive Religious Groups). <u>New Religions and Mental Health: Understanding the Issues</u>. Edited by Herbert W. Richardson. New York: The Edwin Mellen Press, 1980b, pp. 90-105.

697. Richardson, James T. "Conversion, Brainwashing and Deprogramming." <u>The Center Magazine</u> 15 (March/April 1982): 18-24.

698. Richardson, James T. "Economic Policies and Practices of the
      New Religions: A Neglected Research Area." Paper presented
      at the British Sociological Association Conference on New
      Religions, Lincoln, England, 1981.

699. Richardson, James T. "Conversion Careers." Society 17
      (March/April 1980): 47-50.

700. Richardson, James T. "Cult to Sect: Creative Electicism in
      New Religious Groups." Pacific Sociological Review 22
      (1979): 139-166.

701. Richardson, James T. "An Oppositional and General Concep-
      tualization of Cult." The Annual Review of the Social Sci-
      ences of Religion 2 (1978): 29-52.

702. Richardson, James T. "Conversion and Commitment in Contem-
      porary Religion." American Behavioral Scientist 20 (July/
      August 1977): 799-803.

703. Richardson, James T. "Causes and Consequences of the Jesus
      Movement in the United States." Irish Journal of Sociology
      2 (1973): 457-474.

704. Richardson, James T., ed. Conversion Careers: In and Out of
      the New Religions. Beverly Hills, CA: Sage Publications,
      1978.

705. Richardson, James T., and David G. Bromley, eds. The Brain-
      washing/Deprogramming Controversy: Sociological, Psycholog-
      ical, Legal and Historical Perspectives. New York: The
      Edwin Mellen Press, forthcoming.

706. Richardson, James T., and R.B. Simmonds. "Personality As-
      sessment in New Religious Groups: Problems of Interpreta-
      tions." Paper presented at the meeting of the Internation-
      al Association for the Psychology of Religion, Uppsala,
      Sweden, 1977.

707. Richardson, James T., Robert B. Simmonds and Mary W. Harder.
      "Thought Reform and the Jesus Movement." Youth and Society
      4 (December 1972): 185-200.

708. Richardson, James T., Mary W. Stewart and Robert B. Simmonds.
      Organized Miracles: A Study of a Contemporary Youth, Com-
      munal, Fundamentalist Organization. New Brunswick, NJ:
      Transaction Press, 1979. 368 pp.

709. Richardson, James T., Mary W. Stewart and Robert B. Simmonds.
      "Conversion Process Models and the Jesus Movement."
      American Behavioral Scientist 20 (July/August 1977): 819-
      838.

710. Richardson, James T., Jan van der Lans and Frans Derks.
      "Voluntary Disaffiliation, Expulsion and Deprogramming: An

Analysis of Ways of Leaving Social Groups." Paper presented at the annual meeting of the Association for the
Sociology of Religion, Toronto, Canada, August, 1981.

711. Robbins, Thomas. "Cult Phobia." Inquiry, January 1979a, pp.
      2-3.

712. Robbins, Thomas. "Cults and the Therapeutic State." Social
      Policy 10 (May/June 1979b): 42-47.

713. Robbins, Thomas. "Even a Moonie Has Civil Rights." The
      Nation, February 27, 1977a, pp. 238-242.

714. Robbins, Thomas. "Brainwashing vs. Religious Freedom."
      The Nation, April 30, 1977b, p. 518.

715. Robbins, Thomas. "Eastern Mysticism and the Resocialization
      of Drug Users: The Meher Baba Cult." Journal for the Sci-
      entific Study of Religion 8 (Fall 1969): 308-317.

716. Robbins, Thomas, and Dick Anthony. "Brainwashing, Deprogram-
      ming and the Medicalization of Deviant Religious Move-
      ments." Social Problems 29 (February 1982): 283-297.

717. Robbins, Thomas, and Dick Anthony. "Getting Straight with
      Meher Baba: A Study of Mysticism, Drug Rehabilitation and
      Post-Adolescent Role Conflict." In Gods We Trust: New Pat-
      terns of Religious Pluralism in America. Edited by Thomas
      Robbins and Dick Anthony. New Brunswick, NJ: Transaction
      Press, 1981, pp. 191-213.

718. Robbins, Thomas, and Dick Anthony. "The Limits of Coercive
      Persuasion as an Explanation for Conversion to Authoritar-
      ian Sects." Political Psychology 2 (1980a): 27-37.

719. Robbins, Thomas, and Dick Anthony. "Cults vs. Shrinks:
      Psychiatry and the Control of Religious Movements." New
      Religions and Mental Health: Understanding the Issues.
      Edited by Herbert W. Richardson. New York: The Edwin
      Mellen Press, 1980b, pp. 48-64.

720. Robbins, Thomas, and Dick Anthony. "Culture Crises and Con-
      temporary Religion." In Gods We Trust: New Patterns of
      Religious Pluralism. Edited by Thomas Robbins and Dick
      Anthony. New Brunswick, NJ: Transaction Press, 1980c, pp.
      9-34.

721. Robbins, Thomas, and Dick Anthony. "A Demonology of Cults."
      Inquiry, September 1, 1980d, pp. 9-11.

722. Robbins, Thomas, and Dick Anthony. "Cults, Brainwashing, and
      Counter-Subversion." The Annals of the American Academy of
      Political and Social Science 446 (November 1979a): 78-90.

723. Robbins, Thomas, and Dick Anthony. "Sociology of Contempor-
      ary Religious Movements." Annual Review of Sociology 5
      (Fall 1979b).

724. Robbins, Thomas, and Dick Anthony. "New Religious Movements
      and the Social System: Integration, Transformation or Dis-
      integration." Annual Review of the Social Sciences of
      Religion 2 (1978a).

725. Robbins, Thomas, and Dick Anthony. "The Effect of Detente on
      the Growth of New Religions: Reverend Moon and the Unifica-
      tion Church." Understanding the New Religions. Edited by
      Jacob Needleman and George Baker. New York: Seabury Press,
      1978b, pp. 80-100.

726. Robbins, Thomas, and Dick Anthony, eds. In Gods We Trust:
      New Patterns of Religious Pluralism in America. New
      Brunswick, NJ: Transaction Press, 1981. 338 pp.

727. Robbins, Thomas, Dick Anthony and Thomas Curtis. "Youth
      Culture Religious Movements: Evaluating the Integrative
      Hypothesis." Sociological Quarterly 16 (Winter 1975): 48-
      64.

728. Robbins, Thomas, Dick Anthony and James Richardson.
      "Research and Theory on Today's New Religions." Socio-
      logical Analysis 34 (September 1978): 95-122.

729. Robbins, Thomas, et al. "The Last Civil Religion: Reverend
      Moon and the Unification Church." Sociological Analysis 37
      (Summer 1976): 111-125.

730. Robertson, Roland. "Religious Movements and Modern
      Societies: Toward a Progressive Problemshift." Sociological
      Analysis 40 (1979): 297-314.

731. Rosen, Anne-Sofie, and Ted A. Nordquist. "Ego Developmental
      Level and Values in a Yogic Community." Journal of Person-
      ality and Social Psychology 39 (November 1980): 1152-1160.

732. Rubenstein, Richard L. "Who Shall Define Reality for Us?"
      New Religions and Mental Health: Understanding the Issues.
      Edited by Herbert W. Richardson. New York: The Edwin Mellen
      Press, 1980, pp. 6-13.

733. Sargant, William. Battle for the Mind. New York: Doubleday,
      1957. 263 pp.

734. Sawatsky, Rodney J. "Moonies, Mormons and Mennonites: Chris-
      tian Heresy and Religious Toleration." A Time for Consid-
      eration. A Scholarly Appraisal of the Unification Church.
      Edited by M. Darrol Bryant and Herbert W. Richardson. New
      York: The Edwin Mellen Press, 1978, pp. 20-40.

735. Scheflin, Alan, and Edward Upton. The Mind Manipulators.
      New York: Paddington, 1978. 539 pp.

736. Schein, Edgar H. "The Chinese Indoctrination Program for
      Prisoners of War: A Study of Attempted Brainwashing."
      Readings in Social Psychology. Edited by Eleanor E.
      Maccoby, Theodore M. Newcomb and Eugene L. Hartley. New
      York: Holt, Rinehart and Winston, 1958, pp. 311-334.

737. Schein, Edgar H., Inge Schneier and Curtis H. Becker.
      Coercive Persuasion. New York: Norton, 1961. 320 pp.

738. Schwartz, L.L., and K. Kaslow. "Religious Cults, the Indivi-
      dual and the Family." Journal of Marital and Family
      Therapy 15 (April 1979): 80-83.

739. Shapiro, Eli. "Destructive Cultism." American Family Physi-
      cian 15 (February 1977): 80-83.

740. Shupe, Anson D., Jr. Six Alternative Perspectives on New
      Religious Movements: A Case Study Approach. New York: The
      Edwin Mellen Press, 1981. 225 pp.

741. Shupe, Anson D., Jr., and David G. Bromley. A Documentary
      History of the Anti-Cult Movement. New York: The Edwin
      Mellen Press, 1982a.

742. Shupe, Anson D., Jr., and David G. Bromley. "Shaping the
      Public Response to Jonestown: The People's Temple and the
      Anti-Cult Movement." Violence and Religious Commitment.
      Edited by Kenneth Levi. University Park, PA: The Univer-
      sity of Pennsylvania Press, 1982b, pp. 105-132.

743. Shupe, Anson D., Jr., and David G. Bromley. "Apostates and
      Atrocity Stories: Some Parameters in the Dynamics of Depro-
      gramming." The Social Impact of New Religious Movements.
      Edited by Bryan Wilson. New York: The Rose of Sharon
      Press, Inc., 1981a, pp. 179-215.

744. Shupe, Anson D., Jr., and David G. Bromley. "A Role Theory
      Approach to Entrance and Exit From Religious Movements."
      Paper presented at a conference, "Conversion, Coercion and
      Commitment in New Religious Movements," sponsored by the
      Center for the Study of New Religious Movements, Graduate
      Theological Union, Berkeley, CA, 1981b.

745. Shupe, Anson D., Jr., and David G. Bromley. "The Deprogram-
      mer as Moral Entrepreneur." Paper presented to the annual
      meeting of the American Academy of Religion, San Francisco,
      CA, 1981c.

746. Shupe, Anson D., Jr., and David G. Bromley. New New Vigil-
      antes: Deprogrammers, Anti-Cultists, and the New Religions.
      Beverly Hills, CA: Sage Publications, 1980a. 267 pp.

747. Shupe, Anson D., Jr., and David G. Bromley. "Walking a Tightrope: Dilemmas of Participant Observation of Groups in Conflict." Qualitative Sociology 2 (January 1980b): 3-21.

748. Shupe, Anson D., Jr., and David G. Bromley. "Witches, Moonies and Accusations of Evil." In Gods We Trust: New Patterns of American Religious Pluralism. Edited by Thomas Robbins and Dick Anthony. New Brunswick, NJ: Transaction Press, 1980c, pp. 247-262.

748. Shupe, Anson D., Jr., and David G. Bromley. "The Moonies and the Anti-Cultists: Movement and Counter-Movement in Conflict." Sociological Analysis 40 (Winter 1979): 325-366.

750. Shupe, Anson D., Jr., Roger Spielmann and Sam Stigall. "Cults of Anti-Cultism." Society 17 (March/April 1980): 43-46.

751. Shupe, Anson D., Jr., Roger Spielmann and Sam Stigall. "Deprogramming: The New Exorcism." American Behavioral Scientist 20 (July/August 1977): 941-956.

752. Siegelman, Jim, and Flo Conway. "Snapping: Welcome to the Eighties." Playboy, March 1979, pp. 53 ff.

753. Simmonds, Robert. "Conversion or Addiction: Consequences of Joining a Jesus Movement Group." American Behavioral Scientist 20 (July/August 1977): 909-924.

754. Singer, Margaret. "Coming Out of the Cults." Psychology Today, January 1979a, pp. 72-82.

755. Singer, Margaret. "Cults as an Exercise in Political Psychology." Paper presented at the meeting of the International Society of Political Psychology, Washington, DC, 1979b.

756. Singer, Margaret. "Psychological Mechanisms of Cult Affiliation." Paper presented at the meeting of the American Psychological Association, New York, 1979c.

757. Singer, Margaret. "Therapy with Ex-Cult Members." Journal of the National Association of Private Psychiatric Hospitals 9 (1978): 15-19.

758. Skonovd, L. Norman. "Apostasy: The Process of Defection from Religious Totalism." Ph.D. dissertation, University of California, Davis, 1981, 230 pp.

759. Smith, R.E., G. Wheeler and E. Diener. "Faith Without Works: Jesus People, Resistance to Temptation and Altruism." Journal of Applied Social Psychology 5 (1975): 320-330.

760. Solomon, Trudy. "Programming and Deprogramming the Moonies: Social Psychology Applied." The Brainwashing/Deprogramming

Controversy: Sociological, Psychological, Legal and Historical Perspectives. Edited by James T. Richardson and David
G. Bromley. New York: The Edwin Mellen Press, forthcoming.

761. Solomon, Trudy. "Integrating the Moonie Experience: A Sur-
vey of Ex-Members of the Unification Church." In Gods We
Trust: New Patterns of Religious Pluralism in America.
Edited by Thomas Robbins and Dick Anthony. New Brunswick,
NJ: Transaction Press, 1981, pp. 275-294.

762. Sovik, Arne. "A Selected and Annotated Bibliography."
International Review of Mission 62 (October 1978): 474-478.

763. Stark, Rodney. "Must All Religions be Supernatural?" The
Social Impact of New Religious Movements. Edited by Bryan
Wilson. New York: Rose of Sharon Press, 1981, pp. 159-178.

764. Stark, Rodney, and William S. Bainbridge. "Networks of Faith:
International Bonds and Recruitment to Cults and Sects."
American Journal of Sociology 85 (1980a): 1376-1395.

765. Stark, Rodney, and William S. Bainbridge. "Towards a Theory
of Religious Commitment." Journal for the Scientific Study
of Religion 19 (1980b): 114-128.

766. Stark, Rodney, and William S. Bainbridge. "Of Churches,
Sects and Cults: Preliminary Concepts for a Theory of Reli-
gious Movements." Journal for the Scientific Study of
Religion 18 (1979a): 117-133.

767. Stark, Rodney, William S. Bainbridge and D.P. Doyle. "Cults
in America: A Reconnaissance in Space and Time." Sociological Analysis 40 (1979b): 347-360.

768. Strauss, Roger. "Becoming a Scientologist: A Case Study of
Career Development in a Cult-Like Social World." 1979a.

769. Strauss, Roger. "Inside Scientology: Everyday Life in a
Societally Deviant World." 1979b.

770. Strauss, Roger. "Religious Conversion as a Personal and Collective Accomplishment." Sociological Analysis 40 (1979c):
158-165.

771. Streiker, Lowell D. The Cults Are Coming! Nashville, TN:
Abingdon Press, 1979.

772. Sullivan, Thomas J. "Transcendental Meditation, Locus of
Control and Social Isolation." Paper presented at the
meeting of the Society for the Scientific Study of Religion, Chicago, 1977.

773. Sullivan, Thomas J., and David L. Salosky. "Orientations
Toward Transcendental Meditation: Religious and Secular
Aspects of the Movement." Paper presented to the meeting

of the Society for the Scientific Study of Religion,
Milwaukee, WI, 1975.

774. Taylor, David. "The Social Organization of Recruitment in
the Unification Church." M.A. thesis, University of
Montana, 1978.

775. Taylor, David. "Thought Reform and the Unification Church."
Paper presented to the Society for the Scientific Study of
Religion, 1977.

776. Tipton, Steven. "Zen Master and Student: Moral Authority in
a Ritual Context." Atlanta, GA, Emory University, 1982.

777. Tipton, Steven. "New Religions and the Problem of a Modern
Ethic." Religious Change and Continuity. Edited by Harry
Johnson. San Francisco: Jossey-Bass, 1979, pp. 286-312.

778. Ungerleider, J. Thomas. The New Religions: Insights Into the
Cult Phenomenon. New York: Merck, Sharp and Dohme, 1979a,
20 pp.

779. Ungerleider, J. Thomas. "The Programming (Brainwashing)/
Deprogramming Religious Controversy." Los Angeles, CA:
UCLA Center for the Health Sciences, 1979b.

780. Ungerleider, J. Thomas, and David K. Wellisch. "Coercive
Persuasion (Brainwashing), Religious Cults and Deprogramming." American Journal of Psychiatry 136 (March 1979a):
279-282.

781. Ungerleider, J. Thomas, and David K. Wellisch. "Psychiatrists' Involvement in Cultism, Thought Control and Deprogramming." Psychiatric Opinion 16 (January 1979b): 10-15.

782. Verdier, Paul A. Brainwashing and the Cults. Hollywood, CA:
The Institute of Behavioral Conditioning, 1977. 117 pp.

783. Wallis, Roy. "The New Religions as Social Indicators." New
Religious Movements: A Perspective for Understanding
Society. Edited by Eileen Barker. New York: The Edwin
Mellen Press, forthcoming.

784. Wallis, Roy. "Yesterday's Children: Cultural and Structural
Change in a New Religious Movement." The Social Impact of
New Religious Movements. Edited by Bryan Wilson. New York:
Rose of Sharon Press, 1981, pp. 97-134.

785. Wallis, Roy. The Road to Total Freedom: A Sociological Analysis of Scientology. New York: Columbia University Press,
1977.

786. Wallis, Roy. "Observations on the Children of God." The
Sociological Review 24 (November 1976): 807-828.

787. Wallis, Roy. "The Cult and Its Transformation." Sectarianism. Edited by Roy Wallis. New York: Halsted, 1975a, pp. 35-49.

788. Wallis, Roy. "Scientology: Therapeutic Cult to Religious Sect." Sociology 9 (1975b): 89-99.

789. Wallis, Roy. "Societal Reaction to Scientology." Sectarianism. Edited by Roy Wallis. New York: Halsted, 1975c, pp. 86-116.

790. Wallis, Roy. "Ideology, Authority and the Development of Cultic Movements." Social Research 41 (Summer 1974): 299-327.

791. Wallis, Roy. "A Comparative Analysis of Problems and Processes of Change in two Manipulationist Movements." Acts of the Twelfth International Conference for the Sociology of Religion. The Hague: CISR, 1973, pp. 407-422.

792. Wallis, Roy, ed. Salvation and Protest: Studies of Social and Religious Movements. New York: St. Martin's Press, 1979.

793. Weisman, Richard. "Professional vs. Traditional Methods of Influencing Behavior." New Religions and Mental Health: Understanding the Issues. Edited by Herbert W. Richardson. New York: The Edwin Mellen Press, 1980, pp. 65-68.

794. Weldon, John. "A Sampling of the New Religions." International Review of Mission 62 (October 1978): 407-426.

795. West, Louis J. "Contemporary Cults: Utopian Image, Infernal Reality." The Center Magazine 15 (March/April 1982): 10-13.

796. West, Louis J., and Margaret Thaler Singer. "Cults, Quacks and Nonprofessional Psychotherapies." Comprehensive Textbook of Psychiatry III. Volume 3, Third Edition. Edited by Harold I. Kaplan, Alfred M. Freedman and Benjamin J. Sadock. Baltimore, MD: Williams and Wilkins, 1980, pp. 3245-3258.

797. Westley, Frances. "Behind the Faces: Pollution Fears in the Human Potential Movement." Montreal, Canada, McGill University, 1978. 20 pp.

798. Whitehead, Harriet. "Reasonably Fantastic: Some Perspectives on Scientology, Science Fiction and Occultism." Religious Movements in Contemporary America. Edited by Irving Zaretsky and Mark Leone. Princeton, NJ: Princeton University Press, 1974, pp. 547-587.

799. Wilson, Bryan. "The New Religions: Some Preliminary Considerations. New Religious Movements: A Perspective for

Understanding Society. Edited by Eileen Barker. New York:
The Edwin Mellen Press, forthcoming.

800. Wilson, Bryan. "Time, Generation and Sectarianism." The
     Social Impact of New Religious Movements. New York: Rose
     of Sharon Press, 1981a, pp. 217-234.

801. Wilson, Bryan, ed. The Social Impact of New Religious Move-
     ments. New York: Rose of Sharon Press, 1981b. 326 pp.

802. Wolfe-Petrusky, Julie C. "The Social Construction of the
     Cult Problem" Paper presented at the annual meeting of the
     Association for the Study of Religion, Boston, 1979.

803. Wuthnow, Robert. Experimentation in American Religion.
     Berkeley, CA: University of California Press, 1978.
     221 pp.

804. Wuthnow, Robert. "The New Religions in Social Context." The
     New Religious Consciousness. Edited by Charles Glock and
     Robert Bellah. Berkeley, CA: University of California
     Press, 1976, pp. 267-293.

805. Yinger, J. Milton. Religion in the Struggle for Power.
     Durham, NC: Duke University Press, 1946. 275 pp.

806. Younger, J., W. Adnance and R.J. Berger. "Sleep During
     Transcendental Meditation." Perceptual Motor Skills 40
     (June 1975): 953-954.

807. Zaretsky, Irving I., and Mark P. Leone, eds. Religious
     Movements in Contemporary America. Princeton, NJ:
     Princeton University Press, 1974. 837 pp.

808. Zygmunt, Joseph F. "Movements and Motives: Some Unresolved
     Issues in the Psychology of Social Movements." Human
     Relations 25 (November 1972): 449-487.

CHAPTER SIX

THE ANTI-CULT MOVEMENT AND THE LAW

As preceding chapters have documented, the ACM is composed of
several separate components. Religiously based opposition to the
new religions usually has not involved civil or criminal legal proceedings, the Spiritual Counterfeits Project's successful suit to
have Transcendental Meditation declared a religion being the most
notable exception. It has largely been the deprogrammers and anti-
cult association members (along with some public officials) who have
precipitated or initiated various types of legal actions. The central goal of parents, and deprogrammers as their agents, has been to
extricate their offspring from new religious movements. While efforts have been made to warn the public of the danger posed by
cults, restrict their capacity to proselytize and solicit dona-
tions, these have always been secondary interests. The pattern of
parents joining the ACM only after their own children became involved with a new religious movement and withdrawing after resolv-
ing their own family problems belies the claims of civic motivation.

As the cult controversy has broadened and intensified over the
last decade, the courts have been called upon to adjudicate a whole
range of issues. The status of new religious movements as churches
or religions, health practices within these groups, financial considerations ranging from tax exemption to public solicitation of
contributions and the treatment and education of children have all
been sources of litigation. While such issues and outcomes are not
unimportant, it is the constellation of cases associated with the
brainwashing and deprogramming controversy which is most critical.
It is in this area that conflict has been the most intense because
retrieval of offspring has been the central ACM goal, and it is in
this area that the most important new legal precedents are likely to
be set. Therefore, we shall briefly review several legal issues but
focus major attention in this chapter on the legal arguments surrounding brainwashing and deprogramming.

A judicial definition of "religion" has proven to be a complex, perplexing task; indeed up to this time no single definition
has emerged (Dodge, 1969; Boyan, 1968). As Boyan (1968:498) has
observed:
>   ... while courts in recent years have moved toward
>   a non-theistic definition of religion, none has had
>   an occasion either in a single decision, or in a

series of decisions to supply a definition which
is theoretically sound and which is at the same
time comprehensive. Nevertheless, such a definition is important, since legal privileges and ex-
emptions accrue to the status of religion. These
benefits should not be applied in a discriminatory
manner because the definition of religion is inadequate. It is simultaneously necessary that "religion" be limited in such a way that the classifi-
cation does not become meaningless.

Despite the lack of a comprehensive definition of religion the
courts have not been paralyzed, for they have continued to define
what a religion is not, even without a definition of what it is.
Yet the uneasy balance remains, for the executive and legislative
branches of government on all levels also have defined parameters
of "religion" for their own purposes. Often these agencies have
shown less breadth of vision, and some observers have chastened such
potentially precedent setting initiatives. As Whelan (1979:50) put
it, "Congress and the federal agencies should do well to imitate
the reluctance of the courts to engage in definitions of religion."

Although the ACM has challenged the legitimacy of "cults" as
religions, they will find little solace in the pattern of judicial
decisions. The New York University Law Review (Note, 1978:1267-
1268) cited the United States v. Seeger (a claim for exemption from
military service by an atheist on the basis of pacifist convictions) in which the Court concluded that a sincere, meaningful belief that paralleled a belief in more common conceptions of God
qualified as religion as evidence of the broadening boundaries of
judicial conceptions of religion. The court also found for the de-
fendant even in the more extreme case of United States v. Ballard
where practices "involved the solicitation of funds by a few individuals who were unaffiliated with any organized religion and who
claimed to be divine messengers possessing, by reason of supernatural attainments, the power to heal persons of ailments and dis-
eases" (Note, 1978:1268). In comparing the characteristics of contemporary new religions against the standards set in Seeger,
Ballard and subsequent cases, the New York University Law Review
concluded (Note, 1978:1267):

> The Unification Church and other sects like it
> clearly satisfy (such) definitions. In fact an
> organization such as the Unification Church
> would present an easy case even under a more
> narrow definition than those recently offered
> by the judiciary.

Spendlove has concurred (1976:1133):

> It seems clear that the beliefs of most cultists
> would be protected by the free exercise clause.
> The Hare Krishna sect has recently been held to
> be a religion within the meaning of the first
> amendment and the Unification Church would prob-

ably also be held protected, since it completely
meets the criteria set out in Fellowship of
Humanity.

Moore (1980:655), despite a much more openly critical stance toward
new religions, conceded that the same was true for Scientology, citing the Founding Church of Scientology v. United States case:

> Despite an attempt by the United States Attorney
> to condemn the therapeutic process, the publica-
> tions and the marketing thereof, as false and mis-
> leading, the court of appeals found that the
> Scientologists had made out an unrebutted prima
> facie case that they were in fact a religion and
> were not guilty of violating any federal laws.

Health practices and treatment (or lack thereof) have long
been sources of litigation for a variety of religious groups
(Flowers, 1979). For example, the courts have been called upon to
decide whether or not to allow the use of controlled substances in
conjunction with religious services, snake handling and drinking of
poison as part of worship, or refusal of medical treatment based
upon religious belief in life-threatening situations. In the drug-
related cases only the Native American Church has received judicial
sanction for the use of a controlled substance (peyote) on the
basis that regulation would constitute undue intrusion by the state
on religious belief and practice. The courts have ruled against the
snake handling groups even though these practices were central to
the faith of such groups on the basis of danger to the individual
believer and to others witnessing the ceremony. Groups such as the
Christian Scientists and Jehovah's Witnesses have sought exemption
from medical regulations on the basis of religious belief. The
Christian Scientists have refused to innoculate or allow chest
x-rays of children enrolling in school, and Jehovah's Witnesses have
refused blood transfusions. The record in such cases has been
mixed. Cases in which health measures are necessary to a child's
welfare or to the public welfare have almost invariably been decided
in favor of the state. Cases in which adult individuals without
dependents have chosen to refuse blood transfusions on the basis of
religious beliefs, by contrast, have been treated much more favorably by the courts. Similarly, Christian Scientists have sometimes
been granted exemption from vaccination on the basis that they do
not pose a major health threat as long as the majority of individuals are vaccinated. In all of the health related cases the judicial record is far from clear and consistent; outcomes therefore
remain difficult to predict.

Numerous allegations have been made concerning the health and
treatment of members of new religions. Delgado (1977:16-21) has
listed a number of "health-threatening effects" which allegedly are
characteristic of cults, including poor diet, insufficient sleep,
overwork and unhealthy physical conditions. In addition, some individual members reportedly have refused medical treatment for a
variety of physical injuries and ailments, and children allegedly
have been denied medical treatment based on religious precepts of

the group. Even should such allegations prove true, however, any
cases brought before the courts would seem to fall well within the
boundaries of existing precedents. The New York University Law Review (Note, 1978:1278-1279) stated:

> Developments in the area of compulsory medical
> treatment ... support the view that the state
> should not interfere with religious activity
> absent harm to others. Some courts have denied
> the state's power to compel an adult to accept
> medical treatment or blood transfusions against
> his religious scruples. Barriers against such
> intervention have been upheld even when the
> patient's life was in danger.... Sect members are
> competent to make a voluntary decision to practice
> their religion in spite or even because of the
> possible harms to themselves. After all, it is
> not inconceivable that a competent person could,
> of his own free will, choose to endure harm.

Spendlove (1976:1138) put it even more directly:

> In most instances, a state would have no over-
> riding interest in removing a cultist from his
> cult, even if he were getting improper health
> care, food, or clothing, since the cultist would
> be harming only himself by his actions and would
> not affect the public health or safety.

Another major issue has been public solicitation of money by
members of new religions, principally in the Unification Church and
the Hare Krishna. As Johansen and Rosen (1979:125) have noted,
Cantwell v. Connecticut remains the leading case concerning public
solicitation. In that case, Cantwell, a member of Jehovah's Witnesses, was convicted of soliciting money without receiving the ap-
proval of the Secretary of Public Welfare in Connecticut. The
Supreme Court overturned the conviction noting that the Secretary's
licensing power amounted to censorship power. The Cantwell case
became a standard in this area and "the Supreme Court has been un-
willing to tolerate even minimal involvement with a church's financial affairs" (Johansen and Rosen, 1979:127).

The Unification Church has been at the center of public solicitation controversies; it has been involved in over twenty-five
hundred such cases over the last decade. Because the Unification
Church provided theological rationale for fundraising and operated a
nationwide network of fundraising teams (Bromley and Shupe, 1979:
120-124), it quickly became the target of local officials. Public
officials sought either to use restrictive and time consuming application procedures or to strictly limit fundraising activities as
a means of combatting these mobile fundraising teams. However, the
Unification Church and other groups won an impressive string of legal victories, and it became clear that, with the exception of reasonable regulation of time, place and manner of solicitation to insure public safety and order, public solicitation of funds by reli-

gious groups fell well within constitutional safeguards. Bromley
and Shupe (1979:233) cited one such federal ruling in a case involving the Unification Church:

> It is a well established law that distribution
> of literature and solicitation of funds to sup-
> port religious organizations are well within the
> protection of the First Amendment.... The loss
> of First Amendment freedoms, even for minimal
> periods of time, unquestionably constitutes ir-
> reparable injury.

The preceding issues only serve to illustrate the legal conflicts in which new religious movements have been involved. Religious groups have also continually faced tax problems (Beebe,
1979), raised issues concerning the role of educational institutions in religion and religious groups in education (Wood, 1979) and
tested the boundaries of church and state in legislative advocacy
activities (Wogaman, 1979). The new religious movements, like the
more established churches, have become embroiled in these controversies. However, it has been the issue of brainwashing and deprogramming that has presented the greatest potential for legislative
and judicial precedent setting. And it is to that issue that we now
turn.

THE ACM BRAINWASHING AND DEPROGRAMMING POSITION

The ACM has alleged that most if not all new religions fall in
the category of "cults." Such groups are by their very nature (and
by definition) manipulative and destructive. Various ACM supporters have sought to identify the essential characteristics of cults.
Shapiro (1977:83), for example, listed eight such characteristics:

1. Demands complete obedience to and subservience
   to one individual, who purports to be God, the
   Messiah or some form of, or a messenger of, the
   deity.
2. Requires separation from society. Association
   with nonmembers is discouraged, except to gain
   money or to proselytize.
3. Discourages any form of self-development. Education is scorned and the self-image is totally
   destroyed.
4. Teaches hatred of parents, organized religion
   and, sometimes, the U.S. government.
5. Does not have concern for the material body;
   feels only the soul is important.
6. Takes all material possessions (past, present
   and future) for its own use. Members are not
   permitted to own anything in their own names.
7. Makes it almost impossible for a member to leave,
   either through physical restraints or psychologic
   fears.

8. Maintains the member in a "brainwashed" state
through destructive behavior modification techniques.

Marcia Rudin (1979/1980:24-30) has compiled a similar list:

1. Members swear total allegiance to an all-powerful
leader whom they may believe to be a Messiah.
2. Rational thought is discouraged or forbidden.
3. Cult recruitment techniques are often deceptive.
4. The cult psychologically weakens the follower
and makes him believe his problems can be solved
only by the group.
5. The new cults expertly manipulate guilt.
6. Cult members are isolated from the outside world,
cut off from their pasts, from school, job, family and friends as well as from information from
newspapers, radio, and television.
7. The cult or its leader makes every career or life
decision for the follower.
8. To attract idealistic members, some cults promise
to raise money to improve society and help the
poor.
9. Cult followers often work full-time for the group.
10. The cults are anti-woman, anti-child, and anti-
family.
11. Some cult members believe that they are elite members of an "elect" survival group in a world that
is coming to an end.
12. Many of these groups share a philosophy which
allows the ends to justify the means.
13. The cults often are shrouded in an aura of secrecy
and mystery.
14. An atmosphere of violence or potential violence
frequently surrounds the cults.

Based upon these characteristics of "cults" and the implicitly or
explicitly implied dangerous, destructive practices that emanate
from them, ACM spokespersons have advocated a variety of legal, and
sometimes extra-legal, remedies.

ACM Legal Arguments

The primary proponent of legal controls over new religious
movements has been Richard Delgado. He has written extensively on
legal responses to new religions (1982; 1980; 1979-1980; 1979;
1978b; 1977b) as well as the more general issue of brainwashing and
manipulated behavior change (1978a; 1977a). Delgado has attempted
to identify conditions under which legal regulation of religious
practice might be possible and then has sought to demonstrate that
practices characteristic of new religious movements meet those conditions. Delgado has based his assertions largely on evidence provided by psychologists and psychiatrists sympathetic to the ACM,
such as Singer, West, Clark and Galper (cited in Chapter Six) and
other ACM spokespersons (e.g., Rudin, 1979-1980).

Delgado.´s arguments have taken two different tacks. In his
more recent and tangential argument he has asserted that cult practices violate thirteenth amendment prohibitions against slavery. On
the one hand, he has contended (1979-1980:52) that "rigidly hierar-
chical, authoritarian and isolated living arrangements established
by certain religious cults, with the aid of intensive thought manipulation techniques, contravene the thirteenth amendment." On the
other hand, he has derived a second argument that such arrangements
"violate a number of values protected by the thirteenth amendment,
giving rise to a compelling interest in their abatement" even if
they do not constitute slavery. This line of argument was proferred
for several reasons: (1) the issue of initial voluntariness was
avoided and the objective state of affairs evaluated instead, (2)
slavery is prohibited absolutely, (3) medical and psychiatric testimony became unnecessary and (4) the individual member´s apparent
compliance became irrelevant. He concluded this argument by asserting that "Remedies under the thirteenth amendment can and should
be implemented to limit the unique but harmful brand of slavery that
cults impose on their members (1979-1980:67).

Delgado´s primary argument has been that the thought reform
practices of "cults" result in physical and psychological injury.
Major focus has been on harm to individuals since the primary remedies and controls have centered on removing individuals from new
religions. Delgado has asserted that cult membership tends to produce neurotic or psychotic symptoms that potentially are irrevers-
ible. Such symptoms are caused by systematic food and sleep deprivation, lack of opportunity for reality testing and a sensory bar-
rage which narrows the individual´s focus of attention and in-
creases suggestibility. Individuals subjected to this physical and
psychological onslaught are further compelled to break off relationships with non-members (including family), give up educational and
career plans and adopt rigid, stereotypical world views. The result, Delgado has contended, is an individual who is caught up in a
group which stresses dependency, emotional commitment and black and
white thinking over autonomy, rationality and complex, critical
analysis. Individuals have been plagued with feelings of guilt,
worthlessness, apathy and depression. Individuals may be adversely
affected in other ways as well, since groups´ beliefs may lead to
inadequate diet and medical care, forfeiture of money and possessions, and abusive child-rearing practices.

It has been Delgado´s position that intervention by the courts
was both within the scope of judicial powers and consistent with
case law precedent. The essence of Delgado´s argument has been that
"cult" recruitment and socialization tactics have the effect of
diminishing individual free will. There is, he has stated, deliberate manipulation of knowledge and capacity such that an individual
never possesses sufficient amounts of each simultaneously to act
autonomously. As he has put it (1980:28):

> The process by which an individual becomes a member
> of certain cults appears arranged in such a way
> that knowledge and capacity, the classic ingredients
> of an informed consent, are maintained in an inverse

relationship: when capacity is high, the recruits'
knowledge of its practices is low; when knowledge
is high, capacity is reduced.

From Delgado's perspective substantial personal and social injury gives the state a right to legal intervention. He has insisted
that the fact that tactics resulting in such harm have been carried
out under "colorly religious auspices" should not deflect state intervention. First amendment protections have been limited in cases
where behavior is socially harmful, not essential to the group's
system of belief, or motivated by political or economic rather than
religious concerns. Since voluntariness has been substantially reduced, such harms could not be regarded as consensual and hence
protected by constitutional strictures. As he summed it up (1980:
33):

> There appear to be no insuperable constitutional,
> moral or public policy obstacles in the way of
> state or federal action designed to curb the
> abuses of religious groups that utilize high-
> pressure, harmful and deceptive tactics in re-
> cruiting and indoctrinating young members. So
> long as remedies comport with the least restric-
> tive alternative requirements ... and provide
> adequate due process procedures and judicial
> oversight, measures aimed at regulating the
> private use of mind control by religious or
> pseudoreligious groups appear to be fully per-
> missible.

Delgado's own concern about the implications of state intervention
for religious liberty has been reduced since he concluded that
"cults" constitute a special category of groups which "may expose
their indoctrinees to a greater variety of classic mind control
techniques as well as apply these techniques with greater intensity"
(1980:32). Furthermore, he has argued that prohibiting such techniques would not prevent these groups from existing or even from recruiting and continuing to practice their religious beliefs. Finally, he has concluded that other legitimate groups would not be
endangered since intervention against the stronger techniques of
cults would not make imperative action against less serious abuses,
and meaningful distinctions between cults and other groups could be
obtained if means used and results obtained were considered (1980:
33).

Cults have been accused of social as well as individual harms.
Threats to social institutions have included harm to family relationships and potential for violence. Among the alleged violations
of family relationships have been acceptance of minors into cult
membership, deliberate creation of hostility toward parents by sons
and daughters, hiding converts to avoid parental contact or
"rescue," treatment of women as inferiors, marriage or remarriage
without following proper legal procedures or even informing family
members and lack of minimal parental or medical care. Evidence for
potential violence has included the stockpiling of weapons by

certain groups, creation of enemies lists, authoritarian control over followers by leaders and a tendency by members to become converts to other totalistic groups. Naturally, the specter of Jonestown has loomed behind allegations of potential violence. These and other allegations of social injury, while secondary to the main thrust of Delgado's argument, have been used to buttress his contention that legal intervention against new religious movements is warranted.

Based upon such claims of individual and social injury, Delgado has enumerated a variety of remedies for abuses by cults. Recommended remedies have varied with the stage (of the "cult brainwashing experience") at which they are directed and have conformed to the principle of "least harmful available option." Preventive remedies have included self-identification by recruiters, a mandatory cooling off period in which recruits would be required to separate themselves from the group, public education programs which would focus on risks associated with groups employing thought reform techniques, prohibition of proselytization, licensing of individuals permitted to engage in "psychologically intrusive practices" and legal status for statements by individuals that they desired rescue in the event they should become trapped in a cult. Post-induction remedies, all of which were premised upon the assumption that few cult members could exit these groups voluntarily, have included mutual reassessment, conservatorship powers and deprogramming (using "carefully defined guidelines"). Other assorted remedies have involved tort actions for damages sustained while in a cult (e.g., false imprisonment, intentional infliction of emotional distress), civil actions to recover money and possessions donated to cults, and various criminal actions (e.g., unlawful imprisonment, kidnapping, slavery).

LEGAL RESPONSES TO ACM INTERVENTION PROPOSALS

The response by legal scholars to ACM intervention proposals must be understood in the context of generic constitutional guarantees of religious liberty and precedent setting cases which have become guidelines for resolution of contemporary disputes. In general these constitutional guarantees have been broadened as the Supreme Court has expanded the range of groups falling in the "religious" category. The broad parameters of religious freedom in the United States were defined by the first amendment prohibitions on Congress from making any law with respect to an establishment of religion or preventing the free exercise of religion. The establishment clause of the first amendment has constituted a kind of prior restraint on legislatures, prohibiting either advancement or inhibition of religion, while the free exercise clause has constituted a post factum redress for infringement on individual exercise.

Like other constitutionally protected freedoms, the free exercise of religion is subject to legal restraint under some conditions. A distinction has developed between freedom of belief, which is absolutely guaranteed, and freedom of action, which could be constrained. Actions, whether or not they were premised on reli-

gious beliefs, have been restrained when they threatened the
established social order or the rights of other individuals. So,
for example, the Mormon practice of polygamy was not accorded free
exercise protection on the basis that it constituted a threat to
established marriage and family practices and snake handling was
deemed a threat to public safety. It has frequently been observed
that this distinction between belief and action is arbitrary since
it is implausible that deeply held beliefs would not be manifested
in some type of action. Restraint on action, therefore, would almost inevitably involve some degree of restraint on belief. Fortu-
nately, perhaps, the courts have not systematically pursued this
belief-action dichotomy in rendering decisions; rather the courts
have chosen to limit the right of free exercise only when a clash
between free exercise and state interests emerged <u>and</u> a compelling
state interest in restraint could be demonstrated.

Prior to the decade of the 1960´s the courts were relatively
liberal in identifying and ruling in favor of such state interests.
Two landmark cases reversed this priority and shifted the burden of
proof to the state to demonstrate a compelling state interest. The
1963 <u>Sherbert v. Werner</u> case involved a member of the Seventh Day
Adventist Church who was fired for refusing to work on Saturday.
She was refused unemployment compensation benefits by the South
Carolina courts because she had failed to accept work involving
Saturday employment. Upon determining that Mrs. Sherbert was sincere in her belief and that the state was interfering with the
practice of her religion (by forcing her to choose between religious precepts and unemployment benefits) the court concluded that
no compelling state interest had been shown nor had it been demonstrated that alternative remedies were lacking which would avoid
infringement on first amendment rights. The 1972 <u>Wisconsin v.
Yoder</u> case involved prosecution of Old Order Amish and Conservative Amish Mennonites under school attendance laws for refusal to
enroll their children in the post-elementary public education system. The justices ruled that Amish objections to formal education
beyond the eighth grade were rooted in religious precept, that the
state´s enforcement of compulsory education would undermine the
practice of Amish religious beliefs and that the state did not have
a sufficiently compelling interest to override free exercise protections.

Out of these two cases have come the elements of what has come
to be known as the Sherbert-Yoder balancing test. According to
Shepherd (1981:12), the five elements of the balancing test are as
follows:

1. Are the religious beliefs in question sincerely held?
2. Are the religious practices under review germane to
   the religious belief system?
3. Would carrying out the state´s wishes constitute a
   substantial infringement on the religious practice?
4. Is the interest of the state compelling? Does the
   religious practice perpetrate some grave abuse of a
   statutory prohibition or obligation?
5. Are there alternative means of regulation by which

the state's interest is served but the free exercise of religion is less burdened?

It is in terms of these recent precedent setting cases that current ACM intervention proposals must be evaluated.

Conservatorships and Guardianships

The most significant legal issue raised in the contemporary cult controversy has been the issuing of conservatorships to parents of members of new religious groups. The conservatorship issue has become the center of legal conflict for several reasons. First, the primary goal of ACM parents has been extrication of offspring from "cults," and conservatorships would permit this. Existing conservatorship laws have already been used on numerous occasions for this purpose, and broadening conservatorship provisions would constitute a major victory for the ACM. Second, expanding conservatorship powers has been the major legislative thrust of the ACM. Bills passed both houses of the legislature in New York during two consecutive legislative sessions; passage was overturned in both instances by gubernatorial veto. Virtually identical legislation has been introduced in a number of other states although no other comparable success has been achieved. Third, if successful, conservatorship bills would place the state in the position of physically intervening to remove adult individuals from certain religious groups and evaluating their mental health status by virtue of their having joined these groups. Numerous more conventional religious organizations have been drawn into the conservatorship issue as a result of the broad implications of such legislation for religious liberty.

Many states have enacted guardian and/or conservator provisions. Typically such statutes apply to minors, elderly and/or mentally incompetent individuals who have been deemed incompetent to conduct their own affairs. The most common conservatorship powers are financial and are implemented when individuals appear to be in danger of seriously mismanaging their finances or being victimized by "artful and designing persons." More extensive powers are often available if incapacities are more severe. In recent years, parents of converts to new religions have sought to gain legal custody of their offspring through the use of temporary conservatorships (i.e., a few weeks to a few months, depending on the state) for the purpose at least of separating the individual from the group for this period and often for the purpose of deprogramming the son or daugther in their custody. At the same time, the ACM has sought to broaden the scope of conservatorship statutes to explicitly cover affiliation with controversial new religions and to ease the process of obtaining conservatorships in such cases.

Beginning in 1975 conservatorships were used to place members of new religious groups in the custody of family members. A number of ex parte conservatorships were issued in California, for example. As Spendlove (1976:1110) has noted, these conservatorships were not very difficult to obtain:

Temporary conservatorships have been issued upon
petitions which have done nothing but recite the
technical requirements of the statutes—that the
cultist was unable to properly care for his person
or property and is likely to be deceived by artful
and designing persons—and making conclusionary
allegations that the cultist showed abrupt personality changes, had transmitted assets to the leaders
of the religious group, and appeared to be the
victim of mind control through hypnosis, mesmerism,
or brainwashing.

Simply granting conservatorship power to family members without ad-
versarial hearings and without substantiating evidence, however,
raised the possibility of a variety of abuses. Greene (1977:1052)
warned that "Guardianship statutes are subject to abuse if courts
routinely assume that parents invariably have the best interests of
their children at heart, or that membership in particular religious
cults indicates mental incapacity." Other observers were even more
pointed in their concerns; the New York University Law Review (Note,
1978:1289) concluded:

The imposition of conservatorships on members of
unconventional religious groups is uncomfortably
close to the suppression of citizens´ rights to
pursue, join and practice the religion of their
choice. Once it is conceded that the religious
beliefs and practices of one group are the proper
business of another, the opportunities for mis-
chief are limitless.... If conservatorships are
upheld as a legitimate weapon with which to combat unconventional religious beliefs and practices, the courts will be setting off a series
of unjustifiable investigations, accusations and
prosecutions that will go on without forseeable
end, jeopardizing the atmosphere of free discussion of, adherence to, and dissent from religious views that the free exercise clause was
designed to protect.

Interestingly, the current ACM campaign to broaden conservatorship powers has come at a time when states already have begun a move
to restrict them. Recent statutory changes have limited granting of
conservatorships only to situations where extreme self-endangerment
was clearly evident. These developments have confronted the ACM
with a more formidable challenge, for a lifestyle, however bizarre
by conventional standards, would not constitute grounds for legal
intervention unless there was an immediate and extreme danger to the
individual. As Greene (1977:1054) critically observed in a discussion of Hare Krishna:

... the advent of the Hare Krishna religious association, with its emphasis upon chanting, its pristine
values, and the uncommon appearance of its members,
epitomizes a situation in which an unconventional

lifestyle frequently evokes a pejorative psychiatric
labeling of the individual devotee. Embittered or
disappointed parents may obtain the support of a
psychiatrist who could apply his own norms in determining the presence of mental illness.... These proceedings, therefore, allow a select group of individuals to restrict the permissible range of religious
worship, contrary to the fundamental American tradition of religious freedom.

From an ACM perspective the future may be even more bleak since judicial precedents in some states have gone further in the direction
of restricting conservatorships than even the revised statutes.
Spendlove (1976:1118) concluded that, "In light of recent developments in due process as applied to emergency commitment to mental
hospitals, the Arizona temporary guardian statute and the California
temporary conservator statute appear to violate due process." With
respect to the California statute, she asserted (1976:1121-1122) it
is:

> ... unconstitutional on its face and would certainly
> be unconstitutional as used to appoint ex parte tem-
> porary conservators for cultists.... Cultists who
> are put under temporary conservatorships for the
> purpose of being subjected to deprogramming are con-
> demned to suffer grievous loss out of proportion to
> any governmental interest in making sure they do not
> harm themselves or others.

Whatever the degree of restrictiveness involved in the granting
of conservatorships, legal analysts concur that there are numerous
legal and constitutional problems with using conservatorship powers
as a means of extricating individuals from new religions. This
would particularly be the case where conservatorships were granted
so that deprogramming could take place.

One major problem facing the ACM has been (as we have already
noted) that virtually all of the ACM target "cults" possess legal
standing as religions. Under these conditions the possibilities for
legal intervention are dramatically narrowed. It would be virtually
impossible to grant conservatorships or permit deprogrammings without intruding upon the forbidden territory of individual religious
beliefs. Such intrusion occurs when "a court requires a sect member
not only to testify to his sincerity but to prove to the court's
satisfaction that he is not mentally incompetent by virtue of holding his faith" (Note, 1978:1269). Since it has been the lifestyles
and practices within such groups, which are direct outgrowth of beliefs, that have been the sources of complaints from parents, viola-
tion of constitutional boundaries would be most difficult to avoid.
The case would be even clearer with respect to deprogramming.
Spendlove (1976:1135-1136) made the point quite clearly:

> ... deprogramming is a technique the specific aim
> of which is not merely to change a cultist's be-
> havior, but to alter his religious beliefs.... A

court which allowed a parent custody of his child
in order to have him deprogrammed would be vio-
lating the child's first amendment rights.

A second problem concerns demonstrating that coercive mind control practices have been utilized to recruit and retain "cult" members, which has always been the centerpiece of ACM ideology. ·For
example, ACM proponents have used absolute obedience to a "cult"
leader as evidence of thought control. However, since courts must
focus only on sincerity (rather than content) of belief, this argument could easily be turned on its head. As the New York University
Law Review (Note, 1978:1271) put it, "The zealous commitment and un-
yielding devotion displayed by most sect members would make it difficult to argue their beliefs are not sincerely held." Furthermore, as Homer (1974:640) has observed, extreme compliance would be
expected if a devotee believed in a religious leader:

> He may act in accordance with the leader's orders
> unfailingly and unquestioningly from a belief that,
> for example, the leader speaks the will of God. In
> such a case that belief is inextricably bound up in
> the will and thought processes of the member. Inter-
> fering in such a situation would require a prior
> finding that the member's belief that God speaks
> through the cult leader is false and that, therefore,
> the cause of the members' dependence is "thought
> control."

In general, the ACM has not been very successful in substantiating claims of mental coercion that would meet legal standards for
granting conservatorships. As the New York University Law Review
concluded, "Despite the public ballyhoo over and concern about
brainwashing activities, no court that has conducted an evidentiary
hearing has found that any religious organization has subjected its
adherents to mind control, coercive persuasion or brainwashing"
(Note, 1978:1281). Of course, the case could be made in a much
easier and compelling fashion if physical restraint could be demonstrated. However, satisfactory evidence on this point has also been
lacking. As the author observed (Note, 1978:1280):

> Parents requesting conservatorships have been con-
> spicuously unable to furnish proof that their chil-
> dren have been physically restrained. In Katz, for
> example, there was no evidence that the members
> were denied the freedom to come and go as they
> pleased either during the period of their intro-
> duction to the (Unification) Church and inculca-
> tion to its values or thereafter.

Even if ACM protagonists could demonstrate some degree of
thought control, such evidence might well be insufficient given the
necessity of demonstrating an overriding state interest in intervention and the serious intrusion inherent in granting conservatorships. As the New York University Law Review (Note, 1978:1272) has
asserted, conservatorships are not an inconsequential remedy:

Unquestionably, the conservatorship procedure works
a substantial interference. The extreme powers of
temporary conservators ... not only interfere with
but negate the members' free exercise rights....
There is a total and direct denial of the members'
ability to practice their religion and a serious
threat to the freedom of their co-religionists.

The problem of demonstrating compelling state interest is evidenced
by numerous court cases in which, for example, individuals have been
permitted to forego medical treatment on the basis of religious beliefs even in life-threatening situations. Such cases indicate that
courts are unlikely to find self-injury or harm to physical and mental health sufficiently compelling to support the granting of conservatorships. As the author (Note, 1978:1279) concluded:

... the sect members do not engage in conduct that
injures or threatens harm to the legitimate interests of others. The absence of any such injury
distinguishes this case from virtually every
decision in which the courts have found a compelling governmental interest sufficient to out-
weigh a religious claim. The state's interest in
preventing self-endangerment should not, in and of
itself, justify the granting of conservatorships.

This last conclusion anticipates another ACM line of argument.
ACM proponents have attempted to justify conservatorships on the
basis that "cults" are fraudulent (i.e., not religious groups at
all) and do substantial social injury, particularly to the family.
These arguments have fared no better, however. Legal scholars have
pointed out that demonstrating fraud or illicit political activity,
for example, would not specifically help in gaining conservatorships. While a variety of other legal remedies, both civil and
criminal, might be sought for such alleged violations, the sincerity
of devotees' religious beliefs would not be contingent upon the integrity or sincerity of leaders' beliefs and actions. As the New
York University Law Review (Note, 1978:1286-1287) stated:

None of these possible societal harms, however,
need to be combatted by the imposition of temporary conservatorships. Such putative harms
should have no bearing whatsoever on the right
of the devotees to practice their religion.

Assessments of intervention based upon ruptured family relationships
have yielded similar conclusions. The New York University Law
Review (Note, 1978:1285) asserted:

Although the state has an interest in protecting
the family relationship from disintegration, this
interest is overcome by an adult's right to free
exercise of religion.... Here the sect members
involved are emancipated adults, free from parental

authority and free to adopt their own religions
and world views.

Homer (1974:623) reached a similar conclusion:

> While practices such as these may seem extreme
> and inexcusable to some, there would appear to
> be no satisfactory rationale for state interven-
> tion here.... Adherents have joined the particu-
> lar sect voluntarily, have chosen to accept its
> teachings and strictures and when given the
> choice of repudiating parents or family or leav-
> ing the sect, have opted to remain in the sect.
> To justify infringement here, the state would
> seemingly need to establish either that a member
> was being unlawfully imprisoned by the sect or
> that there was no meaningful consent by a member
> to a sect's attitudes and actions against his
> parents.

He went on to make the even broader assertion (1974:637) that "no
cases have been reported in which a court has held that the interest
in affirming parental authority over an emancipated child out-
weighed an individual's interest in the preservation of his religious freedom."

Deprogramming

   Conservatorships or guardianships and deprogramming frequently
have gone hand-in-hand since the former usually have been obtained
to facilitate the latter. Nevertheless, deprogramming must be
treated separately for analytic purposes since conservatorships have
not inevitably been accompanied by deprogramming and deprogramming
frequently has been carried out without benefit of legal custody.
It should be emphasized that what the ACM terms deprogramming in
actuality ranges from voluntary dialogues in which converts to new
religions agree to separate themselves from the group temporarily
and "hear the other side" to forcible abductions. We shall be dealing here only with cases where members have not consented to participate in the deprogramming process.

   Virtually all legal analysts have concurred that forcible deprogramming almost always violates the law. Even those relatively
supportive of controls over "cults" have rejected deprogramming.
For example, Rosenzweig (1979-1980:156) stated:

> As a self-help remedy, deprogramming has been uti-
> lized by parents with the assistance of professional
> deprogrammers to expunge the altered world perspec-
> tive of indoctrinees. The process usually involves
> abduction and physical restraint, and is not only
> potentially illegal but also directly violative of
> the absolute right to religious belief. It entails
> assaults upon the sect members' physical and mental
> integrity.

LeMoult (1978:606) has gone even further in condemning deprogramming, asserting that, "It is far more like brainwashing than the conversion process by which members join various sects."

Precisely what offenses might be involved in any particular deprogramming varies, depending upon jurisdictional statutes and the course of events. Greene (1977:1047) has asserted that both "the forced removal of the worshipper from the group and his subsequent physical detention may constitute false imprisonment or kidnapping." LeMoult (1978:623-625), however, has noted that state kidnapping statutes vary and hence deprogramming may not constitute first degree kidnapping although abduction or deprogramming would be prosecutable as either second degree kidnapping or false imprisonment in most states.

Deprogrammings have continued despite their widely acknowledged illegality for several reasons. First, in successful deprogrammings there simply has been no victim or complainant to initiate legal proceedings. Second, deprogrammers increasingly have arranged to have parents initiate the physical abduction, and victims often have been reluctant to implicate their parents in criminal proceedings. Third, law enforcement agencies have been prone to regard deprogrammings as family disputes and avoid formal involvement. Finally, as LeMoult (1978:622) has observed, cases have not been prosecuted because the "purpose of the deprogramming-kidnapping is not one of the traditional purposes, i.e., ransom, use as a hostage, white slavery or sexual abuse."

Necessity Defense

Even in cases where deprogrammers have been prosecuted for abducting and confining members of new religious movements, conviction has been far from certain. The most systematic strategy that deprogrammers have employed to avoid conviction on criminal charges has been the "necessity defense." Traditionally, defendants have escaped conviction when they have been able to demonstrate that they had "violated a law to avoid a greater evil than the law was designed to prevent" (Pierson, 1981:273). The defense in deprogramming cases usually has rested on two sets of arguments—that parents undertook deprogramming because they had reasonable cause to believe their children were in physical and/or psychological danger and that deprogrammers were necessary agents who rendered vital assistance to parents. Historically, however, the necessity defense has been used where "forces of nature" compelled action (LeMoult, 1978; Greene, 1977), and legal schools have expressed considerable skepticism about its extension to cases involving pressure by other individuals. LeMoult (1978:629), for example, asserted that, "The defense of justification, or choice of evils, is obviously improper in such prosecutions for a violent crime against person—like kidnapping, false imprisonment, or one of the other possible crimes which might arise out of deprogramming." Greene (1977:1047-1048) was even more critical:

> ... the act of necessity which exonerates a
> defendant from criminal liability must be a

lesser harm than that which may have befallen
the victim had no action been taken. The
forced removal and prolonged detention and
depravity of a cultist is at best an equivo-
cal act of parental good faith. At worst, the
experience is a terrifying, violent event
tinged with gangsterism. Thus, the harm in-
flicted by "deprogramming" may in fact be
greater than the harm it avoids. Finally, even
if the "necessity defense" may be appropriately
asserted by parents, extension to the deprogrammer cannot be founded upon theories of agency
law.

By far the most sophisticated analysis of the applicability of
the necessity defense to deprogramming cases has been conducted by
Pierson (1981). He has argued that the legitimacy of a necessity
defense rests on three sets of factors: (1) the harms created by deprogramming, (2) the harms avoided by deprogramming and (3) the
reasonableness of parents´ beliefs that the second set of harms accrue as a result of deprogramming both because of the criminal actions accompanying abduction or restraint and because of the threats
to freedom of religion. As he put it (1981:297):

> Most of the characteristics of cult membership
> on which deprogrammers rely to justify their
> activities—isolation from the rest of society,
> devotion to the cult as a surrogate family, and
> adherence to peculiar beliefs and practices—
> directly affect deprogrammed individuals, and
> also harm the cults. In addition to depriving
> cults of members´ services and support, depro-
> gramming may generate a chilling effect that
> hampers their recruiting efforts.

With respect to harms avoided, Pierson has contended that most
of ACM allegations against new religions would constitute balancing
harms only if an individual could not voluntarily consent to such
conditions. He stipulated that the recruitment and socialization
activities of new religions, which have been termed brainwashing, in
fact constitute advocacy of religious beliefs. He concluded (1981:
302) that:

> The brainwashing argument may assume that there
> are "normal" religious beliefs and "constructive"
> religious practices from which cults deviate and
> that deprogramming allows individuals to appre-
> ciate. It also assumes that some individuals are
> capable of influencing others in a manner so
> clearly contrary to their best interests that it
> is permissible to restrict the influence. It over-
> looks, however, the Supreme Court´s consistent
> rejection of both the former and latter assumptions.

Except in cases of imminent, serious physical injury or damage, therefore, intervention by deprogrammers would not be protected. And, given the force associated with deprogramming, inadequate diet or lack of sufficient sleep would not constitute adequate grounds. Psychological problems would be excluded entirely unless an individual were demonstrably unable to exercise independent judgment.

Finally, Pierson considered the conditions under which defendants might be legally exonerated on the basis of a reasonable belief that the balance of harms justified deprogramming. He asserted that, at a minimum, specific evidence (e.g., correspondence out of character with previous communication, personal contact suggesting incapacity to render independent judgments, blockage of contact with offspring by a "cult") was necessary to legitimate "rescue." Of course, such subjective evidence would be subject to later scrutiny for reasonableness and specificity. In addition, other viable legal alternatives, such as conservatorships, must have been duly considered prior to the undertaking of extra-legal action. He concluded (1981:306) that:

> The choice of evils defense will thus rarely exonerate parents of adult cult members, and will virtually never exonerate professional deprogrammers. Deprogramming constitutes a lesser evil only if the cult member appears incapable of exercising independent judgement or risks severe injury. Even in these situations, courts should reject the defense if viable legal alternatives were available.

Thus, the necessity defense appears to hold little security for deprogrammers in the long run despite a number of successful applications in recent years. As the full legal implications and precedent cases are more widely disseminated, it seems likely that courts will be increasingly less receptive to such arguments.

Based on the preceding analysis the long-term legal prospects facing the ACM appear discouraging. In addition to a general lack of support for ACM legal proposals, however, deprogrammers also run the risk of civil suits (Siegel, 1978:826-828). Civil suits offer a number of advantages such as avoiding the necessity of implicating parents in legal action and offsetting the failure of law enforcement agencies to prosecute deprogrammers. LeMoult (1978:636-637) has identified a number of offenses, including assault and battery, unlawful imprisonment, invasion of privacy and medical malpractice which might be pursued in civil proceedings. Babbit (1979) has suggested that suits under section 1985 (3) of the Civil Rights Act might be viewed favorably by the courts.

In a section 1985 (3) suit a deprogrammed plaintiff has a reasonable probability of success. The plaintiff could clearly show the existence of a conspiracy, an overt act and a class based motivation, and infringement of free exercise of religion and right to travel could be established. As Babbit (1979:254) commented:

If the plaintiff can thus state a cause of action,
trial upon the merits will likely result in vindication of his constitutional right to join the religious group he pleases regardless of public or
private feelings against that religious group.

Disclosure Laws

One suggested alternative to conservatorship legislation or
other highly intrusive controls on religious groups has been disclosure legislation. One supporter, for example, noted the growing
state and federal concern for the protection of consumers in general. She asserted (Siegel, 1978:820-821):

> Surely the marketplace of ideas and religious
> philosophies is as needful of an informed public
> as is the commercial area. It would thus seem
> reasonable to require that religious associations,
> in making representations, conform to a standard
> of disclosure similar to that required in the
> marketing of products. No freedom of activity
> would be sacrificed....

The strongest advocate of such legislation (Rosenzweig, 1979-1980)
has based his defense of such potential statutes on the presumptions
that "cults" widely practice deception in recruitment and that such
practices have been largely responsible for their recruitment success. Recruits, he contends, should have information prior to becoming involved with groups employing thought reform techniques. He
stated (1979-1980:146):

> Absent fraud, the unwitting indoctrinee may never
> have considered sect membership. Therefore, the
> initial deception may be viewed as following the
> newcomer through the indoctrination process,
> vitiating consent to ensuing operation.

From his perspective disclosure laws would be superior to deprogramming because no attack on the beliefs of individuals would be involved. He stated (1979-1980:158):

> Unlike legalized deprogramming, disclosure legis-
> lation does not directly impinge upon the consti-
> tutional rights of religious sects or their mem-
> bers. In addition, it does not unreasonably
> burden a sect´s free exericse of religious worship.

Disclosure issues have not been seriously pursued by the ACM (except
in the case of fundraising) and hence there has been little litigation in this area. However, some doubts have been raised about even
such apparently simple legislation. LeMoult (1978:678-679), for
example, has concluded that:

The constitutionality of this theory is suspect
particularly if one examines the case of Wulp v.
Corcoran in which the court held that the requirements that a newspaper vendor procure and wear a
badge is unconstitutional in the absence of an important governmental interest.

809. Ackerman, David M. "Legal Implications of Taking Religious
     Converts over State Lines for Deprogramming Purposes."
     Washington, DC, Library of Congress, American Law Division,
     June 12, 1977.

810. Anthony, Dick. "The Fact Behind the Deprogramming Contro-
     versy: An Analysis and an Alternative." New York University
     Review of Law and Social Change 9 (1979-1980): 73-90.

811. Babbitt, Ellen M. "The Deprogramming of Religious Sect Mem-
     bers: A Private Right of Action Under Section 1985 (3)."
     Northwestern University Law Review 74 (1979): 229-254.

812. Beebe, Robert L. "Tax Problems Posed by Pseudo-Religious
     Movements." The Annals of the American Academy of Political
     and Social Science 446 (November 1979): 91-105.

813. Boyan, A. Stephen. "Defining Religion in Operational and In-
     stitutional Terms." University of Pennsylvania Law Review
     116 (1968): 479-498.

814. Brandon, Thomas. New Religions, Conversions and Deprogram-
     ming: New Frontiers of Religious Liberty. Oak Park, IL:
     Center for Law and Religious Freedom, 1982. 60 pp.

815. Bromley, David G., and Anson D. Shupe, Jr. "Moonies" in
     America: Cult, Church and Crusade. Beverly Hills, CA: Sage
     Publications, 1979. 269 pp.

816. Buckholder, John. "The Law Knows No Heresy: Marginal Reli-
     gious Movements and the Courts." Religious Movements in
     Contemporary America. Edited by Irving Zaretsky and Mark
     Leone. Princeton: Princeton University Press, 1974, pp. 27-
     52.

817. Clark, J. Morris. "Guidelines for the Free Exercise Clause."
     Harvard Law Review 83 (1969): 327-365.

818. Coleman, Lee, and Trudy Solomon. "Parens Patrie Treatment:
     Legal Punishment in Disguise." Hastings Constitutional Law
     Quarterly 3 (1976): 345-362.

819. Davis, J. Michael. "Brainwashing: Fact, Fiction and Criminal
     Defense." University of Missouri Kansas City Law Review 44
     (1976): 438-479.

820. Delgado, Richard A. "Awaiting the Verdict on Recruitment."
     The Center Magazine 15 (March/April 1982): 18-24.

821. Delgado, Richard A. "Limits to Proselytizing." Society 17
     (March-April 1980): 25-32.

822. Delgado, Richard A. "Religious Totalism as Slavery." New
     York University Review of Law and Social Change 9 (1979-
     1980): 51-68.

823. Delgado, Richard A. "Investigating Cults." New York Times,
     27 January 1979, p. A23.

824. Delgado, Richard A. "Ascription of Criminal States of Mind:
     Toward a Defense Theory for the Coercively Persuaded
     ("Brainwashed") Defendant." Minnesota Law Review 63
     (November 1978a): 1-34.

825. Delgado, Richard A. "The Legal Aspects of Religious Cults."
     Paper presented at the annual meeting of the Southern Cali-
     fornia Chapter of the American Psychiatric Association, Los
     Angeles, CA, 1978b.

826. Delgado, Richard A. "Organically Induced Behavioral Change in
     Correctional Institutions: Release Decisions and the New
     Man Phenomenon." Southern California Law Review 50
     (1977a): 215-270.

827. Delgado, Richard A. "Religious Totalism: Gentle and Ungentle
     Persuasion Under the First Amendment." Southern California
     Law Review 51 (1977b): 1-99.

828. Dodge, Joseph. "The Free Exercise of Religion: A Sociological
     Approach." Michigan Law Review 67 (1969): 679-728.

829. Doog, Lavine. "Retrieving a Cultist Poses Legal Problems."
     National Law Journal, December 11, 1978, p. 19.

830. Dressler, Joshua. "Professor Delgado's Brainwashing Defense:
     Courting a Determinist Legal System." Minnesota Law Review
     63 (January 1979): 335-360.

831. Flowers, Ronald B. "Freedom of Religion Versus Civil Author-
     ity in Matters of Health." The Annals of the American
     Academy of Political and Social Science 446 (November 1979):
     149-162.

832. Fox, Martin. "Cults and the First Amendment." National Law
     Journal, October 14, 1980.

833. Greene, Robert H. "People v. Religious Cult: Legal Guidelines
     for Criminal Activities, Tort Liability, and Parental
     Remedies." Suffolk Law Review 11 (1977): 1025-1058.

834. Homer, David. "Abduction, Religious Sects and the Free Exercise Guarantee." Syracuse Law Review 25 (1974): 623-645.

835. Johansen, R.B., and Sanford J. Rosen. "State and Local Regulation of Religious Solicitation of Funds: A Constitutional Perspective." The Annals of the American Academy of Political and Social Science 446 (November 1979): 116-135.

836. Lauter, David. "Are Churches Under Attack?" National Law Journal, November 1981, pp. 1, 16-17.

837. Laycock, Douglas. "Towards a General Theory of the Religion Clauses: The Case of Church Labor Relations and the Right to Church Autonomy." Columbia Law Review 81 (November 1981): 1373-1417.

838. LeMoult, John. "Deprogramming Members of Religious Sects." Fordham Law Review 46 (1978): 599-634.

839. Levine, Edward M. "Religious Cults: Their Implications for Society and the Democratic Process." Paper presented at the annual meeting of the International Society of Political Psychology, Boston, MA, 1980.

840. Levine, Mark. "The Free Exercise Clause as a Defense to Involuntary Civil Commitment: Bringing Mental Illness into Religion." Albany Law Review 39 (1974): 144-156.

841. Moore, Joey P. "Piercing the Religious Veil of the So-Called Cults." Pepperdine Law Review 7 (Spring 1980): 655-710.

842. "Note. Conservatorships and Religious Cults: Divining a Theory of Free Exercise." New York University Law Review 53 (1978): 1247-1289.

843. Pfeffer, Leo. "Equal Protection for Unpopular Sects." New York University Review of Law and Social Change 9 (1979-1980): 9-16.

844. Pfeffer, Leo. "The Current State of the Law in the United States and the Separationist Agenda." The Annals of the American Academy of Political and Social Science 446 (November 1979): 1-9.

845. Pfeffer, Leo. "The Legitimation of Marginal Religions in the United States." Religious Movements in Contemporary America. Edited by Irving Zaretsky and Mark Leone. Princeton, NJ: Princeton University Press, 1974, pp. 9-26.

846. Pfeffer, Leo. Church, State and Freedom. Boston, MA: Beacon Press, 1967.

847. Pierson, Kit. "Cults, Deprogrammers, and the Necessity Defense." Michigan Law Review 80 (December 1981): 271-311.

848. Poythress, Norman G. "Behavior Modification, Brainwashing,
      Religion, and the Law." Journal of Religion and Health 17
      (1978): 238-243.

849. Reich, Walter. "Brainwashing, Psychiatry and the Law."
      Psychology 39 (November 1976).

850. Robbins, Thomas. "Religious Movements, the State, and the
      Law: Reconceptualizing The Cult Problem." New York
      University Review of Law and Social Change 9 (1979-1980):
      33-49.

851. Rosenberg, Arthur H. "Legal Issues in the Treatment of Cult
      Members." National Association of Private Psychiatric
      Hospitals Journal 9 (1978).

852. Rosenzweig, Charles. "High Demand Sects: Disclosure Legisla-
      tion and the Free Exercise Clause." New England Law Review
      15 (1979-1980): 128-159.

853. Schuman, Eugene R. "Grand Jury Subpoenas and First Amendment
      Privileges." The Annals of the American Academy of Politi-
      cal and Social Science 446 (November 1979): 106-115.

854. Schuppin, Eric. "Areas of Government Involvement in Cults and
      Pseudo-Religious Organizations." Arlington, TX: National
      Ad Hoc Committee Engaged in Freeing Minds, n.d.

855. Shapiro, Robert. "Mind Control or Intensity of Faith: The
      Constitutional Protection of Religious Beliefs." Harvard
      Civil Rights - Civil Liberties Law Review 13 (1978): 751-
      797.

856. Shepherd, William C. "Constitutional Law and Marginal Reli-
      gions." Berkeley, CA, Center for the Study of New Religious
      Movements, Graduate Theological Union, 1982a.

857. Shepherd, William C. "Legal Protection for Freedom of Reli-
      gion." The Center Magazine 15 (March/April 1982b): 30-33.

858. Shepherd, William C. "The Prosecutor's Reach: Legal Issues
      Stemming from the New Religious Movements." Paper presented
      at the Conference on Conversion, Coercion and Commitment in
      New Religious Movements, Berkeley, CA: Center for the Study
      of New Religious Movements, June, 1981.

859. Shepherd, William C. "The New Religions and the Religion of
      the Republic." Journal of the American Academy of Religion
      44 (1978): 509-525.

860. Siegel, Terri I. "Deprogramming Religious Cultists." Loyola
      of Los Angeles Law Review 11 (September 1978): 807-828.

861. Slade, Margot. "New Religious Groups: Membership and Legal
      Battles." Psychology Today, January 1979, p. 81.

862. Spendlove, Gretta. "Legal Issues in the Use of Guardianship Procedures to Remove Members of Cults." Arizona Law Review 18 (1976): 1095-1139.

863. Weiss, Jonathan. "Privilege, Posture and Protection: Religion in the Law." Yale Law Journal 73 (1964): 593-623.

864. Whelan, Charles M. "Governmental Attempts to Define Church and Religion." The Annals of the American Academy of Political and Social Science 446 (November 1979): 32-51.

865. Wogaman, J. Phillip. "The Churches and Legislative Advocacy." The Annals of the American Academy of Political and Social Science 446 (November 1979): 52-62.

866. Wood, James E., Jr. "Religion and Education: A Continuing Dilemma." The Annals of the American Academy of Political and Social Science 446 (November 1979): 63-77.

867. Worthing, Sharon L. "The State Takes Over a Church." Annals of the American Academy of Political and Social Science 444 (November 1979): 136-148.

CHAPTER SEVEN

OPPOSITION TO THE ANTI-CULT MOVEMENT

Among the new religions the Church of Scientology and the Unification Church were particularly active and vocal in combatting
anti-cult allegations as well as the negative images that inevitably flowed out of protracted conflict and controversy. In this
chapter, therefore, we shall concentrate on the responses of these
two groups, along with the reactions of civil libertarians, mainline denominations and scholars engaged in studying new religions.
Some other new religions sought to defend themselves publicly, but
their efforts were less systematic. The Hare Krishna, for example,
issued a publication, A Request to the Media: Please Don't Lump Us
In (International Society for Krishna Consciousness, 1979). Similarly, the Local Church protested its inclusion in Jack Sparks'
critique of "contemporary cults," The Mindbenders (1977), through
a series of publications, such as Who Is the Real Mindbender?
(Ford, 1977) and Mind Bending or Mind Renewing? (Kangas, 1977), and
a civil suit.

The Unification Church issued a great variety of publications
in the form of reports, pamphlets, press releases and policy statements in an effort to shore up its public image. Some of these
publications sought to portray the Church in a favorable light, a
strategy adopted in the wake of continuing negative media coverage.
Illustrative publications of this type include Reverend Moon: A
Vindication for Justice (Unification Church, n.d.f), Rev. Sun
Myung Moon and the Unification Church (Unification Church, n.d.g)
and Charitable and Humanitarian Projects Inspired by Reverend Sun
Myung Moon (Unification Church, n.d.a). These publications, as the
titles suggest, constituted attempts to depict Moon personally and
the Church as an organization as contributors to American religious
vitality and spiritual strength.

Other documents defended the Church against a variety of accusations. Among these were some releases which sought to rebut
general stereotypes of the Church. The Unification Church National
Policy on Fundraising (Unification Church, 1977) was issued in response to continuing charges of deceptive tactics in public solicitation. Allegations that the Church operated surreptitiously
through "front groups" yielded an official explanation, Organizations: Why So Many? (Unification Church, n.d.e). In The New Religions (Durst, 1981), the President of the Unification Church, sought
to convince the public that all new religions encountered persecu-

tion, and therefore allegations should be kept in perspective. Additional publications of this genre include Commonly Asked Questions (Unification Church, n.d.b) and Help - We Are Being Persecuted (Unification Church, n.d.c).

Most of the publications were reactions to specific events that the Church regarded as critical to its interests and welfare. For example, then president Neil Salonen issued a series of "statements" in response to what was deemed prejudicial news coverage, in this case in the New York Daily News and in the New York Times (Salonen, 1976a, 1976c). He issued similar statements in response to the "Dole Hearings" (informal hearings conducted by Senator Robert Dole which provided anti-cultists with a public opportunity to record their litany of allegations against the Unification Church), including "Our Response to Persecution: A Report by President Neil Salonen" (Salonen, 1976d). Other such reports included a denial of anti-Semitism in the Divine Principle, Statement on Jews and Israel (Moon, 1976), following a highly critical report issued by the American Jewish Committee, Jews and Judaism in Reverend Moon's Divine Principle (Rudin, 1978), and a long rebuttal of allegations that Moon was linked to (and possibly an agent of) the Korean government and KCIA (see Bromley and Shupe, 1979a:221), Our Response to the Report of October 31, 1978 on the Investigation of Korean-American Relations (Ad Hoc Committee of Members of the Unification Church, 1979).

The Church of Scientology has issued a parallel set of publications. There have been reports countering a whole range of accusations made against Scientology, such as Common Falsehoods About Scientology and Docmentation to the Contrary (Church of Scientology, n.d.b) and A Correction of Common False Rumors Heard About the Church of Scientology (Church of Scientology, n.d.c). These reports rebut charges related to Scientology's legal or tax exempt status, the nature of E-meters, conflict with psychiatry, exploitation of members and "Fair Game" policy through documentation in the form of organizational records, evidence from outsiders, letters from Church members and affidavits. Other reports have focused on "distorted" media coverage of Scientology, Black Propaganda: A Smear Campaign Against a Reform Church (Church of Scientology, n.d.a), and "prejudicial" legal proceedings, Freedom of Religion Denied (Church of Scientology, 1981a). Finally, there have been a number of reports issued to attack specific allegations such as Paulette Cooper's expose, The Scandal of Scientology (1971) and McBeth's, Strange New Religions (1977), False Report Correction: The Scandal of Scientology by Paulette Cooper (Church of Scientology, n.d.f), The Paulette Cooper Tapes (Church of Scientology, 1981b) and False Report Correction of Strange New Religions (Church of Scientology, n.d.e).

The Church of Scientology and the Unification Church both gradually compiled lists of civil libertarians, public officials, church leaders, academicians studying new religions and even some family members of converts who were sympathetic with their position. These individuals were informed through memoranda, letters and newsletters when major legal victories or defeats were registered, threatening legislation was pending, anti-cult sponsored hearings were being conducted or members were deprogrammed. The Unification Church was particularly active in this regard as the conferences it sponsored through the International Conference on the Unity of Science and the New Ecumenical Research Association brought numerous contacts with sympathetic outsiders. Many of these individuals, although ambivalent about the Unification Church, at least felt that the group constituted a bona fide religion and deserved equal protection under law.

When Moon was convicted on charges of tax evasion, for example, the Unification Church sent out a letter to "friends and colleagues" prior to Moon's sentencing requesting supportive letters to be delivered to the judge. Information on the case was provided in an accompanying memorandum, "Statement on the Tax Case of Reverend Sun Myung Moon" (Unification Church, 1982b); and a press release was enclosed announcing that Harvard law professor Laurence H. Tribe had become chief defense counsel in the case (Unification Church, 1982a). Following a second abduction and deprogramming of member John Abelseth, the Church sent out a packet of materials containing an affidavit (Abelseth, 1982), press clippings ("A Moonie Eclipsed: Kidnappers Nab John Abelseth Again," Alberta Record, 11 December 1981; "Rescue by Kidnapping: A Cultist Charges His Parents as Deprogramming Turns Violent," Alberta Report, 22 May 1981; and "A Case of a Kidnapped Moonie," Alberta Report, 14 August 1981), a resolution on deprogramming issued by the National Council of Churches (28 February 1974) and a list of indictments and convictions against deprogrammers. These materials were widely disseminated because Unification Church leaders thought this case would help to discredit deprogramming. Abelseth was thirty-three years of age, married, operated his own business, was forcibly abducted on two separate occasions, was transported across both international and state boundaries and withstood prolonged confinement and deprogramming sessions. There was hardly a better case to illustrate the excesses of deprogrammers. The Church of Scientology made similar appeals. When certain political leaders in Clearwater, Florida, who had long opposed the location of Scientology's international headquarters there, organized public hearings on Scientology, the Church appealed for letters of protest. A letter and packet of materials including newspaper accounts of the hearings ("Anti-Scientology Strategy Urged," Clearwater Times, 15 September 1981; "Curb Scientology with Ordinances, Lawyer Suggests," Clearwater Times, 12 September 1981; "Taxing Nonprofit Groups Is Studied," Clearwater Times, 15 September 1981) and the names of officials who should be contacted. Newspaper clippings frequently were enclosed in such packets to validate claims of discrimination in accompanying letters and memoranda. In this case supporting materials indicated that an outspoken Scientology critic (Michael J. Flynn, a Boston attorney) who was handling a number of civil suits against Scientology had been selected to conduct the probe. Such documentation eased the fear of sympathetic but wary outsiders that they might become drawn into defending new religions when abuses by them had indeed taken place.

Both the Church of Scientology and the Unification Church also created and sponsored organizations which linked their own particular struggles to broader issues of religious liberty, minority

rights and constitutional safeguards. For instance, the Church of
Scientology established the Citizens Commission on Human Rights.
Among its activities were investigatory reports such as one produced on prominent anti-cult psychiatrist John Clark, Investigation
of John G. Clark, Jr., M.D. (Citizens Commission on Human Rights,
n.d.a). The Commission complained in this case that Dr. Clark was
providing testimony concerning mental or emotional injury of converts to new religions without having met in person with the individuals in question. In this case, the Commission was successful in
gaining a letter of admonition from the Board of Registration and
Discipline in Medicine of Massachusetts which stated in part:

> ... it is not good medical practice to certify a
> patient as mentally ill and dangerous without
> setting forth the factual bases of those conclu-
> sions. It is also improper and unlawful to base
> a finding of mental illness solely on membership
> in a religion, regardless of one's personal opin-
> ion as to the merits of that religion.

The Unification Church formed Minority Alliance International (MAI)
and the International Coalition Against Racial and Religious Intolerance (ICARRI). The goal of Minority Alliance International was
stated as the "total eradication of racial, religious and sexist
bigotry" (Johnson, 1982; see also Stevin, 1982). ICARRI was concerned with similar issues and sponsored civil liberty conferences
with the New Ecumenical Research Association.

CIVIL LIBERTIES ALLIES

A number of civil liberties organizations took up the cause of
new religions in response to extra-legal deprogramming, conservatorship bills and formal or informal cooperation of public officials
with the anti-cultists. There was considerable diversity in the nature of the civil liberties groups. Several of the most active
groups were directly spawned by the new religions controversy and
were closely related, although independent of, the contemporary new
religions. First Freedom, for example, was formed after the Attorney General of California placed the Worldwide Church of God in
receivership (Worthing, 1979). An interdenominational group, First
Freedom has closely monitored legislative activity impacting upon
churches and religious liberty, primarily in California. The organization has issued periodic "legislative updates" (e.g., Barnhart,
1982) calling attention to relevant pending legislation and sponsored conferences designed to spotlight major threats to religious
liberty. The 1982 conference held in San Francisco, for example,
addressed the issues of tax exemption (following on the heels of the
Bob Jones University case) and "anti-conversion laws."

Another such group, the Alliance for the Preservation of Religious Liberty (APRL) concentrated a great deal of its energy and resources on the new religious controversy. Both Scientology and the
Unification Church were extremely active in APRL. APRL corresponded
regularly with "friends of religious liberty," issued reports and a

newsletter and lobbied against anti-cult sponsored legislation.
APRL's newsletter, for example, featured articles which attacked
anti-cult ideology, such as "Cults Pose No Dangers Declare Religious
Scholars" (Alliance for the Preservation of Religious Liberty,
1979a) and "Psychiatry and the Brainwashing Myth" (Alliance for the
Preservation of Religious Liberty, 1981b). Other articles called
attention to struggles over anti-cult oriented legislation, such as
"Jeremiah Gutman Calls Richard Delgado Proposals Blatantly Unconstitutional" (Alliance for the Preservation of Religious Liberty,
1979c) and "House Resolution #20 Attacked by Prominent Leaders" (Alliance for the Preservation of Religious Liberty, 1979b). In longer
publications, APRL sought to focus public attention on the religious
implications of deprogramming by emphasizing the physical abduction
and restraint involved, the spread of deprogramming to more conventional religious groups and the inevitable challenging of specific
religious beliefs in the deprogramming process (Alliance for the
Preservation of Religious liberty, n.d.). A related organization
based in Canada, Canadians for the Protection of Religious Liberty,
engaged in similar activities and issued similar reports (e.g.,
Bryant, 1979b).

Other more conventional civil liberties organizations also became involved in defending the new religions, particularly with respect to deprogramming and conservatorship legislation. Civil liberties officials in the National Council of Churches, for example,
issued a resolution opposing deprogramming (National Council of
Churches, 1974) and actively spoke out against it in other forums
(Kelly, 1977). The American Civil Liberties Union co-sponsored a
conference on deprogramming which resulted in a report, Deprogramming: Documenting the Issue, containing extensive evidence on the
legal and religious liberties violations of deprogrammers (Alliance
for the Preservation of Liberty and American Civil Liberties Union,
1977).

Religious groups and civil libertarians banded together most
cohesively when conservatorship legislation was pending since many
groups recognized the generalized threat posed by such bills. Conservatorship legislation was introduced in a number of states, but
New York affords the best single illustration of the coalition that
formed in opposition. The New York legislation was extremely significant because that bill served as a model for legislation in other
states, success in New York would have been a major political victory and conservatorship bills twice passed both houses of the legislature before being vetoed by the governor. Opponents to the New
York conservatorship bill (Montano, 1981a, 1981b) included the
American Jewish Committee (1981), the New York Bar Association
(1980), the New York State Catholic Conference (Davitt, 1980), Americans United for Separation of Church and State (Sumner, 1980), the
New York State Council of Churches (1981), the Congress of Racial
Equality (Innis, 1981), the New York Civil Liberties Union (1980),
noted constitutional attorney Leo Pfeffer (1980) and the Commissioner of the New York State Office of Mental Health (Prevost, 1981).

Spokespersons for the various organizations expressed opposition to conservatorships. There was a general concern about the

implications for conversions to virtually any religious group. As
Charles Sumner put it on behalf of the Americans United for Separation of Church and State (1980):

> A man named Saul claimed he was walking down the
> road toward Damascus when he was blinded by a
> bright light and heard the voice of God. He has
> now changed his name to Paul and is active in the
> cult of an obscure Jew called Jesus of Nazareth.

The American Jewish Committee made a similar observation (1981):
"Under the standards adopted by these bills, the transformation of
Moses upon seeing the burning bush would have been grounds for the
appointment of a temporary guardian by a court, since that experience was not a gradual change resulting from maturation or education."

Specific concerns were registered about the vagueness of characteristics which would serve as the basis for the granting of conservatorships. The New York State Council of Churches (1981) observed that the stipulated characteristics would fail to distinguish
between coercive persuasion and conversion:

> The aforementioned characteristics are sometimes
> present in many people who experience a religious
> conversion to any faith or from one faith to an-
> other. When a religious conversion takes place, it
> can be seen as coercive persuasion by those who
> stand outside of the actual experience. Therefore,
> we see this as an anticonversion bill.... If the
> bill becomes law, it may be used by the judicial
> system and parents to remove a young person from a
> genuine faith conversion experience.

The American Jewish Committee (1981) put the matter simply: "The
proposed legislation is unconstitutionally vague and provides un-
workable standards for the determination it would require of the
courts."

Other interest groups clearly were concerned about issues
which transcended religious liberty. Speaking for the Congress of
Racial Equality, for instance, Roy Innis (1980) stated that the bill
"can be used not only against religious converts but against members
of unpopular political and ideological followings." He went on to
assert that "it is directed against people who think differently
from the status quo" and that "it undermines the American tradition of free thought by labeling it psychological deterioration."
The New York State Bar Association (1980) objected to the lack of
due process, to the conservatee's being required to pay for attorneys and the bill's targeting victims rather than perpetrators. The
New York Civil Liberties Union (1980) observed the inevitable intrusion into the validity of the content of belief:

> The bill empowers a court to inquire into the be-
> liefs and practices of a religious group, to make

a judgement as to the validity or acceptability of
those beliefs and practices and to punish one of
its adherents accordingly. In considering a peti-
tion for temporary conservatorship, a court must,
for example, determine whether the group in question
uses "deception in the recruitment of members."
What constitutes such "deception"? Many religions
promise their followers eternal salvation. Others
allege that they can heal the sick and wounded. To
non-believers, these claims are often viewed as
"deceptive."

The Commissioner of the New York State Office of Mental Health
(Prevost, 1981) was concerned both about using the color of mental
health laws to gain legal leverage on religious groups and about the
negative consequences for mental health professionals in being used
in this way. With respect to the first point he asserted: "This
bill goes beyond focusing on the need of the individual by linking
intervention to an evaluation of the practices of a group with which
the individual is associated." Because it would be necessary to
demonstrate that an individual´s "psychological deterioration resulted from coercive persuasion by a deceptive individual or group,"
he concluded that the bill "contemplates a trial of the practices of
a group which has attempted to influence the thinking of the respon-
dent." On the second issue, he warned that:

I do not believe that it is possible for psychiatrists to offer competent testimony on the issue of
the effect of an alleged course of conduct might
have on an individual they may not have met prior to
the temporary guardianship proceedings.... This testimony will only heighten the public mistrust of
mental health professionals. This mistrust inevitably carries over to our legitimate efforts to
assist people who are truly mentally ill.

THE MEDIA AND CIVIL LIBERTIES

Media coverage of the new religions was largely negative; the
anti-cultists´ allegations received widespread coverage (Bromley,
Shupe and Ventimiglia, 1979). Nevertheless, the new religions were
not without defenders, particularly when anti-cult legislation was
pending which threatened to abridge civil liberties. On such occasions editorials appeared across the country which warned of the
consequences of making exceptions in the area of civil liberties.
The following titles illustrate the flavor of such articles: "Religious Freedom Applies to All" (Ft. Worth Star Telegram, 16 October
1975), "Do Unto Others" (Council Bluffs Nonpareil, 19 March 1977),
"Defending Your Right to Be Weird in America" (Lancaster Intelligencer Journal, 31 March 1977), "A Right to Be Wrong" (Plainfield
National Courier, 16 April 1976), "Whose Rights Next?" (Rockford
Register-Republic, 27 August 1976), "Leave the Moonies Be" (White
River Valley Herald, 27 January 1977), "Fair Is Fair" (Ottumwa
Courier, 24 March 1977), "When Children Aren´t Children Anymore"

<u>Ft. Wayne Journal Gazette</u>, 7 April 1977), "Witch Hunts Are an Old
American Tradition" (<u>Philadelphia Inquirer</u>, 7 February 1979).

     Most of these writers made it clear that they had little sympa-
thy for the new religions and were defending them solely on a civil
libertarian basis. As one editorial (Goss, <u>Philadelphia Inquirer</u>,
27 March 1977) put it:

> I don't have much use for the array of religious
> movements that have swept our country the past
> several years. I don't like a lot of what they
> stand for, I don't like their on-the-street pro-
> selytizing, harassment and begging and I'm sus-
> picious of their motives.... These movements are
> using the alienation, bewilderment and uncertainty
> of young adults for their own benefit.... I don't
> like any of it. But that doesn't make them illegal.
> It doesn't make these movements wrong.

These articles typically echoed the concerns of church leaders and
civil libertarians. One common concern was the applicability of new
laws to conventional religious groups. Heagney (<u>Levittown Courier
Times</u>, 30 March 1977) stated:

> And if we start with the Moonies, who is to say
> we won't end up with Methodists? If we begin de-
> programming religious cultists, how far are we from
> deprogramming communists or socialists or a myriad
> of people who don't adhere to the social, religious
> or political norms of this country?

There was similar opposition to conservatorships ("Moonies Saved;
Some Salvation," <u>Dayton Daily News</u>, 29 March 1977): "That won't work
as a legal proposition, and ... is scarier than a legion of vacant-
eyed Moonies cadging dimes to keep their man in an earthly splendor
even real Gods would envy." And there was concern about allowing
parents to exercise legal control over their adult offspring ("A
Time to Let Go," <u>Tulsa Tribune</u>, 30 March 1977):

> There comes a time in every parent's life to stand
> back and let the children's judgement be proven.
> An adult ... should be well on the road toward
> finding his own way or making a complete mess of
> his life. In either case, it shouldn't be a judi-
> cial matter.

BEHAVIORAL SCIENCE SUPPORT

     A great deal of social science research has had the effect of
debunking anti-cult claims concerning new religious movements. Indeed, with the exception of a relatively small group of behavioral
science professionals, the anti-cultists garnered relatively little
support from the findings of most social science research. Nevertheless, the anti-cult supporters achieved considerably greater

visibility since their claims were buttressed by the widespread publicity accorded parents of converts to new religions and atrocity
stories recounted by apostates (Bromley, Shupe and Ventimiglia,
1982). A number of behavioral scientists, academicians and practi-
tioners, attempted to counter the extreme allegations of the anti-
cultists and to point out the implications of acting on the premises
of anti-cult ideology. Several themes ran through this literature:
(1) parallels between the response to contemporary new religious
movements and similar movements which appeared during earlier periods of American history, (2) the implications of efforts to define
the controversy over "cults" in medical terms and (3) the political
consequences of allowing anti-cult initiatives to prevail.

New religious movements have received heavy-handed treatment
throughout American history, scholars have pointed out. Those familiar with American religious history have insisted, therefore, that
current polemics should be kept in perspective. For example, Kelly
(1977:28) observed:

> Most, if not all, of the behavior associated with
> so-called cult religious movements will seem bi-
> zarre and mystifying only to those largely innocent
> of any knowledge of church history or, indeed, of
> human history. What we are seeing in these groups
> today is not something new, but something old; a
> phenomenon sometimes labeled <u>conversion</u>. Thirty or
> 40 years ago, similar anxieties were stirred by the
> Jehovah's Witnesses and their aggressive proselyti-
> zing. The Mormons were widely feared and despised
> in the nineteenth century.... The early Quakers
> were detested and persecuted for their persistent
> efforts to persuade others to their beliefs.

Bromley and Shupe (1979b), for another example, noted the similarities between the socialization process experienced by novitiates in
a cloistered Catholic convent and converts to Hare Krishna. In the
former case, the process is viewed as spiritual training; in the
latter it is labeled brainwashing. Elsewhere (Shupe and Bromley,
1981:255-256), they observed the parallels between allegations of
brainwashing and satanic possession and between deprogramming and
exorcism. Furthermore, a list of stigmata that allegedly characterize "cultists" (truncated vocabulary, monotonic voice, fixed smile,
glassy eyes, body odor, hyperactivity) is strikingly similar to
"marks of the devil." Robbins and Anthony (1979a) have noted the
historical parallels in literatures of countersubversion which
emerge to legitimate countermovements such as the ACM. They have
identified five common themes in this type of literature: (1) subversion myths, (2) violence, (3) enslavement, (4) over-generalized
stereotypes and (5) apostates. First, there is the "subversion
myth," a belief that a new religion poses a clear and present danger
to the social order, particularly if it continues to gain strength.
Such movements are portrayed as conspiratorial and inherently un-
American. Second, there is the specter of violence. New religions
are portrayed as fanatical and vindictive, willing to go to any
lengths to achieve their ends. Particularly in the wake of Jones-

town, these allegations evoke considerable fear. Third, individual
members are viewed as duped, corrupted or enslaved by unscrupulous
leaders. The contemporary brainwashing metaphor simply constitutes
the most recent version of this theme. Fourth, over-generalized
stereotypes emerge. In the nineteenth century, Mormons, Masons and
Catholics became indistinguishable from one another in the counter-
subversion literature; today it is Moonies, Premies and Krishnas.
Finally, new religions in every historical period have been confronted by disgruntled apostates. As we have discussed in earlier
chapters of this volume, such individuals have had a disproportion-
ate influence in shaping the public image of new religious movements.

   Another major concern of behavior science professionals has
been the intrusion of psychiatry into the arena of religious
choices. When converts to new religious movements have been alleged
to be brainwashed, psychologists and psychiatrists usually have been
designated the appropriate experts to pass judgment on their mental
or emotional state. Robbins (1979b:241) succinctly formulated the
implications:

>   When the state endorses the seizure and forcible
>   deprogramming of adults ... authority to use coer-
>   cion is conferred upon vigilantes more fanatic and
>   more brutal than the sectarians they persecute.
>   Whatever coercive deprogramming is tolerated, a
>   psychiatrist or psychologist has been mystifying
>   the community with tales of "mind control." The
>   real danger lies more in the encroachments of psy-
>   chiatry-psychology than in the depredations of
>   vigilantes. The doctors now presume to arbitrate
>   between legitimate and illegitimate religions.

The involvement of mental health professionals in conflicts over religious conversion is problematic particularly in light of the hostility of psychiatry toward religion. As Anthony and Robbins (1980:
10) observed:

>   Modern psychiatry has been a primary vehicle for
>   extending secular values in modern society. Be-
>   ginning with Freud´s The Future of an Illusion,
>   conventional psychotherapy has attacked religion
>   as a force inimical to the triumph of objective
>   rationality. Humanity can be delivered into a
>   modern secular utopia only if we become free of
>   the irrational forces expressed in religious life.

In essence, then, there is very real conflict between mental health
professionals and new religions. On the one hand, the subjection of
reason to the demands and standards of faith, trust in emotionality
over rationality and an unwillingness to accept affective and in-
strumental compartmentalization of life all put new religions at
odds with traditional psychotherapists. On the other hand, a number of new religions offer services which directly compete with
those offered by mental health professionals. Scientology, for

example, essentially involves an alternative therapy that is premised on spiritual principles. It is fundamental to the lifestyle
of members of Hare Krishna and the Unification Church that mankind's
problems, both individual and social, are attributable to spiritual
malaise and hence not redressable in any meaningful sense through
secular, rational means. All such groups therefore offer very different routes to mental health and authorities for their solutions.
If there is such a natural antagonism between mental health professionals and new religions, therapists can hardly be treated as neu-
trals in assessing the meaning, significance and value of participation in new religious movements. As outspoken critic and psychiatrist, Lee Coleman (1982:35) put it:

> ... the anti-cult movement is asking society to do
> the very thing it claims "cults" are doing. It asks
> society to turn over independent thinking to gurus.
> But in this case the gurus are psychiatrists. I see
> no difference between the outlandish claim that Jim
> Jones could cure cancer and the equally outlandish
> claim that a psychiatrist can tell a washed brain
> from an unwashed one. As long as we persist in ele-
> vating psychiatrists to the position of godlike wis-
> dom, we will be guilty of the same mistake made by
> those who turn over their independent thinking to
> someone else.

A third theme in the writings of behavioral science professionals has been the implications for religious liberty of political
initiatives ostensibly directed against cults. Various writers have
pointed out the importance of minority rights in protecting majority
rights. For example, Anthony and Robbins (1980:9) asserted:

> Our civil libertarian tradition owes much to the
> struggles of relatively authoritarian groups for
> their "freedom of conscience" against the power of
> a state proposing to intervene on behalf of commun-
> ity standards. Religious liberty and "freedom of
> conscience," which are sometimes thought to apply
> only to tolerant, nondogmatic groups, were in fact
> initially developed through the claims of groups
> such as the Puritans and the Jehovah's Witnesses.
> Controversial sects have contributed substantially
> to the building of America.

Bromley and Shupe (1981:220) sought to make the same argument in a
somewhat different fashion:

> ... these small religious groups are just as much a
> part of the reality of American religious life as
> are the mainline denominations. To the extent that
> legislatures create laws rejecting the legitimacy
> of certain forms of religious organization and ex-
> pression, for whatever excuse, they are essentially
> declaring that these groups are alien to us. The
> closer we as citizens move toward considering only

the beliefs and practices of certain dominant, established segments of our society as legitimate,
the closer we move toward the destruction of democratic pluralism.

These writers emphasized the vulnerability of new religious movements to repression. Popular conceptions of religious conversion
emphasized cognitive change, considerable stability in membership
and strictly individual choices. However, in the cases of a number
of new religious movements conversion involved emotional commitment
and peer group support. Minority definitions of reality and major
reorientations of lifestyle require emotional impetus and substantial, continuing social reinforcement. Thus, new religions were
particularly at risk because separation from peer group support
could lead to a questioning of faith. Such questioning in turn led
those unsympathetic to new religions to presume that conversions
were counterfeit. For this reason (among others) "brainwashing" became a formidable allegation against new religions; and behavioral
science professionals sought to warn of the open-ended dangers of
such metaphors. Robbins (1977:519) stated, for example:

> The term "brainwashing" is an ideal weapon for
> legitimating repression because: (1) it can never
> be disproved (how is abdication of free will meas-
> ured?); (2) it implies that authorities are con-
> cerned, not with the content of a belief but with
> the manner in which it was induced (they're not
> suppressing opinion); (3) it implies that devotees
> are passive victims of conditioning rather than
> seekers of meaning exercising their constitutional
> rights.

These were among the most important but certainly not the only
themes to be found in the civil liberties oriented literature produced by behavioral science professionals. There also were numerous
critiques of media coverage of the new religions (Bromley, Shupe and
Ventimiglia, 1982; Bryant, 1979a; Testa, 1979) which contributed to
public hysteria. None of these themes distinguish this literature
from newspaper editorials. In most cases the writings of behavioral
scientists were more analytic and sophisticated, and frequently they
appeared in publications with more limited circulation. Thus, these
writers were more likely to reach "opinion leaders" than mass audiences and therefore such publications probably had a greater long-
term than short-term impact.

ALTERNATIVES TO CONFLICT

New religions, civil libertarians and leaders of some established churches sought alternatives to potential state intervention
in religious affairs. Both defenders and opponents of new religions
recognized that in many cases of conversion to a new religious movement family relationships were strained, particularly in the communally organized high-demand groups. The ACM's strategy was to remove
converts from such groups. Defenders of religious liberty sought to

prevent illegal abductions and deprogrammings and to block legaliza-
tion of such tactics through conservatorship legislation. However,
civil libertarians would be tactically outflanked if ACM initiatives
were rejected without any constructive counterproposals in light of
admittedly frayed family relationships. In order to avoid this awk-
ward situation, civil libertarians proposed voluntary, family con-
ciliation services which were designed to reduce family conflicts
without allowing state intrusion. There were several such programs
proposed or in operation by the early 1980´s.

The Alliance for the Preservation of Religious Liberty established one such service which it named Conciliatory Dialogue (1977).
Under this plan if APRL was contacted by a family member with a request for communication with a son or daughter, pressure was to be
exerted on the new religious group to arrange some kind of dialogue
(1977:9):

> The meetings can start at the request of a parent,
> spouse or sect member. The Alliance for the Pre-
> servation of Religious Liberty will act as an in-
> termediary to set up the meetings.... In the event
> that a child refuses to attend such a meeting, an
> appeal is made to the leaders of the religious
> group to instruct the child that it is in the best
> interest of that group to attend the meeting. Any
> refusal or non-cooperative attitude on behalf of a
> group is noted and continuous moves that stifle
> communication efforts are reported and the relevant
> community leaders are so informed.

APRL assumed this relatively strong stance in order to head off parental "desperation." The proposal admonished, "The child who re-
fuses to enter into peaceful dialogue with his parents to iron out
differences is betraying not only himself, but the religion of which
he is a member."

A second service was established by the Berkeley Interfaith
Council. The Council sought neutrality in defining its ground rules
(Berkeley Interfaith Council, n.d.):

> Berkeley Area Interfaith Council will act as a
> referral service to connect parents and young
> people with one of these mediators, who will then
> contact both parties and arrange for a get-together
> in a neutral place away from the young person´s
> religious group. The mediator will maintain strict
> neutrality in any disagreement between family mem-
> bers. He is not there to persuade the young person
> to leave his religious group, nor to persuade the
> parents to accept his remaining there. His sole
> concern is to help restore family harmony through
> frank and open communication.

The most ambitious proposal for establishing family dialogue
has been the Family Consultation and Communication Service initiated

by Dean Kelly on behalf of the National Council of Churches (National Council of Churches, 1982). The prospectus asserted that families should be able to obtain help from their own churches "rather than having to turn to lawyers, psychiatrists or kidnappers." The service was designed as a communication rather than a mediation device. The proposal stipulated:

> The service is not a mediation or conciliation service in the sense that it does not try to reconcile the differences between family members; it will simply try to help them to understand each other.... Its aim is not to get the converts out of the "cults" or keep them in, but to protect their right to make their own religious choices, wherever they may lead.

Each of these services sought to position itself a little differently, but all had in common the objective of reopening the lines of communication among family members. Only the Berkeley Area Inter-faith Council had any substantial experience in this area by 1982, and demand for their service had dropped off considerably. Given the imperative neutrality of such services, neither side in the controversy could be wholly enthusiastic. The new religions were more likely to support such proposals since mediation was preferable to repressive legislation; the ACM had much less to gain. As a result, such services held unfulfilled promise and constituted good faith efforts as much as viable solutions to the continuing controversy surrounding new religious movements.

868. Abelseth, John. "Statement." Oakland, CA, February, 1982.

869. Ad Hoc Committee of Members of the Unification Church. Our Response to the Report of October 31, 1978 on the Investigation of Korean-American Relations Regarding Reverend Sun Myung Moon and Members of the Unification Church. New York: The Holy Spirit Association for the Unification of World Christianity, 1979. 271 pp.

870. Alexander, Brooks. "What Is a Cult?" Liberty 74 (May/June 1979): 10-11.

871. Alliance for the Preservation of Religious Liberty. "Faith-breaking, 1980's-Style." San Francisco, CA, January, 1981a.

872. Alliance for the Preservation of Religious Liberty. "Psychiatry and the Brainwashing Myth." APRL News (July 1981b): 3-4.

873. Alliance for the Preservation of Religious Liberty. "Cults Pose No Threat Declare Religious Scholars." APRL News 2 (March 1979a): 1, 4.

874. Alliance for the Preservation of Religious Liberty. "House
      Resolution #20 Attacked by Prominent Leaders." Philadel-
      phia, PA, May 31, 1979b.

875. Alliance for the Preservation of Religious Liberty. "Jeremiah
      Gutman Calls Richard Delgado Proposals Blatantly Unconstitu-
      tional." APRL News 2 (March 1979c): 3, 6.

876. Alliance for the Preservation of Religious Liberty. "Reli-
      gious Freedom Group Attacks Anti-Cult Conference." Phila-
      delphia, PA, May 18, 1979d.

877. Alliance for the Preservation of Religious Liberty. "Concil-
      iatory Dialogue." Los Angeles, 1977.

878. Alliance for the Preservation of Religious Liberty. The Anti-
      Religion Movement: An Abstract of Contemporary Terrorism,
      Kidnapping and Violation of Religious and Civil Liberties in
      America. Los Angeles, CA: Alliance for the Preservation of
      Religious Liberty, n.d. 45 pp.

879. Alliance for the Preservation of Religious Liberty and Ameri-
      can Civil Liberties Union. Deprogramming: Documenting the
      Issue. New York, 1977.

880. American Jewish Committee, New York Chapter and American
      Jewish Congress. "Statement in Opposition to Proposed
      Bills A. 7912 and S. 5119." New York, 27 May 1981.

881. Anthony, Dick, and Thomas Robbins. "A Demonology of Cults."
      Inquiry, September 1, 1980, pp. 9-12.

882. "Anti-Scientology Strategy Urged." Clearwater Times (St.
      Petersburg, FL), 15 September 1981.

883. Barnhart, Brent. "Legislative Update," First Freedom, Sacra-
      mento, CA, 28 May 1982.

884. Berkeley Area Interfaith Council. Mediation as an Alternative
      to Deprogramming. Berkeley, CA: Berkeley Area Interfaith
      Council, (1978). 2 pp.

885. Bromley, David G., and Anson D. Shupe, Jr. "Moonies" in
      America: Cult, Church and Crusade. Beverly Hills, CA: Sage
      Publications, 1979a. 269 pp.

886. Bromley, David G., and Anson D. Shupe, Jr. "The Tnevnoc
      Cult." Sociological Analysis 40 (Winter 1979b): 361-366.

887. Bromley, David G., Anson D. Shupe, Jr., and Joseph M.
      Ventimiglia. "The Role of Anecdotal Atrocities in the
      Social Construction of Evil." The Brainwashing/Deprogram-
      ming Controversy: Historical, Sociological, Psychological
      and Legal Perspectives. Edited by James T. Richardson and
      David G. Bromley. New York: Edwin Mellen Press, 1982.

888. Bryant, M. Darrol. "Media Ethics: The Elimination of Perspec-
      tive." Religious Liberty in Canada: Deprogramming and Media
      Coverage of New Religions. Edited by M. Darrol Bryant.
      Toronto, Canada: Canadians for the Protection of Religious
      Liberty, 1979a, pp. 56-60.

889. Bryant, M. Darrol, ed. Religious Liberty in Canada: Depro-
      gramming and Media Coverage of New Religions. Toronto,
      Canada: Canadians for the Protection of Religious Liberty,
      1979b. 68 pp.

890. "A Case of a Kidnapped Moonie." Alberta Report (Alberta,
      Canada), 14 August 1981.

891. Choate, Martin P. "The Case Against Government Regulation of
      Religious Cults." Speech at the Sunday Morning Forum, First
      Unitarian Church of Berkeley, CA, April 8, 1979.

892. Choate, Martin P. "He Loved Big Brother": Toward a Theory of
      Mind Control, N.p.:n.d. 33 pp.

893. Church of Scientology. Freedom of Religion Denied. Portland,
      OR: Church of Scientology of Portland, 1981a. 20 pp.

894. Church of Scientology. The Paulette Cooper Tapes. Church of
      Scientology of California, 1981b. 12 pp.

895. Church of Scientology. Black Propaganda: A Smear Campaign
      Against a Reform Church. Church of Scientology, Department
      of Public Relations Information, n.d.a. 28 pp.

896. Church of Scientology. Common Falsehoods about Scientology
      and Documentation to the Contrary. Church of Scientology,
      n.d.b.

897. Church of Scientology. A Correction of Common False Rumors
      Heard About the Church of Scientology. Church of Scientol-
      ogy, Department of Public Relations Information, n.d.c.

898. Church of Scientology. Evidence on Religious Bona Fides and
      and Status of the Church of Scientology. Church of Sci-
      entology, Department of Archives, U.S. Ministry of Public
      Relations, n.d.d.

899. Church of Scientology. False Report Correction of Strange New
      Religions. Church of Scientology, Department of Public Re-
      lations Information, n.d.e.

900. Church of Scientology. False Report Correction: The Scandal
      of Scientology by Paulette Cooper. Church of Scientology of
      California, U.S. Ministry of Public Relations, n.d.f. 56
      pp.

901. Church of Scientology. Scientology: A World Religion Emerges
      in the Space Age. Church of Scientology Information

Service, Department of Archives, n.d.g. 155 pp.

902. Citizens Commission on Human Rights. Investigation of John G. Clark, Jr., M.D. Boston: Church of Scientology of Boston, (n.d.a).

903. Citizens Commission on Human Rights. A Twentieth Century Inquisition: Warning to the Citizens of Boston, Preliminary Report. Boston: Church of Scientology of Boston, (n.d.b).

904. Clines, Francis. "Religious Freedom vs. Parental Care." New York Times, 1 November 1976.

905. Coleman, Lee. Psychiatry the Faithbreaker: How Psychiatry is Promoting Bigotry in America. Sacramento, CA: Printing Dynamics, 1982. 40 pp.

906. Coleman, Lee. "New Religions and Deprogramming: Who's Brainwashing Whom?" Berkeley, CA, N.p.: n.d.

907. Connecticut Civil Liberties Union to Connecticut General Assembly. "Substitute Bill #1429 – An Act Concerning Temporary Guardians." Hartford, CT, 4 May 1981.

908. Cooper, Paulette. The Scandal of Scientology. New York: Tower, 1971.

909. Cox, Harvey. "Playing the Devil's Advocate, As It Were." New York Times, 16 February 1980.

910. "Curb Scientology with Ordinances, Lawyer Suggests." Clearwater Times (St. Petersburg, FL), 12 September 1981.

911. Davitt, J. Alan, Executive Director of the New York State Catholic Conference, to Richard A. Brown, Counsel to the Governor of the State of New York. "Relative to the Appointment of Temporary Conservators." Albany, NY, 1 July 1980.

912. "Defending the Rights of Religious Cults." Civil Liberties (April 1979): 4.

913. "Defending Your Right to be Weird in America." Lancaster (PA) Intelligencer Journal, 31 March 1977.

914. "Deprogramming and Religious Liberty." Church and State 29 (November 1976): 4-5, 8-9.

915. "Do Unto Others." Council Bluffs (IA) Nonpareil, 19 March 1977.

916. Durst, Mose. The New Religions. New York: Unification Church, 1981. 3 pp.

917. "Fair Is Fair." Ottumwa (IA) Courier, 24 March 1977.

918. Flinn, Frank. "Deprogramming and the Deprogramming Network."
      Religious Liberty in Canada: Deprogramming and Media Cover-
      age of New Religions. Edited by M. Darrol Bryant. Toronto,
      Canada: Canadians for the Protection of Religious Liberty,
      1979, pp. 3-10.

919. Ford, Gene. Who Is the Real Mindbender? Anaheim, CA: Gene
      Ford, 1977. 80 pp.

920. Goss, Ela. "While Another Harasses Moonies." Philadelphia
      (PA) Inquirer, 27 March 1977.

921. Harmgaal, Ya´agov. "Deprogramming: A Critical View."
      American Zionist 68 (1977): 16-19.

922. Heagney, John. "The Hazards in Shooting for the Moon."
      Levittown (PA) Courier Times, 30 March 1977.

923. Innis, Roy, Chairman of the Congress of Racial Equality, to
      All New York State Assemblymen and Senators. "Memorandum
      concerning Assembly Bill 7912." New York, 18 May 1981.

924. International Society for Krishna Consciousness. A Request to
      the Media: Please Don´t Lump Us In. Los Angeles: Interna-
      tional Society for Krishna Consciousness, 1979.

925. Johnson, Calvin. "Reverend Moon Inspires Minority Alliance
      International." Unification News, 22 February 1982, p. 1.

926. Judah, J. Stillson. "New Religions and Religious Liberty."
      Understanding the New Religions. Edited by Jacob Needleman
      and George Baker. New York: Seabury Press, 1978, pp. 201-
      208.

927. Kangas, Ron. Mind Bending or Mind Renewing? Anaheim, CA:
      Gene Ford, 1977. 51 pp.

928. Kelly, Dean. "Deprogramming and Religious Liberty." The
      Civil Liberties Review 4 (July/August 1977): 23-33.

929. Lauter, David. "Are Churches Under Attack?" The National Law
      Journal, 2 November 1981, pp. 1, 16-17.

930. "Leave the Moonies Be." White River Valley Herald (Randolph,
      VT), 27 January 1977.

931. Lemoult, John E., to the Privacy Committee of the American
      Civil Liberties Union, "Kidnapping Members of Religious
      Groups - Deprogrammers," 1 December 1976.

932. Lucksted, Orlin D., and D.G. Martel. "Cults: A Conflict Be-
      tween Religious Liberty and Involuntary Servitude?" (Part
      I.) FBI Law Enforcement Bulletin (April 1982a): 16-20.

933. Lucksted, Orlin D., and D.G. Martel. "Cults: A Conflict Between Religious Liberty and Involuntary Servitude?" (Part II.) FBI Law Enforcement Bulletin (May 1982b): 16-23.

934. Lucksted, Orlin D., and D.G. Martel. "Cults: A Conflict Between Religious Liberty and Involuntary Servitude?" (Part III.) FBI Law Enforcement Bulletin (June 1982c): 16-21.

935. Maher, Frederick. "Mind Control and Religious Liberty." Paper presented at the Annual Meeting of the Society for the Scientific Study of Religion, Chicago, October, 1977.

936. Marson, Charles C., Margaret C. Crosby, and Alan L. Schlosser. "On the Civil Liberties of Sect Members." Science, Sin and Scholarship: The Politics of Reverend Moon and the Unification Church. Edited by Irving Louis Horowitz. Cambridge, MA: The MIT Press, 1978, pp. 193-197.

937. McBeth, Leon. Strange New Religions. Nashville, TN: Broadman Press, 1977.

938. Montano, Armando, Assemblyman representing the 77th Assembly District, to "Friend of Religious Liberty." "News from Assemblyman Armando Montano." Albany, NY, 2 June 1981a.

939. Montano, Armando, Assemblyman representing the 77th Assembly District, State of New York, to "Friend of Religious Liberty." "News from Assemblyman Armando Montano." Albany, NY, 3 June 1981b.

940. Moon, Rev. Sun Myung. Statement on Jews and Israel. Tarrytown, NY: Unification Church, 1976. 5 pp.

941. "A Moonie Eclipsed: Kidnappers Nab John Abelseth Again." Alberta Record (Alberta, Canada), 11 December 1981.

942. "Moonies Saved; Some Salvation." Dayton (OH) Daily News, 29 29 March 1977.

943. National Council of the Churches of Christ. "News Alert," 2 February 1982a.

944. National Council of the Churches of Christ. "Prospectus for a Family Consultation and Communication Service." New York, 1982b.

945. National Council of the Churches of Christ. "Resolution on Deprogramming: Religious Liberty for Young People Too," 28 February 1974.

946. New York Civil Liberties Union, Legislative Department. "1980 Legislative Memorandum #21." New York, n.d.

947. New York State Bar Association, Committee on Mental Hygiene. "Report No. 11122-A." New York, 23 June 1980.

948. New York State Council of Churches. "New York State Council
      of Churches Position Paper: Temporary Guardianship."
      Albany, NY, 18 May 1981.

949. Nixon, Robert W. "Congressmen Look at Cults." Liberty 74
      (May/June 1979): 12-13.

950. "No Job for Congress." Trenton (NJ) Evening Times, 30
      September 1975.

951. O'Connell, Joseph. "The Breakdown of Family Trust." Reli-
      gious Liberty in Canada: Deprogramming and Media Coverage
      of New Religions. Edited by M. Darrol Bryant. Toronto,
      Canada: Canadians for the Protection of Religious Liberty,
      1979, pp. 11-18.

952. Pak, Col. Bo Hi. Truth Is My Sword: Testimony of Col. Bo Hi
      Pak at the Korea Hearings, U.S. Congress. International
      Exchange Press, n.d. 68 pp.

953. Pfeffer, Leo. "Statement on 11122-A Conservators Bill."
      Brooklyn, NY, 11 June 1980.

954. Prevost, James A., Commissioner of the New York State Office
      of Mental Health to Assemblyman Armando Montano, Assembly
      Mental Health, Alcoholism and Substance Abuse Committee.
      "Memorandum concerning Assembly Bill 7912." Albany, NY, 27
      May 1981.

955. Price, John L. "Witch-hunts are an Old American Tradition."
      Philadelphia (PA) Inquirer, 7 February 1979, p. 11-A.

956. "Religious Freedom Applies to All." Ft. Worth (TX) Star Tele-
      gram, 16 October 1975.

957. "Rescue by Kidnapping: A Cultist Charges His Parents as Depro-
      gramming Turns Violent." Alberta Report (Alberta, Canada),
      22 May 1981.

958. Richardson, Herbert W. "The Psychiatric State." Religious
      Liberty in Canada: Deprogramming and Media Coverage of New
      Religions. Edited by M. Darrol Bryant. Toronto, Canada:
      Canadians for the Protection of Religious Liberty, 1979, pp.
      23-26.

959. "A Right to Be Wrong." Plainfield (NJ) National Courier, 16
      April 1976.

960. Robbins, Thomas. Civil Liberties, "Brainwashing" and "Cults."
      Berkeley: Center for the Study of New Religious Movements,
      1981. 48 pp.

961. Robbins, Thomas. "Religious Movements, the State and the Law:
      Reconceptualizing the Cult Problem." Review of Law and

Social Change 9 (1979-1980): 33-50.

962. Robbins, Thomas. "Cults and the Therapeutic State." Social Policy 10 (May/June, 1979): 42-47.

963. Robbins, Thomas. "Brainwashing and Religious Freedom." The Nation, April 30, 1977, p. 518.

964. Robbins, Thomas, and Dick Anthony. "Harassing Cults." New York Times, 16 October 1980.

965. Robbins, Thomas, and Dick Anthony. "Cults, Brainwashing and Counter-Subversion." The Annals of the American Academy of Political and Social Science 446 (November 1979a): 78-90.

966. Robbins, Thomas, and Dick Anthony. "Cult Phobia: A Witch Hunt in the Making?" Inquiry, January 1979b.

967. Robbins, Thomas, and Dick Anthony. "Cults vs Shrinks: Psychiatry and the Control of Religious Movements." Paper presented to the Association for the Sociology of Religion, 1979c.

968. Robbins, Thomas, Dick Anthony and Jim McCarthy. "Legitimating Repression." Society 17 (March/April 1980): 39-42.

969. Rudin, A. James. "Jews and Judaism in Reverend Moon's Divine Principle." Science, Sin, and Scholarship. Edited by Irving Louis Horowitz. Cambridge, MA: The MIT Press, 1978, pp. 74-83.

970. Salonen, Neil Albert. "A Statement by Neil Albert Salonen, President, Unification Church of America." January 12, 1976a. 9 pp.

971. Salonen, Neil Albert. "A Statement by Neil A. Salonen, President, Unification Church of America." February 23, 1976b. 7 pp.

972. Salonen, Neil Albert. "A Statement by Neil Albert Salonen, President, Unification Church of America." July 23, 1976c. 10 pp.

973. Salonen, Neil Albert. "Our Response to Persecution: A Report by President Neil Salonen." New Hope News, 8 March 1976d.

974. Sawatsky, Rodney. "Mennonites, Mormons, Moonies: Christian Heresy and Religious Toleration." Religious Liberty in Canada: Deprogramming and Media Coverage of New Religions. Edited by M. Darrol Bryant. Toronto, Canada: Canadians for the Protection of Religious Liberty, 1979, pp. 27-42.

975. Scott, Osborne, Chairman of the Committee Against Racial and Religious Intolerance, to Members of the Connecticut State Senate. Letter in opposition to Senate Bill 1429. New

York, 14 May 1981.

976. Shupe, Anson D., Jr. "Deprogramming: The New Exorcism."
     American Behavioral Scientist 20 (Summer 1977): 941-956.

977. Shupe, Anson D., Jr., and David G. Bromley. "Witches, Moonies
     and Accusations of Evil." In Gods We Trust: New Patterns of
     Religious Pluralism in America. Edited by Thomas Robbins
     and Dick Anthony. New Brunswick, NJ: Transaction Press,
     1981, pp. 247-262.

978. Sparks, Jack. The Mindbenders. New York: Thomas Nelson,
     Inc., 1977. 283 pp.

979. Stanford, Phil. "The Quiet War on Cults." Inquiry, October
     15, 1979a, pp. 6-7.

980. Stanford, Phil. "Spying Back." Inquiry, December 24, 1979b.

981. Stevin, Jonathan. "New Minority Alliance Vows Fight for Jus-
     tice." The News World, 17 January 1982, p. 4A.

982. Sumner, Charles H., New York State Chairman of Americans
     United for Separation of Church and State, to Hugh L. Carey,
     Governor, State of New York. Letter in Opposition to As-
     sembly Bill #11122-A. Rochester, NY, 25 June 1980.

983. "Taxing Nonprofit Groups Is Studied." Clearwater Times (St.
     Petersburg, FL), 15 September 1981.

984. Testa, Bart. "It Would Have Been Nice to Hear from You."
     Religious Liberty in Canada: Deprogramming and Media
     Coverage of New Religions. Edited by M. Darrol Bryant.
     Toronto, Canada: Canadians for the Protection of Religious
     Liberty, 1979, pp. 61-68.

985. "A Time to Let Go." Tulsa (OK) Tribune, 30 March 1977.

986. Unification Church. "Internationally Famed Constitutional
     Specialist, Laurence H. Tribe, to Represent Reverend Sun
     Myung Moon." New York, 1982a.

987. Unification Church. "Statement on the Tax Case of Reverend
     Sun Myung Moon." New York, 1982b.

988. Unification Church. The Unification Church National Policy on
     Fundraising. New York: Unification Church, 1977. 3 pp.

989. Unification Church. Charitable and Humanitarian Projects In-
     spired by Reverend Sun Myung Moon. New York: Unification
     Church, n.d.a.

990. Unification Church. Commonly Asked Questions. New York:
     Unification Church, n.d.b. 5 pp.

991. Unification Church. Help - We Are Being Persecuted. Berkeley, CA: Unification Church, n.d.c. 10 pp.

992. Unification Church. In 1952 This Was Reverend Moon's Church. New York: Unification Church, n.d.d. 2 pp.

993. Unification Church. Organizations: Why So Many? Berkeley, CA: Unification Church, Office of Public Affairs, n.d.e. 1 p.

994. Unification Church. Reverend Moon: A Vindication for Justice. New York: Unification Church, n.d.f. 16 pp.

995. Unification Church. Rev. Sun Myung Moon and the Unification Church. New York: Unification Church, n.d.g. 26 pp.

996. "When Children Aren't Children Anymore." Ft. Wayne (IN) Journal Gazette, 7 April 1977.

997. "Witch Hunts Are An Old American Tradition." Philadelphia Inquirer, 7 February 1979.

998. "Whose Rights Next?" Rockford (IL) Register-Republic, 27 August 1976.

999. Wiley, Jerry. "Post-Guyana Hysteria." Liberty 74 May/June 1979): 3-9.

1000. Willoughby, William. "Religious Journalism and New Religions." Religious Liberty in Canada: Deprogramming and Media Coverage of New Religions. Edited by M. Darrol Bryant. Toronto, Canada: Canadians for the Protection of Religious Liberty, 1979, pp. 43-55.

1001. Worthing, Sharon L. "The State Takes Over a Church." The Annals of the American Academy of Political and Social Science 446 (November 1979): 136-148.